Protection and Security on the Information Superhighway

D1476059

Protection and Security on the Information Superhighway

Dr. Frederick B. Cohen

John Wiley & Sons, Inc.

New York • Chichester • Brisbane • Toronto • Singapore

Publisher: Katherine Schowalter

Senior Editor: Diane D. Cerra

Managing Editor: Maureen B. Drexel

Text Design & Composition: Integre Technical Publishing Co., Inc.

Designations used by companies to distinguish their products are often claimed as trademarks. In all intances where John Wiley & Sons, Inc. is aware of a claim, the product names appear in initial capital or all capital letters. Readers, however, should contact the appropriate companies for more complete information regarding trademarks and registration.

This text is printed on acid-free paper.

This publication is designed to provide accurate and authoritative information in regard to the subject matter covered. It is sold with the understanding that the publisher is not engaged in rendering legal, accounting, or other professional service. If legal advice or other expert assistance is required, the services of a competent professional person should be sought.

Library of Congress Cataloging-in-Publication Data:

Cohen, Frederick B., 1956–
    Protection and security on the information superhighway /
Frederick B. Cohen.
        p.   cm.
    Includes bibliographical references (p.   ).
    ISBN 0-471-11389-1 (acid-free paper)
    1. Computer security.   2. Data protection.   3. Computer networks–
Security measures.   I. Title.
QA76.9.A25C59   1995
005.8—dc20   94-40488
                                                          CIP

Printed in the United States of America

10 9 8 7 6 5 4 3 2 1

About the Author

Dr. Frederick B. Cohen is world renowned for his ground-breaking work in protection for information systems and networks. In 1974, he developed and prototyped the first timed permutation lock based on musical patterns. In 1976, he developed protocols for secure digital networks carrying voice, video, and data to be used in the next generation of computer networks. In 1981, he helped develop and prototype the first electronic cashwatch system for implementing personal digital money systems. In 1984, he was the first author to publish scientific work on transitive integrity corruption mechanisms and defenses against them, and he coined the term *computer virus* at that time.

Since 1984, Dr. Cohen has authored over 50 invited, refereed, and other scientific research articles on mechanisms for enhancing integrity, availability, and privacy in information systems and networks. He has authored seven graduate-level texts on information science, several of which have been used to teach graduate students in universities. In 1989, he won the prestigious international Information Technology Award for his scientific work on integrity protection. He has developed several key technologies and products in use throughout the world, and today, over half of all computers sold world wide contain integrity protection mechanisms first published and prototyped by Dr. Cohen.

As a nationally recognized authority on information infrastructure, Dr. Cohen regularly provides consulting services for top management. His clients include many Fortune 500 companies, government agencies, universities, and professional corporations. He has participated in corporate studies ranging from designing the next generation of cable television and telephone systems, to securing global financial institutions as they attach to the National Information Infrastructure. He has taught graduate level courses at several universities, implemented protection for office automation systems in several small companies, and helped several public access Internet service providers.

Beginning in 1984, Dr. Cohen performed significant research and analysis for U.S. Government Agencies. In 1984, he performed studies in conjunction with a missile defense program on the feasibility of attacking multilevel secure operating systems with computer viruses. Throughout the late 1980s, Dr. Cohen participated in DoD sponsored conferences and training and education programs to help raise awareness of vital infrastructure issues. In the last several years, Dr. Cohen has performed significant work in the area of defensive information warfare, including acting as a principal investigator on studies for the Defense Information Systems Agency, the Office of the Secretary of Defense, and the U.S. Air Force.

Dr. Cohen is also on the editorial boards of the IFIP TC-11 Journal *Computers and Security*, the DPMA, IEEE, and ACM Computer Virus and Security Conference, and the ACM/SigSAC Annual Student Paper Review Board. He has reviewed scientific papers for IEEE, ACM, IFIP, and other professional society publications, and has participated in other public service activities throughout his career.

Acknowledgments

I want to give my deepest and most sincere thanks to two people without whose efforts I would not have been able to write this book. They are exceptional people who I have found to be members of the rare breed who place personal integrity and honesty above money, fame, and other worldly things. Not only have they spent many hours debating minute details that most of my readers will probably never appreciate, but they have also kept me well grounded in reality, prevented me from making statements that stretch the truth, and pressed me to convince them in writing that my views are well supported. In alphabetical order by last name, they are Ron Knecht and Charles Preston.

Ron is one of those people who can listen to me communicate technical details of information protection at or around full bandwidth. I would place him in the top ten or twenty people in the world in his field. His demand for precision in some of the work that supported this book, his understanding and guidance in considering many of the national and international issues, and his comprehension of technical matters has been an invaluable aid in this work and in this book. He has also taken time on weekends, evenings, and early mornings to read and review some of my analysis, which is certainly going above and beyond the call of duty.

Charles is just plain helpful. Charles doesn't believe anything I tell him without checking it out for himself. The availability of a fact checker who sincerely wants to know the truth about a field is one of the best things an author of a technical book can have. For example, if I used the number $100 million somewhere and didn't cite the correct page number, Charles would not only find that the dollar value was incorrect and should be $300 million, but he would (he did) also find the correct page number and send me a copy of the source material on Sunday night of a holiday weekend via facsimile. Without Charles, this book would probably have only half of the hard facts and citations it now has, and for my money, that's worth more than I can express.

I should also take the time to thank Diane Cerra, who is the person I deal with at John Wiley and Sons. Diane says that I am very easy to work with, which probably means that other authors are really hard to work with. She is, of course, very easy for me to work with because she eliminates every obstacle before I even know it was there. I send her a partially completed book, and she tells me that we should change the title to this or that, or that I could use a chapter on some other topic. I either say okay or tell her why it's a bad idea, and after a few minutes, we are back to talking about how many sales we will need for me to buy a condominium in New York. So far, we have sold enough to almost make one monthly payment.

There are so many other people who have provided information and assisted in the development of this book in various ways that I cannot possibly remember them all or list them here. Also, many of them would probably rather I didn't mention them. To all of you, a collective thank you will have to do.

Contents

CHAPTER 1   Introduction and Overview   **1**

   1.1   PREVIEW   4
   1.2   THE NATIONAL INFORMATION
         INFRASTRUCTURE   9

CHAPTER 2   A Growing Dependency   **13**

   2.1   TECHNOLOGY MARCHES ON   14
   2.2   SURVIVAL DEPENDENCIES   18
   2.3   PERSONAL AND BUSINESS DEPENDENCY   20
   2.4   NATIONAL SURVIVAL DEPENDENCIES   24
   2.5   INDIRECT DEPENDENCY   27
   2.6   THE INFORMATION SUPERHIGHWAY   28

CHAPTER 3   The Disrupters Are Among Us   **33**

   3.1   COMPUTER ACCIDENTS   33
   3.2   INTENTIONAL EVENTS   40
   3.3   A CLASSIFICATION OF DISRUPTIONS   54
   3.4   THE DISRUPTERS   56
   3.5   MOTIVATION   71
   3.6   THE MAGNITUDE AND SCOPE OF
         THE PROBLEM   74
   3.7   ADDING IT ALL UP   78

CHAPTER 4   Asleep at the Switch   **79**

4.1   A HISTORY OF SECRECY   80
4.2   IGNORANCE IS NOT BLISS   82
4.3   THE BIRTH OF THE PERSONAL COMPUTER   83
4.4   A SUPPRESSED TECHNOLOGY   87
4.5   THE UNIVERSITIES FAIL US   90
4.6   AN INDUSTRY OF CHARLATANS   91
4.7   INFORMATION ASSURANCE IGNORED   93
4.8   CURRENT DISRUPTION DEFENSES DEPEND
      ON PEOPLE   100
4.9   THE REST OF THE WORLD RESPONDS   104

CHAPTER 5   Protecting Your Information Assets   **107**

5.1   INFORMATION PROTECTION   108
5.2   INFRASTRUCTURES ARE DIFFERENT THAN
      OTHER SYSTEMS   110
5.3   A PIECEMEAL APPROACH   113
5.4   AN ORGANIZATIONAL PERSPECTIVE   132
5.5   SOME SAMPLE SCENARIOS   146
5.6   STRATEGY AND TACTICS   148
5.7   THE COST OF PROTECTION   151
5.8   AN INCREMENTAL PROTECTION PROCESS   159

CHAPTER 6   Protection Posture Case Studies   **165**

6.1   HOW TO DO A PROTECTION POSTURE
      ASSESSMENT   165
6.2   CASE STUDY 1: A MA AND PA BUSINESS   172
6.3   CASE STUDY 2: A (NOT-SO) SMALL BUSINESS   179
6.4   CASE STUDY 3: A BIG BUSINESS   185
6.5   CASE STUDY 4: A MILITARY SYSTEM   187
6.6   CASE STUDY 5: THE DOD AND THE NATION
      AS A WHOLE   193

CHAPTER 7   Summary and Conclusions   **197**

APPENDIX A   Details of the NII   **199**

A.1   INFORMATION CHANNELS   199
A.2   THE EVOLUTION OF THE INFORMATION
      INFRASTRUCTURE   199
A.3   THE NII TODAY   202

A.4 INFORMATION SERVICE PROVIDERS 204
A.5 POSSIBLE FUTURES 204

APPENDIX B Case Studies **207**

B.1 CASE STUDY 3: XYZ CORPORATION 207
B.2 CASE STUDY 4: THE ALMA SYSTEM 234
B.3 CASE STUDY 5: THE DOD AND THE
NATION AS A WHOLE 257

References **269**

Glossary **291**

Index **295**

CHAPTER 1

Introduction and Overview

Have you been to the bank lately? If the computers weren't working, could you get any money from them? How about the supermarket? Would they be able to check you out without their checkout computers? Does your car have computers to control the fuel mixture? How about at the office? Does your company use computers to get you your paycheck? Does the gas station where you get gas use computers in their gas pumps?

The United States as a nation and its citizens as a people depend on information and information systems as a key part of their competitive advantage. This is common knowledge. But the dependency doesn't stop there. Without properly operating information systems, the national banking system, electric power grid, transportation systems, food and water supplies, communications systems, medical systems, emergency services, and most businesses cannot survive.

Operation Desert Storm was an object lesson in the critical importance of information in warfare, in that it demonstrated the ability of the United States to obtain and use information effectively while preventing Iraq from obtaining and using comparable information. But it was also a lesson in what happens to a country that only moderately depends on information when that information is taken away. The vast majority of the destruction in Iraq was to systems that provided the communications required for command and control of forces. The effect was the utter destruction of the Iraqi economy, and as a nation, Iraq is now at or below par with most third-world nations.

These object lessons were observed and understood by other nations and organizations. The world has seen the effect of removing the information infrastructure from a country that was only marginally dependent on it, and the effect was devastating. But what about the effect on a nation that is highly dependent on its information infrastructure?

The United States is rushing headlong into the information age. But the world is a dangerous place. People are regularly attacking the information highways already in place. Here's a good statistic to show you what I mean. Something like 900 million attacks take place on the Internet each year.

Financial loss is often cited as the rationale behind enhanced information protection, and a lot of figures fly around. As an example, AT&T claims that its toll fraud losses added up to $2 billion in 1992. Meanwhile, FBI figures claim that computer crime losses range from $164 million to $5 billion annually. [21] That's quite a range! It also seems to indicate that the FBI figures don't include the AT&T figures.

And financial loss is not the only form of loss encountered in our society. Businesses have confidential information stolen and patented by competitors, individuals end up in jail and inmates are released because of disruptions in law enforcement computers, IRS computer failures have caused thousands of small companies to be put out of business, corporate telephone switches have regularly had hundreds of thousands of dollars worth of telephone calls stolen through them over a weekend, and the list goes on almost without end.

The more information that flows through the information highways, the harder it is to protect people from accidents and abuse. The more places the information highways go, the more people are susceptible to harm. A good example is the Internet, one of the largest information networks in the world. The Internet connects more than 2 million computers together today. Compare this to the fall of 1988, when there were only about 60,000 computers on the Internet. The reason to choose the fall of 1988 for comparison is because that is when the Internet Virus was launched. In that incident, one person essentially stopped all work on 60,000 computers for two days. In 1994, another Internet incident was discovered that, at a minimum, involved the theft of passwords to more than 100,000 computer systems. The perpetrator has not been found, and this estimate of the magnitude of the damage could be low by as much as a factor of 25. Nobody knows for certain what the perpetrator did with those passwords, but it's a good bet that they were used to examine or modify some of the estimated billion megabytes of information available on those systems.

But let's face it. If you're going to live in the modern age, you are going to have to deal with the risks of modern life. When people started using automobiles, there were no speed limits on the open road, traffic cops, or parking meters. Some people got killed in early automobiles, but it wasn't until the 1960s, almost 50 years after automobiles became popular, that the government and manufacturers started to really get serious about safety. Airbags only became mandatory on new automobiles in the United States in 1994. Cars have been used in robberies since the early part of the twentieth century. Drunk drivers have killed hundreds of thousands of people. Drive-by shootings are now commonplace.

You are probably going to have to get on the information superhighway if you want to get anywhere in the information age, and there are going to be accidents and crimes on that highway just as there are accidents and crimes on our automotive highways. There are no safety belts in most modern computers, and the computer criminals know how to break into your computer over the network just as their compatriots know how to break into your car in a parking lot.

So how do you protect your information assets? If I could answer that question in a sentence, this would be a very short book indeed. Fortunately, the basic plan can be outlined pretty quickly:

- Recognize your dependency on information. Everyone has always depended on information to one extent or another, but in the information age, the dependencies are more extreme, and the implications of those dependencies are more far-reaching. The information industry has created tools for dealing with information. Almost everyone who depends on information now depends on those tools as well. In many cases, people literally cannot live without them. Dependencies on the information infrastructure are presented in depth in Chapter 2, "A Growing Dependency."
- Recognize the weakness of the infrastructure you depend on and the extent to which it is being exploited. Most people believe that most computers work most of the time, and that when they occasionally have problems, they can be easily fixed. Of course, that is what the people who exploit information systems probably want you to think as they steal billions of dollars a year, win military conflicts, gain advantages in negotiations, ruin other peoples' reputations, and on occasion, kill people. Infrastructure weaknesses are addressed in Chapter 3, "The Disrupters Are Among Us." The historical roots of these problems and some of the issues we face in addressing them are discussed in Chapter 4, titled "Asleep at the Switch."
- Recognize that protection is something you do, not something you buy. What do I mean when I say that? Suppose I want to protect my house from water damage. It doesn't matter how good a roof I buy for my house, it's not going to protect my house forever. I have to maintain the roof to keep the water out. It's the same with information protection. You can't just buy it, you have to do it.

Most people in the United States today believe that money can cure their problems. But in this particular area, it is your time and effort that makes the difference. No matter who you are or what you do, you are a part of the solution to the information protection problem, and it affects you personally. From the person who uses an automated teller machine (ATM) to get cash on a weekend, to the top technical expert at the largest information technology provider in the world, everyone must play their part in order for protection to be effective. To play our parts properly, each of us must know what to do and how to do it. The techniques used to address information protection are discussed in Chapter 5, "Protecting Your Information Assets."

- Pursue information protection with appropriate priority. Most people ignore information protection issues completely most of the time and treat them as a very high priority item over a short period of time during crisis periods. This results in higher costs and greater losses. The most effective strategy, and the one that costs the least in the long run, is a slow and steady approach that achieves reasonable levels of protection in reasonable time frames for reasonable costs. Case studies show this point most effectively and are provided in Chapter 6, "Protection Posture Case Studies."

A caution before you read on: The gap between reality and the widespread perception of our technical community is so vast that many so-called experts who read this book may claim that the threats described here are overblown. I want to give you at least one example of just how far the majority view can be from the reality. In September of 1988, I submitted a proposal to the National Science Foundation (NSF) to perform research into defenses against computer viruses. The response I got from the technical reviewers (which arrived in late October) was, in essence, that there was no such thing as a computer virus, and that such a thing was impossible in modern computer systems and networks. About three weeks after I got that response, the Internet Virus incident occurred, and more than 60,000 networked computers were infected for a period of two days. The chances are very good that the very researchers who claimed it was impossible in their review of my proposal were harmed by that "impossibility" only a few weeks later. Today, there are several thousand known computer viruses spreading through the information systems of the world.

1.1 PREVIEW

This book is about the risks that arise from mixing computers with communications and how to remain safe in that environment. The overall organization of this book follows a progression first developed in a study done for a government agency in which I was one of the principal investigators. [63] The core position taken in this book can be summarized as:

> - We all depend on information and information systems.
> - These systems are highly vulnerable to disruption.
> - A lot of people can and do disrupt these systems.
> - It is in our best interest to protect ourselves.
> - Protection is something you do, not something you buy.
> - We all need to know what to do to protect ourselves.

The remainder of the book details what organizations of various sorts can do, should do, and actually do to protect themselves.

We All Depend on Information Systems

I presume that you understand by now that we all depend on information systems in our daily lives, but perhaps you don't know how deep the dependency really is. Our telephone systems, cable systems, electrical power grid, much of our transportation and delivery systems, and almost every other element of our National Information Infrastructure (the NII) is controlled by computers. Most NII information systems are networked. In effect, the whole nation and much of the world is interconnected. Even the U. S. military heavily depends on the civilian information infrastructure for major aspects of command, control, logistics, payroll, training, and other operations.

> In short, our national dependency on the National Information Infrastructure is so extreme that our nation and our way of life literally could not continue without this infrastructure operating properly.

Information Systems Are Highly Vulnerable

When you buy a car, the salesperson doesn't normally tell you about how many people get killed each year in automobile accidents. It's the same way with computers. The salespersons tell you about how much you can do with them, how easy they are to use, how useful they can be for storing, manipulating, and presenting information, and how easily they connect to other computers throughout the world.

In the case of cars, there is plenty of publicity about crashes and the government requires safety features to help prevent accidents and mitigate the harm when accidents happen. Incidents of people running each other over with cars on purpose are fairly rare, and when people do, they are charged with vehicular homicide. Computers, on the other hand, have little or no protection. No protective features are mandated, there are few laws about what you can or cannot do with a computer, and interconnected computers are generally wide open to accidental or malicious disruption.

The lack of mandatory protection requirements means that those features are an added expense for computer hardware, software, and service providers that can only be justified by consumer demand. But demand is largely driven by marketing, and history has shown that marketing safety when there is little or no perceived risk paints a negative image on the product or service. Thus, there is no economic benefit to the supplier to provide for protection at this time, except where it may save on warranted maintenance costs. The result is that modern information systems are almost completely devoid of meaningful protection.

> Today's information systems are so vulnerable to attack that this book contains hundreds of examples of actual attacks with effects ranging from financial loss to death. I don't want to minimize them by trying to give just one example here.

A Lot of People Disrupt Information Systems

There are a lot of people in the world who know how to disrupt information systems. More than 30 countries have sponsored concerted efforts in both attack and defense technologies related to disrupting information systems. Many of those countries create or produce the technologies we now depend on for the NII. But nation states are only a small part of this story.

> There are hundreds of individuals and organizations throughout the world with the capability of disrupting large portions of our NII.

Groups capable of disrupting the NII include terrorist organizations, economic rivals, hacker groups, drug cartels, organized crime cartels, and knowledgeable individuals. Furthermore, the disruption of some portions of the NII can cause cascading effects that impact other NII components. For example, the power grid is controlled by telephonic communications, while the telephone system gets its power from the power grid. If an attacker could take some portions of the power grid off-line for about 10 days, it could cause a massive telephone failure that could result in the electric utilities being unable to get the power grid back up.

But if you are not concerned about a national collapse, you should be concerned about the far larger number of people who know how to cause disruption within smaller organizations. There are at least several thousand people who know how to remotely access and disrupt internal information systems and networks at almost any modern organization. Even those who use special *firewall* computers to protect themselves from this sort of attack can be easily defeated by a sufficiently knowledgeable attacker.

The losses from these sorts of attacks are quite startling. Some figures cite as much as 4 percent of the gross domestic product of industrialized nations as being lost due to information system disruption. There are several well-documented and publicized losses in excess of 100 million dollars. Some incidents have produced losses in the billion-dollar range.

We Need to Protect Ourselves

The NII is comprised, in essence, of all of the interconnected information systems in the United States and all of the interconnection mechanisms used to make those connections work. This currently includes more than one half of all of the computers in the country, all of the telephone systems, all of the cable television systems, all of the satellite communications systems, and many other elements.

> If the NII as a whole is disrupted, or if the NII is exploited to disrupt some of the systems that are a part of it, the harm to the people of the United States may be staggering.

It is clearly in the best interest of everyone in the United States to assure that adequate protection is provided both for the NII as a whole and for the elements that comprise it.

Protection Is Something You Do, Not Something You Buy

The key element in understanding information protection is getting a solid grasp of the concept that protection is something you do, not something you buy. A good example of how many people misperceive this is the recent flurry of interest in using firewall computers to protect internal networks that are connected to the Internet.

> It is not unusual for people who sell or promote products to claim that their product is the solution to all of your problems but, unfortunately, in information protection, no product can solve all of your problems.

The Internet firewalls now being pushed into the market may provide a valuable technical tool that allows a competent team of experts to prevent and detect certain classes of attacks that originate from other sites. They are not universal products that keep you from harm of all sorts. There are literally hundreds of ways of bypassing any such protection scheme, ranging from human engineering to fraudulent software update disks.

In order for the firewall technology or any other protection technology to be effective, the technology has to be properly managed, skilled professionals must operate it, users must be trained on how to use it, changes to it have to be properly controlled, it must be physically protected, it must be tested, auditing must be done on a regular basis, and this is only the beginning of the story.

Protection Requires Knowledge

At the heart of the protection activity is the problem of getting the knowledge needed to properly carry out that activity. Because the value of information is pervasive in modern life, so must be its protection. Anywhere valuable information goes, protection must also go. That means that everyone who deals with valuable information must also be involved in the information protection function at some level.

My daughter Megan is only 11 months old, but she is already learning not to touch the buttons on the VCR in the living room. Her older brother David is five, and he already knows not to touch other peoples' computers, that wires are not to be fooled with, that fingers don't touch the shiny parts of floppy disks, that you don't tell strangers about yourself without permission from your parents, and on and on. My six-year-old knows to read the instructions on the computer screen before pressing the keys, and she even knows which directories and files are not hers. My eight-year-old knows that overheated computers break more often, she has files with private information, she has a user ID and a password, and she knows to turn the laser printer off when it's not going to be used for a while.

In order to be effective in information protection over the long run, as a nation, we have to start to teach our children about computer ethics and other information protection issues, and we have to help them understand that computers are not always right or trustworthy. Our children need a healthy respect for both the power and the limitations of our information technology, and the same thing applies to all of the rest of us.

How to Protect Yourself

In order to be involved in the protection function, people at all levels of an organization must be aware and knowledgeable about the protection issues they will encounter and understand how and why these issues involve them. From the chairperson of the board of the largest corporation in the world to the person who cleans the toilets at the local restaurant, some degree of understanding of information protection must be embedded in their job function if protection is to be effective.

> Effective protection requires a combination of people with expertise from different fields working together to provide an appropriate mix of operational solutions that meet the need.

For ma and pa businesses, this may mean restricting the use of the NII or using services that provide protection functions. For larger businesses this may mean a shift in operating policies and procedures and a long-term commitment to protection in line with the long-term commitment to information technology. For large multinational firms, this may mean even more commitment and resources, and cooperation by people from all around the world. For military organizations and governments, this may mean sacrificing some efficiency in exchange for effectiveness.

Summary

If you are buying computer security products or using quick fixes for every protection problem you encounter or hear about—stop. Start forming a reasonable and responsible information protection plan using high quality, well-qualified experts to help you. Then follow the plan and you will have long-term, effective protection at a justifiable cost.

1.2   THE NATIONAL INFORMATION INFRASTRUCTURE

The term *Information Superhighway* was coined by the press in 1992 as a way to talk about the emerging *National Information Infrastructure* (NII) described by Vice President Al Gore in his call to action for the nation. The use of this term follows a long tradition of talking about computers in the frame of reference of automobiles. For the remainder of this book,

I will use the term NII or National Information Infrastructure to describe this evolving entity.

To understand the issues that come up in the NII, it's helpful to understand what the NII is comprised of, how it operates, how it came to be, and what the future is likely to look like. Unfortunately, nobody can actually describe the NII at any given time because it is constantly changing, is not centrally controlled, and is evolutionary in its makeup.

In a recent talk, I used a series of 10 overhead viewgraphs representing different viewpoints on the NII, ranging from cable television, to telephone systems, to information services, to satellite maps, to fiber optics, and so on. After describing all of these components, I put all of the slides up on the screen at one time and declared "This is the NII." Of course, with that many network maps on the screen, it is impossible to see much more than a jumble, which is an accurate depiction of the state of the NII today.

With such a complex jumble of independently changing technical components, it is impossible to get a good understanding of the NII without some technical knowledge. Furthermore, understanding the issues of information protection requires a solid understanding of the state of information technology. Even from an executive level, some amount of technical understanding may help in understanding the language of protection and the rationale behind protection decisions.

On the other hand, most people understand the NII in terms of the services it provides. Today's providers provide a wide range of information services. Over time, people will learn to use increasingly sophisticated information services, and the user-level information service providers will grow into a massive component of the industry.

> There is essentially no limit to the sort of information that can be provided in a general purpose information system like the NII. In fact, this may lead to the real problem with such a system. With all of the information available, it may become difficult to separate the signal from the noise.

Right now, the range of services available for $10 to $30 per month (plus special fees for some services) includes but is not limited to:

- Business Information: Business registries, lists of trademarks and patents, universal industry codes (UIC), universal product codes (UPC), lists of products and prices, on-line shopping, and store fronts.
- Financial Information: Current market information, on-line trading, financial news, investment advice, consulting, interest rates, dates

and deadlines for market events, federal regulations, and proposed operational changes.

- News, Weather, and Sports: Associated Press (AP) and United Press International (UPI) wire services, newspaper articles from the last 100 years, current and historical weather and predictions from around the world, current and historical results of athletic events, event schedules, and tickets.
- Computing: Mailing lists of people who own or are interested in any computer hardware and software of interest, on-line copies of thousands of shareware products, bulletin boards about all sorts of issues in computing, low cost computers and parts, access to consultants, reports of computer risks, and reports of recent computer viruses.
- Personal Information: Motor vehicle information, results of court cases, credit history, names and addresses of relatives, telephone numbers, where you work, what you get paid, where you live, what kinds of things you buy, where you shop, what clubs you belong to, where you go on vacation and when you are gone, who you call, who calls you, how long your calls last, when you make those calls, what kind of car you drive, your driving record, where you buy gas, how much you travel by car, what books you read, your age, hair color, eye color, height, weight, how much and what brand of shampoo and birth control you use, and what magazines you subscribe to.
- Reference and Education: On-line encyclopedias, dictionaries, reference libraries, upcoming lectures and speeches, scheduled media events, proposed legislation, congressional records, summaries of news and magazine articles, detailed technical information on all sorts of systems, disease statistics, population statistics, farm reports, building codes, pictures from NASA, and traffic regulations.
- Entertainment and Games: On-line real-time adventure games with live opponents, games against computers like chess and checkers, video games and simulations, humorous articles and jokes, announcements of concerts and other events, news of international tournaments, and bridge and chess player ratings.
- Travel and Leisure: Reservations, ticketing, travel brochures, world maps, on-line communication with people from faraway places, science fiction groups, people who like novels, book clubs, on-line books and videos, and tips on how to mow your lawn.
- Groups and Clubs: You name it, it's in there. Thousands of on-line groups are commonly available, covering everything from quilting to skydiving.
- Electronic Mail: To anywhere in the world with a network address, 24 hours a day, 7 days a week, mail arrives in seconds between many locations.

- File Sharing and Remote Access: On-line access to remote files with any of the information listed here and much more, remote access to millions of computers for those authorized to use them, World Wide Web service and Gopher to locate information throughout the network based on a word or words describing it.

Other services are also available. For example, you can connect your local area network (LAN) directly to the National Science Foundation network (NSFnet) by leasing a high-speed telephone line from your site to the local public access point. You can get a satellite dish and lease time slots on satellites for private communication. Video teleconferencing capability is provided by many telecommunications providers to enable sites around the world to have meetings by video phone. Teleconferencing is now widely used by geographically distributed companies to have meetings. Cable systems can be used to form metropolitan area networks by leasing some of the unused bandwidth and putting proper equipment on the cable.

Information services in the NII may eventually be tailored to each individual.

> Consider the effect on advertising when enough personal information becomes available to be able to send each individual a custom-tailored advertisement for just the items that person is most likely to buy at the highest price he or she is likely to be willing to spend for them.

The pitch may even be so customized that people believe it's their old friend or someone from their local religious group on the other side of the wire, when in fact, it's only a machine.

The NII holds great promise, but it also holds great risks. Success on the information superhighway will depend on our ability to properly manage it so as to balance the risks with the benefits.

CHAPTER 2

A Growing Dependency

Information has been critical to the survival of nations and individuals throughout recorded history.

- More than 5,000 years ago, there were spies gathering information for their governments, systems for calculating and assessing taxes, inventory and supply systems, documented strategic planning, and mechanical cryptographic systems. [121]
- Numerically inferior forces with an information advantage have historically dominated in military conflict [11] because of what is now called the force multiplier provided by that advantage.
- When Paul Revere declared that the British were coming, it was based on the integrity of an information system (one lantern if by land and two if by sea).
- When John Kennedy initiated a blockade of Cuba, it was based on information systems that showed nuclear missiles had been placed there.

> Information has had a significant role in the survival of societies from Biblical times [233] to today, [33] and will likely continue to affect national survival for the indefinite future. [41]

In the October, 1993 crisis in Russia, the members of the dissolved parliament escalated to military action by ordering their supporters to take over the mayor's office across the street, the television station across town, another major telecommunications center, and the Kremlin a few blocks away, in that order. The takeover of the mayor's office in downtown Moscow was essentially unopposed (only warning shots were fired), but when it came to the television station, the battle became fierce. The other targets were never even threatened. Can there be any question that the Russian leadership on both sides understood the import of information as the key to victory?

2.1   TECHNOLOGY MARCHES ON

If information has played a crucial role throughout history, why is there a pressing need to reconsider this issue in a different light today? The answer lies in the fundamental changes in information systems and the new ways in which people have come to depend on them over the last several years. Just as the industrial age led to fundamental changes in the way the world worked, the information age is now leading to fundamental changes in the way the world works. [214]

If you were a tailor near the beginning of the industrial age, you might have gotten involved with technology when the first sewing machine came out, or you might have waited a while. If you waited a while, you might not have been on the leading edge of tailoring, but it wouldn't have hurt your business. But over time, almost all tailors came to use sewing machines because there was a definite advantage in terms of the time required to make a similar quality item. It eventually became necessary in order to compete. But some holdouts remain even today. In China, they still hand sew some goods, but even there, the machine is proving more cost-effective and the transition is underway.

Compare this to the information age. In the beginning, computers were exotic. Some companies had them, but very few companies were put out of business because they lacked computers. Over time, more and more companies found that the savings obtained in using a computer over people operating adding machines made computers cost-effective. Today, even many of the least technology-oriented businesses have fax machines, computerized telephone systems, answering machines, voice mail, and even PCs. I once stated that people really knew they were in the information age when most people used information systems at least once a day. Today, most people who work use some form of information system more than once per hour and millions of people use information systems almost all of their working day.

The information age is not just about computers. Consider the way cable television has changed your life. Although radio news has been almost instantaneous for a long time, as recently as the mid-1980s, much of the news was reported hours or even days after it happened and videos from war zones were rarely available right away. By the 1990s, the people of the world saw the Gulf War live from Bagdad on their home television sets. In less than a decade, our country went from 4 network channels to 40 cable channels. And this is only the beginning. In the 1980s, going out to the movies was a major source of entertainment. In the 1990s, movies are watched on cable television more than in the movie theaters. Just as news reels were primarily seen in theaters in the 1940s and moved to network television news shows in the 1960s, the movies themselves are moving out of the theaters and into your home.

And how about telephones? By the 1980s, computer systems were commonly being sold with modems, those boxes that let you dial into on-line information services. It started with a few services, but by the 1990s, on-line information services were providing professional services to tens of thousands of doctors, lawyers, scientists, educators, and other professionals.

By the early 1990s, the small international business became a major force, primed to a large extent by the low-cost fax machine. The fax machine was a rarity in the mid-1980s, but by 1990, almost any business could have a fax machine. For the small international business, this meant that contracts could be closed and deals made via international telephone calls at low cost and in short time frames. Whereas the high cost of getting involved in international business was limiting in the early 1980s, by 1990, cost factors made it possible for even the smallest companies with unique products to communicate and do business with networks of people all around the world. In the mid-1990s, fax machines have become so common that many people have them in their homes and use them in place of the mail to send letters.

> With the inclusion of fax-modems in computers, more and more documents are generated, transmitted, received, viewed, edited, and returned in purely information form.

In addition to reducing costs, emerging information technology is rapidly eliminating the drudgery of once routine tasks, such as data entry and hand calculation. Accountants don't add a lot of numbers any more. A data entry clerk enters the numbers into a computer and the accountant spends time figuring out different ways to use them. Some day soon, optical character recognition (OCR) systems and voice input systems will eliminate the data entry component. Even today, a lot of accounting uses direct data fed from computer to computer. Reading many pages of typed text into a computer is now faster, cheaper, and more accurate using OCR technology than using people for data entry.

Another information phenomena of the late 1980s was the automated telephone attendant. The early, and often obnoxious, high-tech telephone answering machines granted the caller the ability to select from many different options when a person was unavailable to take a call or when the information being provided could easily be summarized into a few hours of digitally recorded speech. For many people, this was going too far. Some backlash resulted and many companies chose to return to providing personal service to their customers rather than making them interact with a computer to get assistance. But after the short-lived backlash, automated attendants became widely used in place of individual answering machines and, as speech understanding technology improves, computers are taking on more and more telephone tasks for people.

The real turning point for speech input to computers probably came with the VCR Voice product that revolutionized speech interaction with information systems. This hand-held device took one of the most complex technical problems of our day (programming a VCR to record a program) and turned it into child's play. You simply say *record—channel 2—9PM 10PM* and the information system programs the VCR for you. The telephone companies rapidly followed with voice-activated telephone dialing, and the Japanese even developed an automated translation device for handling multilingual calls in real-time. The day may soon come when typing into a computer, pressing buttons on a telephone, and other similar information system interaction nearly disappears in favor of speech input and video output.

Another major information technology that has dramatically affected people is the optical disk. In the late 1980s, high-volume storage was primarily done with magnetic tape, which is slow to access but could typically handle hundreds of millions of bytes of digital information and several hours worth of analog video information. More recently, digital audio tape (DAT) has been used to store several thousand megabytes of digital information, but again, access time is relatively slow. In the early 1990s, optical disks came into their own with compact disks (CDs) replacing phonograph records throughout the audio industry. With computers as the controllers, CD–read–only–memories (CD-ROMs) and rewritable optical disks have dramatically changed the very nature of information systems.

One very good example of this change is in the on-line dictionaries and encyclopedias that have recently appeared. In these new forms of books, the user can literally watch and listen to famous speeches while reading the text and supporting information. The multimedia aspects of these new systems make learning a very different experience. It is likely that multimedia presentations will soon replace most written documents used for marketing purposes in the information industries.

> It is even possible that within 10 to 15 years, the printed book will become widely replaced by digital books.

Consider this. Suppose you ask the library to provide you with all of the published works analyzing Shakespeare's tragedies in terms of character development, and the library transmits the information to you over the cable television system for a fee. The research results (some 10,000 articles) are loaded into a rewritable optical disk in your electronic book and you walk away with the book in your hands just like any other book you would buy off-the-shelf. As you sit under a tree in the park, you open the book and ask it to select an article of possible interest. If you like the article, you tell the book to keep it, otherwise, you tell the book to throw it away. In a few hours, you have done enough searching and selecting for your purposes, so you start to dictate your article into the book, automatically including citations to the other articles. After a few hours, you produce a draft of your multimedia report.

All of the elements of this technology are available today. Optical disks are small, store hundreds of books worth of information, are resilient relative to other storage technologies, and have the capacity to hold photographs, text, and voice for rapid recall. In a book-like technology, you could carry around a typical library of several thousand books in a package with the same size, weight, and shape as a paperback book now takes. Computerized speech understanding in limited domains has been available since the early 1970s, and today, there are commercially available speech understanding systems for taking dictation using personal computers. And all of this technology is still progressing at a rapid rate.

Every technology just described has a common component that produces great efficiency. That component is the computer. Information technology is not just about computers, but the core technology that allows modern information technology to be flexible and to automatically communicate is the computer.

As technology delivers more complex systems with more automation and smoother interfaces, people will become even more dependent on computers. When people no longer need to write or type because automated voice input has made that technology unnecessary, they may lose the ability to do those things. How much longer will handwriting remain a vital skill when our voice boxes provide the same information in typed form without the risk of carpal tunnel syndrome or the inconvenience of finding a keyboard? I for one will not miss the keyboard, and as soon as the voice-input replacement is cheap enough, I will be getting sore throats instead of finger aches.

> As new technologies enable new processes, the new processes drive out old processes. The dependencies we once had on ourselves and other people shift toward dependencies on these new technologies.

Infrastructure has been a major military target at least since World War II, when the allies targeted German ball bearing factories. [76] This was not only because ball bearings were used in tanks, aircraft, and naval craft, but also because they were used in the machinery that made machinery.

Information and information systems are the ball bearings of the information age. Both military and civilian activities depend on this technology at almost all levels. [108] Information technology is used to design information systems, to direct the transmissions used to implement the information infrastructure, and to control the manufacturing and delivery of new information systems that comprise the ever-changing infrastructure. We are now at the point where we cannot produce more advanced information systems without using existing information systems.

2.2   SURVIVAL DEPENDENCIES

Many people depend on information systems for their very lives. For example, every pacemaker today is a small piece of information technology that delivers electrical waves of the right shape to the right place at the right time. When that information technology fails, an individual may die.

When my grandmother was a young woman of only 85 or so (she is now more than 100 and going strong), she started to feel tired one day, and told my uncle she didn't feel like getting up to come over and visit. My uncle, who is a doctor, went over to visit her (yes, he makes house calls) and found that her pacemaker was running at a rate of only four beats per minute. They rushed her to the hospital, replaced the battery, and she was back to her old self again. Now I must say that I would feel very tired indeed if my heart was only beating four times per minute, and I naturally wondered about what went wrong. When I found out, I was amazed. It turns out that the battery they put in when they installed the pacemaker was supposed to last about 12 years. Since the technique was fairly new at the time and the patients were all quite old, nobody figured that anyone would last long enough to need a battery replacement. She has had several replacements since that time, and the periodic replacement of pacemaker batteries is now part of the regular process.

Whereas the pacemaker constitutes a truly intimate individual dependency, other forms of information technology are less intimate, but just as vital to individual survival. One example is the air traffic control system that millions of people depend upon every day. The air traffic control system is an information technology that forms a vital component of our national transportation infrastructure. As an information system, the air traffic control system includes radio and wired communications equipment, a multitude of sensor arrays to detect everything from aircraft to weather conditions, a large number of widely distributed computer systems, and of course a lot of people.

In our air traffic control system, there are many examples where people have died because the system was unable to respond adequately to the circumstance. I don't mean to say that the system didn't respond as it was designed to respond (which it almost always does), but rather that the system was not designed to respond to circumstances that cause some of the fatal crashes.

One example of this sort of failure is when a pilot doesn't behave in strict accordance with the wording required to invoke emergency response. The air traffic control system basically ignores the circumstance. In one case, a commercial airliner crashed killing all aboard because the pilot stated that the fuel was almost empty and that it was extremely urgent that they have priority to land. He did not, however, *declare an emergency* in the proper wording because he was not a native English-speaking pilot and was apparently unable to recall the proper word sequence. Similarly, when the pilot of a plane loses bearings, which can easily happen in many weather conditions, one of the common modes of response is to ask air traffic control for help. A typical scenario is that the pilot says something like, *I need a place to land,* and the air traffic control response is something along the lines of, *Please advise us what you are going to do.* If you declare an emergency and properly ask the controller to vector you to the nearest airport for landing, you will probably get the advice you need, but, when you are confused by circumstances and overloaded by the burdens of keeping the plane flying, it is easy to fail to say the magic words that get you safely on the ground.

The point of this is not to critique the air traffic control system, but rather to point out a problem in the nature of interacting with a complex information system on which you depend for your survival. The problem is that, even though there are people in the loop, the system is designed to operate the way it operates and not to flex in emotive response to systems that don't interact properly with it. Thus, our survival needs force us to learn how to interact with the information systems on which we depend, the better we are able to interact, the better our chances are for survival.

Our survival dependency goes a lot deeper than this, of course. For example, many of us now depend on information systems to work the brakes in our cars, to open up air bags in case of accidents, and to operate the traffic lights on our streets. People also use information systems to determine and deliver proper doses of medicine in hospitals, to control electrical power, and to connect us to emergency services. The use of the 911 telephone number to call for emergency services is a good example of an infrastructure-level survival dependency in the United States (different numbers are used for emergency services in other countries). Failures in any of these systems could cause death.

2.3   PERSONAL AND BUSINESS DEPENDENCY

On a personal level, dependency on automated information systems may seem to have begun fairly recently, but from an infrastructure standpoint, the United States and its population have depended on automated information systems to a high degree for some time. At first, the dependency was limited, and these systems were highly diverse, distributed, and independent. But over time, technology advanced, and designers began to consolidate and centralize for efficiency.

But efficiency is not always the best solution. For example, the Space Shuttle is dynamically unstable during reentry into the Earth's atmosphere. That means that if the computer fails for more than about one thousandth of a second, the shuttle will literally break up into thousands of pieces (or more). To assure that this does not happen, the shuttle has redundant computers. If one fails, another takes over. It would be more efficient to use a single computer, but the designers chose redundancy to provide added assurance. In today's NII, there is plenty of redundancy, but it is rarely used to enhance assurance.

Every individual, company, government agency, and other entity in the United States depends on information systems to one degree or another. For example, almost every entity in the United States today uses the telephone as a key communications device. If telephones no longer functioned, you and I would no longer be able to call 911 in an emergency, we could no longer use modems to communicate, our fax machines would be useless, we could not call our relatives and friends, or quickly do business at a distance. The economy would move back from a global one to a local one, centralized information systems would be useless because there would be no efficient way to gather or redistribute the information, and all of the companies that depend on these services would have a severe problem.

This is the nature of a universal dependency. Everyone in our society depends on information in many of its forms, and without automated information systems, our society would revert, as did that of Iraq, back to the sort of society the United States had in the early half of this century. Along the way, many of us would die, and the United States would be so weakened as a nation that it would likely become susceptible to many forms of political and economic change.

Very Small Business

My definition of a very small business is a business with only a few employees or with gross sales of less than a million dollars per year. Another term would be a Ma and Pa business. To me and most other people I have talked to, this is what a small business is; but the U.S. government has a much broader definition, so I make the distinction here.

In very small businesses, computers are a rarity. There may be as many as two or three PCs in such a business, and these computers are usually run by the owner or one trusted employee. If a computer was stolen, these businesses would, for the most part, continue with at most a minor disruption. This is, of course, changing as younger people introduce more automation into these businesses, but the change is slow, and the computer is rarely the core of the business. The main exception is the small computer software firm; but then if you live by the computer, you die by the computer.

Many very small businesses depend on the post office more than any other information-processing facility, and many depend heavily on the telephone. Professional offices tend to depend on computers for billing, but they often send unpaid bills to collection agencies. Small collection agencies in turn use paper tracking systems, telephones, and the mail. Very small law offices use computers to produce letters, but for little else. They depend heavily on paper filing systems.

Very small businesses tend to depend on manual rather than automated information systems and, for that reason, they have little to lose from a business standpoint if the automated information systems of the world collapse. Of course, the big exception to this rule is that very small businesses tend to depend on other businesses for supplies, services, and the like.

Small Business

In stark contrast to the very small business, the average small business (by U.S. government standards) depends heavily on information systems for every aspect of its operation. These businesses include engineering firms, restaurants, large stores, professional offices, regional chain stores, distributors, manufacturers, car dealers, trucking companies, telephone answering services, and telemarketing companies. One of the things many of these businesses have in common is the physical proximity of their employees. Most small businesses are in one building, fewer are spread across one city, still fewer are spread across a region, and very few are spread across the nation or over the world.

Physical proximity is important in that it tends to make communication efficient and reduces the dependency on long distance communications services. For example, many small businesses have one local area network and a simple internal telephone system that serve the entire corporation's internal automated information system requirement. The advantages of physical proximity do not usually extend to external information exchange, which remains highly dependent on telephone companies. For example, electronic data interchange (EDI) is playing an increasing role in gaining efficiencies in business-to-business order processing, and without external voice communications, many of these businesses would quickly go out of business.

Internally, most of these businesses use computers for tracking customers, employees, payroll, inventory, payables, receivables, and almost all other facets of business operations. The more automated information systems are exploited to run the business, the more likely the officers are to be able to make prudent decisions, and the more dependent they become. Annual reports, advertising, letters, memos, and all other corporate communications tend to depend on automated information systems.

In most cases, these companies cannot meet payroll, ship or receive goods, maintain accurate inventory, or otherwise operate efficiently without computers. However, in a pinch, they usually get by, even if the computers all fail for a week or more. Costs go up, but almost anything most of these businesses do in terms of office work can be done without a computer. Unfortunately, this is not all these companies tend to do.

Many successful small companies have automated more than office functions. In many small manufacturing plants, numerically controlled machines and assembly lines are vital to operation. Automation has replaced many workers in jobs where it is cost-effective due to economies of scale. The automation, in turn, tends to depend on information systems. Companies that have moved to just-in-time delivery schedules (delivery schedules where the goods required to do a job arrive just as the job requires them) have used information systems as a lever to reduce inventory costs and increase efficiency. When the lever fails, the company can no longer attain the efficiency, and collapse is almost always inevitable.

Big Business

Big businesses tend to be more physically distributed, have more managers and administrators, and use more specialization of job function than small businesses. As a result, the need to coordinate the efforts of many people is greatly increased, and the efficiency level of individuals tends to go down. In a typical dealing with a large corporation, no single individual can make a substantial decision, so more people get involved, and the same decision takes longer and costs more to make. Compare this to a very small business where every decision is made by an individual. On the other side of the coin, the redundancy provided by the corporate legal staff, the executive corps, the secretaries, the administrative assistants, and other staff members provide big business with a lot of checks on decisions that prevent many of the mistakes made in smaller companies. Yet with all of this redundancy, big companies still make mistakes and, quite often, they are big mistakes.

From an information technology standpoint, the physical distribution of big business, the specialization of staff, and the large number of employees leads to greater dependency on information technology and greater exploitation of its leverage. In most big businesses, information system failure translates directly into business failure. Payroll cannot be done without computers, receivables and payables cannot be tracked without computers, contracts cannot be generated without computers, sales people cannot get assignments or process orders without computers, the telephones don't work without computers, letters can't be sent without computers, and on and on. In a corporation with tens of thousands of employees, it is literally impossible to use an alternative manual system to get these things done. It's not just a matter of cost—there are simply too many things to do to get them all done in the time frame required in the space available. It would take months or years for most big businesses to adjust to life without information technology, and the costs of this sort of change would be so extreme that almost no big business could survive it.

Big business has also made the largest investment in automation of factories, of inventory control, in just-in-time delivery, in electronic data interchange, and in all the other leverages created by information technology. As a result, they depend even more heavily than smaller businesses on this leverage and collapse even more quickly when it is removed. A good example of the dependency on just-in-time delivery was the three-day strike in August of 1994 by 3,500 employees of the General Motors plant that manufactured lights and bumpers. More than 46,000 workers were temporarily laid off as a side effect of this strike because the just-in-time delivery system makes every part of the operation highly dependent on all the other parts. [6] The same result could have been caused by computer problems. If you don't believe that, look at the case of the Denver airport, which, as of this writing, has been unable to open for more than six months because they can't get the computers that run the automated baggage handling system to work properly.

Big business tends to spend adequate resources on information technology (IT) and those who support the information technology function. In almost every big business today, there are hundreds of IT staff members who keep the systems running properly. Most big businesses also employ a substantial number of outside consultants in the IT area, and they can be called in on an emergency basis to help get through problem periods. Most big businesses have suffered through several substantial computer failures and have come to realize that their dependency on information technology is high. As a result, they have started to plan for many of the events they have seen in the past in order to mitigate future effects.

2.4 NATIONAL SURVIVAL DEPENDENCIES

Nations need information systems in order to survive in much the same way as individuals and businesses. There are commonly two sides of government that operate very differently from an information dependency standpoint: the civilian side and the military side.

Civilian Government Dependency

Governments are some of the largest organizations found on this planet, and for the most part, they are extremely information-intensive. They gather more data, process more records, and produce more output than almost any other sort of organization. Storage requirements are enormous, because they tend to store a lot of historical data about a lot of people. Fetching any particular piece of data can be a mammoth task. Getting a single file commonly takes weeks and involves several hours of individual effort. A lot of information is lost or misplaced. If you are unlucky enough to be affected by such a thing, you may find that this enormous information system is very unforgiving.

In recent years, the U.S. government has made a substantial effort to reduce the complexity of this system by storing more and more information on computer systems, but the process of data entry is inherently error-prone, and the redundancy necessary to remove the errors is simply not there. As a result, errors are most often found by the people they affect.

The process of removing errors is an inherently difficult one for the affected individual. As automation has increased, so has the use of records for multiple purposes. The result has been fairly dramatic. In several recent cases, government computers have identified innocent people as criminals and the police have arrested and held them because they believed the computers, despite clear evidence to the contrary. [181] In some cases, correcting the error takes weeks or months and, by the time the problem is corrected in one computer, it has spread to other computers via information interchange. The victims of this kind of problem can wage a David and Goliath battle that takes years to resolve and results in the individual changing names rather than the government repairing the errors.

The U.S. government has become so dependent on information technology that all non-critical functions are shut down when information technology becomes unavailable. In the winter of 1993–1994, the weather was so bad that rolling blackouts were necessary to control power usage in the Washington, D.C. area. The result was the total shutdown of the majority of the Federal government. The government simply could not operate. People may have been able to answer the telephones in some cases, but what would they tell the caller? *My computer is down, so I can't help you.*

If you look at the pattern, you will find that this high dependency is related to the highly distributed physical location of government sites, the large number of employees, and the enhanced efficiency provided by these information systems. The Hudson, Ohio government, for instance, is not substantially dependent on information systems, because it is small, physically in one building, and has very few employees. The national government of the United States is at the other extreme.

DoD Dependency

The Department of Defense (DoD) is dependent on information for all aspects of its operation. Historically, components of the DoD have implemented *stovepiped* information systems designed to fulfill special needs. These systems are called stovepiped because they perform all of the information requirements of a particular task by themselves, from sensors, to communications, to storage, to analysis, to presentation. They are special purpose because they are specially designed to the particular task.

This has resulted in a coordination problem in joint operations because integrating the diverse information stored in these stovepiped systems is difficult and time-consuming, and thus limits the tempo of operations. To fully exploit the advantages of information in warfare and to reduce the costs associated with information processing, duplicative systems, and redundant data entry, the DoD has made the doctrinal and policy decision to move toward a globally integrated Defense Information Infrastructure (the DII). [155]

The complexity, scope, and timeliness requirements of DoD information processing are exemplified by some of the applications supported by the DoD. While some of these examples also provide insight into other organizations, it is important to realize that in the DoD, lives are at stake.

- The inventory, supply, and logistics systems of the DoD and their service providers are now automated to the point where they cannot locate or deliver inventory in a timely fashion without properly functioning information systems. Joint forces coordinated logistics operations—like the logistics effort used to coordinate Operation Desert Storm—now require that a large number of physically distributed heterogeneous (i.e., dissimilar) information systems operate properly together. [155] Increased demands on the information systems supporting the DoD's supply and logistics systems are produced by reduced lift (i.e., long distance transportation) capacity, [26] and just-in-time delivery requirements called for in current DoD doctrine.

- The DoD now trains personnel at all levels to work in unison by using a geographically distributed network of simulators that communicate with each other in real-time to emulate complex battle situations. This is how the DoD prepares soldiers, sailors, airmen, and marines for the sort of joint and coordinated efforts required to win a more rapidly paced war with fewer people. [127]
- The use of *Command and Control Warfare* both to paralyze the enemy and to enhance friendly speed and agility has become a theme in DoD doctrine. [31] This capability requires reliable, available, accurate, real-time, globally interlinked, robust information systems. [171]

The accomplishment of military functions, both direct combat operations and support, depend to varying degrees upon the availability and accuracy of information. For example, most activities in modern warfare depend on the reliable communication of command and control and situational information. Many military activities rely on timely, assured access to accurate position, environment, logistics, medical, personnel, or financial information. This dependency is not static based on the content of the information. Rather, employment of particular military weapons or operational tactics at a particular operational tempo (i.e., rate) depends on the assured availability of a certain quantity and quality of information at a particular time.

By analogy, information requirements are equivalent to petroleum budgets required to maintain a particular operational tempo. If either the information or the petroleum is unavailable, the desired operational tempo will not be obtained. (This analogy is not perfect in that once petroleum is used, it is gone, while information is not consumed in its application.)

> In short, nearly every component of the U.S. military and the infrastructure upon which it depends are highly dependent on information and information systems.

There are many publicly available examples of the U.S. dependency on both military and commercial information technology, including recently published examples from wartime military operations.

The U.S. Army's Chief of Staff called Desert Shield/Storm the *knowledge war*. [33, p.ix] The House Armed Services Committee said "... acquiring support systems consistent with high-tech weapons may be more important than buying the next generation plane or tank." [33, p. xxi] According to another author, "... it is very surprising that very extensive use had also to be made of the international commercial networks, Intelsat and Inmarsat." [10] Still another author wrote "DISA and CENTCOM learned a valuable lesson: A viable information systems architecture requires the total integration of commercial and military communications systems ... ". [201]

Logistics data passing over local and wide area computer networks also became vital. Regarding Marine Corps operations: "Supply and maintenance information, ... soon came to be seen as critical to the success of the operation ... these systems had to operate in the same environment as the systems that [performed command and control] functions." [168]

2.5   INDIRECT DEPENDENCY

Suppose someone changed the computer-controlled temperature setting of the sterilization phase of the manufacturing process used to make meals ready to eat (MREs) for the U.S. military so that it was not hot enough to kill botulism. The end result could be military defeat, since many troops in the field might get sick.

I use this example to demonstrate how we all depend on each other. Any dependency any of us have, the rest of us may share through our interdependency. In some cases, extremely subtle dependencies can make an enormous difference. When commercial airliners crash, you may hear the term *chain of events* used to describe the improbable set of circumstances that combined to cause a crash. The same sorts of improbable chains of events can cause information systems to operate incorrectly.

I am not aware of this particular thing ever happening with MREs, but there certainly have been times when wells were poisoned in military conflicts to try to attain a similar effect. The rationality of the attack is quite compelling. For one thing, the risk is minimal because the MRE manufacturing plant doesn't have the same protections in place as a munitions factory. For another thing, MREs are distributed throughout the military and only widely used in real combat situations. This makes it unlikely to be detected before a real incident. Even though MREs are tested extensively in production and botulism might be detected in these tests, there are certainly other toxins that could have a similar effect that are not detected in standard testing, and which could be triggered by environmental conditions specific to a particular region where a conflict is taking place. This is a very effective information-based attack since the dependency on the information system is so subtle that even if the effect were noticed, it might be a long time before the root cause was discovered.

It turns out that almost every small business depends indirectly on some larger businesses, and vice versa. Consider how even the largest business gets its plumbing fixed when there is a leak. The vast majority of these cases are handled through very small businesses, even in companies with internal maintenance staffs. But those very small businesses in turn depend on not-so-small distributors for their parts, which depend on medium-sized and big businesses for the manufacturing of those parts, all of which depend on those small plumbing businesses for their plumbing.

So what does plumbing have to do with the information infrastructure? It's simple. Without properly working information infrastructure, the big businesses that make the parts the plumber uses would likely be unable to continue operating. The plumbers would not be able to get parts, and thus would not be able to fix the leaks. If no plumbing could be done, we would all be in (to quote a recent government official) deep doodoo. The leaks and plumbing problems would result in failures in electrical systems (due to short circuits), water damage, and eventually, air conditioning failures. Now this is key. Air conditioners depend heavily on plumbing, and the bigger the air conditioner, the more it needs to be plumbed regularly. The really big air conditioners are used to cool large office buildings, and without those cooling systems operating, the temperature increases inside those buildings by as much as 50 degrees in the summer. Now, in addition to the obvious side effect that it is uncomfortable to work in extreme heat, the effect of heat on computers is particularly devastating. At around 120 degrees, most computers will only run for a matter of an hour or two before breaking down with a hardware failure. So, as all of the computers fail, the phone system no longer works, the information infrastructure begins to fail, and as a result, operators can no longer call in a plumber to fix the air conditioners.

Now this may seem a little bit like a Rube Goldberg setup, and that's part of my point. We live in an age where we all depend on each other.

2.6   THE INFORMATION SUPERHIGHWAY

In the great depression of the 1930s and 1940s, the government of the United States created the Works Progress Administration (WPA) to employ jobless workers in the task of building up the national infrastructure. This government program not only kept millions of U.S. citizens working and eating, it also built a great deal of the transportation and recreation infrastructure our people now depend on. One of the results was greatly improved efficiency in transportation over the last 60 years, reducing the costs of goods, enabling many businesses to form and prosper that could not have existed without the infrastructure, and affecting the lives of hundreds of millions of people for the better. It is a legacy that has passed the test of time. It's not that highway development stopped when the WPA stopped. In fact, after World War II, many of the highways we use today were built over or near the sites used for the highways of the 1930s and 1940s. This infrastructure investment was the beginning of the replacement of the rail transportation system with the automotive transportation system that dominates in the United States today.

Perhaps as a part of the effort to help end the great recession of the late 1980s and early 1990s, the government of the United States has decided to support and encourage another infrastructure. This time, it is an information infrastructure.

> Just as transportation was a key component of success in the industrial age, communication is and will continue to be a key component of success in the information age.

Just as the transportation capabilities built in the 1930s and 1940s made many things possible that would have been impossible without that infrastructure, the communication capabilities built in the 1990s and 2000s will make things possible that would be impossible without this infrastructure. The improved efficiency will be reflected in dramatic changes in the way our society operates.

Communication Replaces Transportation

Some speculate that the urbanization of the twentieth century will be replaced by a more and more rural economy in which people can live in beautiful country settings, own substantial amounts of land, and yet work for a large corporation whose nearest office is hundreds of miles away. If this seems hard to believe, consider that for the last eight months, I have worked most of my time from my home for a billion-dollar corporation whose nearest employee's office is more than 100 miles away from me. I have never been to that office, but I have visited offices all over the United States and in Europe for short periods for various reasons. Most of these visits would not have been needed if a good videoconferencing facility were available.

Some speculate that communication between people will replace transportation of people to a large extent. The almost universal availability of video conferencing and distributed computing that will begin in the second half of the 1990s will allow many, if not most, information workers to work from home more of the time. The resulting effect on the environment, the reduced loading on the transportation infrastructure, the increased time available for workers with their families, and the increased flexibility in work schedule, will produce dramatic and fundamental changes in the way our society works.

Of course, transportation will not be completely eliminated. For example, it will still be necessary to transport food and other goods. Service-oriented jobs will require increased transportation to get to the customer base. People who want to go shopping will have further to travel, and regional stores will probably provide delivery services much as delivery services thrived in the earlier part of the century.

It is possible, likely, perhaps even closer to certain that this facet of this issue will have the most dramatic and vitally important effect on all of our lives of anything discussed so far. And yet the reason is so far afield that to even mention it may seem bizarre. Since the beginning of recorded history, there have been plagues that have wiped out on the order of 90 percent of the human race in a locality. These diseases have sprung up seemingly overnight, ravaged a society till near destruction, and then gone away as the population was so diminished that nobody susceptible was left to kill.

These plagues killed more than 90 percent of the American Indians when they first interacted with the Europeans, killed more than 90 percent of the citizens of some cities in the 1800s, and killed more than 90 percent of the people in the small villages they hit in the 1980s in Zaire. In the case of the Ebola Zaire virus, the difference between killing 90 percent of the people in a few cities and killing ninety percent of the people in the whole world, was very likely the remoteness of those populations relative to the rest of the world population at those times. [39]

But with modern transportation making the distance between people so short, an airborne disease in Australia may be carried to the United States on a 747 in a matter of a day. With the movement of those 400 passengers to other flights when they arrive in the United States, in a matter of 48 to 72 hours, such a disease may reach the vast majority of the population of the U.S.

So how does this relate to the information superhighway? As the world moves toward replacing transportation with communication, people will also be dramatically curtailing the spread of biological disease. If the airline steward who seeded so much of the AIDS epidemic in the United States had not been travelling, perhaps hundreds of thousands of lives would have been saved.

If the change is dramatic enough, information technology could prevent the next major plague from wiping out much of the population of our country. On the other side of this coin, increased exposure to diseases causes increased immunity for the survivors. The reason so many American Indians died when the Europeans came was, at least in part, because the Europeans had been exposed to such a high degree that they were all immune. In the cases of pneumonic plague and Ebola Zaire, immunity is not likely to play a very big factor, since each is so fatal so quickly.

Efficiency Trades with Adaptability

In a technologically driven field under rapid change, there is a very heavy penalty for being unable to adapt quickly. Take for example the large mainframe users of today. Even six years ago, most of these organizations had few options to using a mainframe to perform their large scale computations, but today, they are stuck paying several million dollars per system and several hundred thousand dollars per year in maintenance to support computers that could be replaced for about $10,000 if it weren't for the software investment in the old computers. Over the last six years, the hardware cost has gone down by a factor of 64, while the software and maintenance costs have not substantially changed. Even going to a lower-cost mainframe only partially resolves this issue because mainframes still don't support many of the new applications and capabilities that have emerged in the last several years.

This problem is related to the astounding improvements in information technology over more than 20 years. Every two to three years, the cost of information technology has dropped by about a factor of 2, while the performance of that technology has multiplied by about a factor of 2. That comes to an effective increase in the *bang-for-the-buck* of about a factor of 2 per year. In terms of value for your dollar, performance that cost 1 million dollars six years ago now costs 1/64 of that, or only about ten thousand dollars.

Meanwhile, the Internal Revenue Service (IRS) still forces you to write off computer equipment as a capital expense over a five-year period, even though two-year-old computers are obsolete in many business applications today. For example, in 1992, a PC with 500 megabytes of disk space cost about $5,000, and was a rarity. By 1994, most computers sold included more than 250 megabytes of disk space, cost less than $2,000, and systems with more than 1 gigabyte of disk space were common. Most of the systems sold in 1992 cannot support the disk requirements of the software sold for systems in 1994.

Investment with falling prices, rising performance, and rising capabilities must be shortened to reduce momentum and enable change to be handled more quickly and efficiently. To do this, I return to a law of physics, $f = ma$. To change more quickly, either more force must be applied, weight must be reduced, or both. When you increase force in organizations (e.g., by applying more money or pushing people to change), it puts more pressure on people. You can only push so far before the organization cracks under the strain of these pressures. The only alternative is to reduce the mass, or in other terms, reduce the dependency on the leverage provided by any specific technological element. In the process, _rease your adaptability, but reduce efficiency, and thus introduce inefficiency in exchange for the flexibility.

Dependency Effects of the Information Superhighway

The Achilles heel of building our society to run on the information superhighway is our increased dependency and our lack of adequate protection. It is likely that over time, the people who design information systems, schools, government agencies, businesses, military organizations, and infrastructure will build even more dependency on information infrastructure into our society. As we have seen, the people of the United States are so dependent today that in some cases, we literally cannot survive without information systems. As we follow this new road, we may soon reach the point of no return.

People have always had dependencies, but rarely have people depended so much on something so fragile as today's information systems. We must all take great pains to understand the nature of this fragility and to address it effectively, if we are to survive.

"The benefits of the NII for the nation are immense. An advanced information infrastructure will enable U.S. firms to compete and win in the global economy, generating good jobs for the American people and economic growth for the nation. As importantly, the NII can transform the lives of the American people—ameliorating the constraints of geography, disability, and economic status—giving all Americans a fair opportunity to go as far as their talents and ambitions will take them." [153]

But this will only be true if the NII can get the right information to the right place at the right time. Recent studies have shown that U.S. industries lose billions of dollars per year because of disruptions in their information systems, [16, 58] and the loss is increasing year by year.

"In addition, it is essential that the FEDERAL government work with the communications industry to reduce the vulnerability of the nation's information infrastructure. The NII must be designed and managed in a way that minimizes the impact of accident or sabotage. The system must also continue to function in the event of attack or catastrophic natural disaster." [153]

The U.S. economy now depends for its very survival on the information infrastructure. With the inclusion of new services including national health care, access to state and local government information, financial records, and health records, under the promise of the NII, that dependence will grow.

CHAPTER 3

The Disrupters Are Among Us

When I talk about problems in information systems, one of the most common responses I get is that my depiction is inherently pessimistic. If systems are as vulnerable as I say they are, why isn't there already a global collapse? My best responses are:

- There is a global collapse, you just aren't aware of it.
- The crooks haven't caught up yet, but they will soon.
- They don't want to kill the goose that laid the golden egg.

I personally try to understand this issue by studying the causes of information system failures in detail, classifying the causes and effects, and trying to understand how and why things are the way they are. Many experts also use lists of incidents to consider the efficacy of protection. To give an idea of the sorts of incidents that may cause disruption to components of the NII, I have included a broad but not comprehensive set of descriptions of accidents, attacks, motives, perpetrators, and effects.

In order to interpret descriptions of this sort it is vital to understand that these lists are not exhaustive. They represent only a small portion of the things encountered in a typical career in this field. These descriptions are intended to give a general sense of the breadth and magnitude of the problems in information protection in the NII and an understanding of why the issues of protection need to be carefully examined.

3.1 COMPUTER ACCIDENTS

Information system problems are commonly broken down into accidental and intentional acts. Most information technology managers recognize that accidents happen and consider protection from accidents to be part of the cost of doing business. It is common to differentiate accidents into acts of God or nature and acts or inaction by human beings, but I will not explicitly differentiate them here.

As an example of the impact of disruption on organizations, a survey of denial of services identified about 4 billion dollars of losses in 1992 alone. [16] This survey doesn't even begin to address the sources of disruption or differentiate intentional from accidental disruption, but it should give an idea of the extent of the problem.

Errors and omissions This is probably the most widely recognized disruptive phenomena today. Everyone makes mistakes, and when these mistakes affect information systems, even a small mistake can be severe. More than one rocket has blown up because of a + sign instead of a − sign in a computer program. [181] In one case, there was a jet aircraft automatic pilot that flipped the plane upside down when it went south of the equator because of such an error. It would have been a fun flight if the flaw wasn't detected in a simulation run. Errors and omissions have been responsible for many other incidents, including several cases where lives were lost.

> Examples of loss of life include overdoses of radiation due to programming errors in medical equipment with only software safety provisions and several commercial airline crashes related to autopilot problems. [181]

Power failure Power failures have caused major outages in information system operations ever since computers became more reliable than the power system. A typical home computer operates for several years without a hardware problem, while power failures happen several times per year for short periods of time in most U.S. locations. If your computer is on and writing to the disk when the power fails, you could lose the entire contents of the disk. In larger systems, the problem is far more severe. In one incident in the 1970s, the power to the computers in the computer science department at Carnegie-Mellon University failed, even though they had two separate power lines coming into their computer center. It turned out that a backhoe cut the wire between where the two power sources entered the university and the point of presence in the building. Backhoes may be the single most dangerous weapon of the information age. Power disruptions capable of interfering with computer operations in my company's data centers have averaged between one per week and one per month over a 10-year period, and these figures are not unusual.

Cable cuts The rare power failures caused by a cable cut are only a symptom of the backhoe disease. Cases of communication cables being cut seem to be almost epidemic. When a communications cable is cut, it physically disrupts communications that would otherwise operate over that cable. For example, if the cable to an office building is cut, the entire building may lose communications. With the increased bandwidth of cables caused by technological advances, we have used fewer cables to carry more data, which makes this problem far worse. For example, a fiber optic cable can carry about 375,000 telephone calls, so a fiber optic cable cut may disrupt all of the calls taking place at any one time in a major city. Recent famous examples include a cable cut in New York City that disconnected air traffic control for much of the northeastern United States and a cable cut in upstate New York that disconnected the 18 supposedly redundant Internet connections between New England and the rest of the United States. All 18 connections ran through the same fiber-optic cable. There are also many less spectacular cable cuts, and it is almost certain that every organization will experience at least one incident every few years.

Fire Fire has been a leading cause of death and destruction ever since cities became popular. Legend has it that Nero played the fiddle while Rome burned several thousand years ago. [159] Although Nero was apparently not involved, Rome did indeed burn. Fire physically destroys equipment and inventory of all sorts, including backup tapes, communications wires, switching equipment, and information systems. It also tends to make repair very difficult because all traces of the previous configuration are lost in a typical fire.

In Chicago, in the spring of 1990, a telephone company central office fire resulted in lost telephone service to tens of thousands of customers for a period of several months. [160] If you were in the telephone-based mail-order business in the affected area, you were almost certainly out of business fast. Insurance may cover fire damage, but few policies cover the consequential damage resulting from loss of use of information systems affected by fire.

Flood Floods have a tendency to happen in low-lying areas and stream beds, and few natural floods since the one Noah was in have had a severe effect on the second story of buildings on hillsides. On the other hand, the Johnstown flood which involved a broken dam in Johnstown, Pennsylvania, did destroy many two-story buildings on the hillsides downstream of the dam. Floods tend to short out electrical connections, which are the heart of information systems. Although many parts of many information systems can survive water, almost all systems are at least temporarily disrupted. The major floods in the midwest in 1993 disrupted information systems in many buildings. But an even more interesting flood from my perspective was the Chicago flood of 1992. In this case, underground waters were held back from the nineteenth-century underground tunnel system of Chicago by walls that were poorly maintained. When one particular wall broke down, there were major power and telephone outages throughout the city. Almost everyone was caught unaware because they never thought of Chicago as being very susceptible to floods.

Earth movement In zones where earthquakes are common, it is also quite common to have earth movement produce outages in information systems. Earth movement causes vibrations that disrupt internal connections between information system components, disrupt power, cause disk drives to physically destroy themselves, and disrupt wiring. In the Los Angeles earthquake of 1993, telephone service and electrical power were unavailable to hundreds of thousands of people for several days. The effect on information systems was obviously severe, but it didn't get much press coverage because next to the human suffering, it wasn't considered very important. Many businesses may have taken a long time to recover their information systems. Other forms of earth movement include mud slides, sink holes, and other similar phenomena. Although these forms of earth movement are comparatively local, they can still cause significant disruption.

Solar flares Solar flares increase background radio frequency noise which interferes with communication. Solar flares also increase the number of cosmic rays, which collide with computer memory elements and sometimes cause transient bit errors. In one case, solar flares interfered with the Global Positioning System (GPS), causing errors in displayed position. [181] With a GPS receiver, you can locate your position in the space around Earth to within about ten meters. With some careful calibration, you can get within about two meters, and by using enough statistical information, you can get an even more exact location. GPS is now used in military operations and has been accepted by the Federal Aviation Administration (FAA) for use in commercial aircraft guidance.

Volcanos Volcanic eruptions are fairly rare events in most of the world, but there are still many active volcanos. Most active volcanos generate lava flows on an ongoing basis, but when the rare one blows, it can change a lot of things in the environment that affect information systems. The Mt. St. Helens eruption in the 1980s was an example of a catastrophic eruption, while Hawaii deals with lava flows all of the time. The major problems for information systems in volcanic eruption come when physical destruction from the volcano interferes with parts of the infrastructure being used to support information systems and when small ash from the volcano becomes widely disbursed and causes physical damage to disk drives and other similar devices.

Severe weather, static electricity, air conditioning loss, etc. Severe weather causes many effects on information technology. For example, high temperatures tend to make air conditioning fail, which in turn causes overheating, which destroys computers very quickly. Low temperatures tend to make relative humidity low, which increases static electricity, and this can also destroy computers. Thunderstorms cause lightning, which strikes buildings and causes power fluctuations that destroy information systems. Extreme weather also affects other aspects of the infrastructure which cause indirect effects on information systems. Hurricanes are one severe example of how weather can damage information systems. Large hurricanes tend to disrupt substantial portions of the power grid, telecommunications, and other infrastructure elements. They also physically destroy computer centers and other elements of the information infrastructure of individuals and organizations.

Relocating computers Relocating computers sometimes causes enough vibration to disrupt the delicate alignment of disk drives, which in turn makes disks unusable. In one case at a major university, a computer system was moved only a few feet and yet sustained total loss of disk storage. Fortunately, backups were done just before the move to cover this contingency, and the loss was minimal. Although computer components are increasingly designed to sustain movement without substantial damage, there are still physical forces that can damage components and their interconnections.

System maintenance In another incident at the same university, a hardware maintenance person came in and realigned the tape heads of a tape drive to compensate for mechanical skew as a part of regular maintenance. After the maintenance person departed, old tapes could no longer be read. The cure was to properly misalign the tape head so the improperly written tapes could be read, read in the tapes, realign the tape heads to the proper setting, and rewrite the tapes.

> Many disruptions occur from system maintenance, but without maintenance, many other disruptive factors might go undetected.

Testing The whole point of testing is to find problems before they impact users. Once problems are found, they can be fixed. A common problem encountered today is that test modes are often available at times when they should not be. When this happens, many undesired side effects are possible. In one incident, a test of computer viruses at AT&T resulted in the accidental infection of the master copy of AT&T's supposedly secure version of the UNIX^{TM} operating system. [75] It seems the testing mode was being used in that system, and it introduced a vulnerability. In a similar incident, the Internet Virus entered through a testing capability that was left enabled in a standard distribution of Sun's version of the UNIX operating system. [115] [114] It is fairly common for people to test uninterruptable power supplies, but it is also fairly common to forget to turn off the information systems they support before testing. If the power supply fails, so do the information systems it supports.

Inadequate maintenance Inadequate maintenance can be just as hazardous as inappropriate maintenance. The whole purpose of maintenance is to find and correct problems before they have a serious impact on operations. Many modern information systems cannot operate over an extended period of time without maintenance. As a simple example, sophisticated information systems often produce audit records. If these audit records are never examined or deleted, they are of no value, and they may cause the system to fail by consuming so much space that the information system runs out of storage.

Humidity High humidity causes electronics to fail because it causes short circuits, but perhaps it is more dangerous to paper, which absorbs the water from the air, weakens, and rots. On the other hand, if paper is kept too dry, it will become brittle and crack. In humid environments, microorganisms thrive, and they tend to eat everything from the rubber in cars to the plastic in computer circuit boards. In dry environments, many materials become very brittle and misshaped. For example, the circuit boards used in computers may crack, disk drives may warp, power supplies may change characteristics, fan lubrication may dry up, static charges may accumulate in video displays, mechanical switches on pointing devices may fail, and wires connecting components may break. Needless to say, this can cause serious problems.

Smoke Smoke often causes more damage than fire. In the case of information systems, smoke causes serious damage in unsealed components. For example, a floppy disk drive has an electromagnetic read-write head with tolerances about the width of a human hair. If smoke gets in the system, the disk head may fail. Even the fans used to cool systems become less reliable when smoke comes along, because it causes friction in the bearings and can gum up air filters, causing cooling to become inefficient, and producing heat-related damage. Other components, such as integrated circuits, depend on air flow for cooling. Smoke may deposit added insulation that reduces the cooling effect and increases thermal damage.

Dust If you've ever opened a computer that has been running for a few years without an internal cleaning, you have found an enormous amount of dust. Dust accumulates because the fan typically blows air through a system to cool the components which have higher failure rates at higher temperature. As the dust enters the system, it is trapped in areas with low air flow, and it accumulates, causing larger areas of low air flow, and so on. Over time, a computer can accumulate so much dust that cooling becomes ineffective and failure rates go up.

Gasses, fumes, and cleaning chemicals But don't rush in with a regular cleaning person to clean all your computers. I made the mistake of letting a cleaning person come in and clean my dusty computers one day, and nearly paid the price in a big way. It turned out that the cleaning chemicals used on the dust rag got into the electronics and caused a temporary short circuit resulting in a system failure. After the fluids dried, the system worked again, but it was a bit scary to have the system go down from disk failures just as the cleaning person sprayed cleaning chemicals into the disk-drive enclosure. Various gasses and fumes cause plastic enclosures to fail. Among the effects are damage to sealed disk drives and loosened connections. In some cases, the chemicals are changed by the increased temperature inside a computer and this can cause chemical reactions that cause other damage.

Heat Several of the previous examples relate to heat. Increased heat causes failure rates in electronic and mechanical components to rise fairly dramatically. In studies of electronics done in the 1970s, it was found that for every 10 degrees celsius increase in temperature over the normal operating range of an integrated circuit, the mean time to failure was cut in half. In other words, on the average, a computer running at 15 degrees celsius that fails only once per 10 years will fail once per 5 years if operated at 25 degrees celsius. Mechanical systems have similar problems because as bearings get hot, they deform. This causes more friction, which increases the heat, which increases the deformation, and so forth. If you run a disk drive at a higher temperature, on the average, it will crash sooner.

Temperature cycling Lest you decide to keep turning your computer off to reduce heat damage, you should be aware that temperature cycling also causes damage. Metallic components expand and shrink as temperature changes, causing mechanical stresses which eventually cause breakage in the same way as bending a coat hanger back and forth will eventually break it. When you turn a computer on for several hours and then turn it off again for several hours, temperature cycling is most pronounced.

Electronic interference In several recent cases, signals from airport radar and similar sources have caused computers to fail and the interaction of emanations from information systems has been cited a number of times as a cause of system failures. [13] This is the reason the FAA now requires airline passengers to turn off personal computers and some other electronic equipment during takeoff and landing.

Vibration Electronic equipment that is shaken is subject to the same physical stresses as any other device. Under enough stress of the right characteristic, the equipment will fail. Most information systems are not designed for extensive shaking, dropping, or other such things, but there are components designed to handle such stresses. These components cost more, but in an environment where these stresses are common, they are well worth the price difference. For example, military equipment specifications require hardening against shaking and falling, and palmtop computers such as the HP-100 can fall from six feet onto pavement without significant damage.

Corrosion Anyone who has spent much time fixing computers or other electronic equipment is familiar with the effects of corrosion. The contacts between integrated circuit boards and the computer's backplane corrode, and this causes transient errors and, eventually, permanent faults. The common cure is to *reseat* the boards by removing them and putting them back in. Corrosion is usually caused by environmental factors.

3.2   INTENTIONAL EVENTS

Several authors have reported that once detection was put in place, over one incident per day was detected against their computers attached to the Internet. [19] [35] [179] Other people have placed detection systems on the Internet to detect attacks and have privately reported similar figures. There are about 2.5 million computers on the Internet, so simple multiplication tells us that something like 900 million attacks per year take place on the Internet alone.

   With that amount of computer crime underway, you might well ask where the superhighway patrol is. Unfortunately, it is a lot harder to patrol the information superhighways than the automotive superhighways, and unlike the highway patrol, there are no information police to speak of and they don't have information patrol cars.

The situation today in the infosphere is much the same as it was in the goesphere in the wild west. It's easy to steal from the weak and it's easy to avoid being caught. There are some law enforcement people out there, but they are few and far between and they have almost none of the tools required to get the job done. Information system users end up hiring private police that are often inadequate to the task.

Many of the most common attacks are listed here to give a flavor for the sorts of things people do to attack information systems. This list is by no means comprehensive, but it gives a flavor of the variety of events that may occur.

Trojan horses A Trojan horse is a hardware or software component that has an unadvertised side effect. The term is normally used to indicate a malicious side effect, and comes from an ancient war in which the Greeks were being defeated on the battlefield by the Trojans. In desperation, the Greeks gave a giant wooden statue of a horse to the Trojans. The Trojans took the horse into their walled fortress, and that night, the Greeks hiding in the statue came out and opened the gates to the fortress. The Greeks entered and massacred the Trojans—thus, the expression, *Beware of Greeks bearing gifts*. In computers, a Trojan horse can be used to deny services, to corrupt information, or to leak secret information. Many examples of Trojan horses appear every day in the information business.

Time bombs A time bomb in an information system is just the analogy of a physical time bomb. Once the time bomb is activated, it detonates at a later time, resulting in some damaging effect. A time bomb can potentially deny services, corrupt information, and/or leak secrets. A software time bomb might try to delete all of the files on a system, while a hardware time bomb might cause a component to fail. Another way of looking at this is by considering planned obsolescence. In products warranted for one year, it is common to have hardware failures just after the end of the warranty period. This is either because product testing shows that failures begin at that time, or because the parts used to make the system are selected for their low cost, and the price is set by the quality of the component. It is also possible to design systems to have very sharp changes in reliability after a well-defined point in time by exploiting the known failure characteristics in combination. [196] [102]

Use or condition bombs A use or condition bomb is just like a time bomb except that it is triggered by a number of uses or some other condition of the state of the environment. This practice has been used by some consultants to assure payment or to cause damage when they are fired. [211] A typical condition might be that the consultant's last login was more than three months ago. The effects of such an attack are often limited to the consultant's work product, but not always. In some cases, consultants who were not paid for a job claimed that a use or condition bomb was their way of assuring payment. The courts have consistently ruled against these consultants.

Dumpster diving A lot of people in today's society throw away a lot of things without realizing their potential value. Information is commonly discarded when stored in paper form, and even old magnetic tapes and floppy disks are commonly thrown in the garbage when they have outlived their usefulness to the owner. The information contained in these forms may be quite helpful to an attacker. In trying to break into systems, it is now a common practice for attackers to go to the dumpsters used for disposal of waste in search of information that may lead to easier entry or more successful attack. Similarly, some waste disposal companies have been accused of selling waste paper to people in search of information. The police also commonly search garbage for evidence, and this is certainly not beyond the scope of work for a spy. Some of the most famous AT&T attacks came about as a result of dumpster divers getting copies of manuals for systems. In exceptional cases, listings of user IDs and passwords are found in dumpsters.

> In many organizations, old backup tapes are thrown out when they begin to have faults during backups. Under these circumstances, a dumpster diver may get a full on-line copy of a lot of corporate information, including password files and details of internal controls.

Fictitious people In the current Internet, it is fairly easy to create as many personas as desired. Little authentication is done to verify the identity of anyone willing to pay for services. One author suggested that there is a risk of people taking on multiple fictitious identities and providing several different viewpoints that all combine to recommend the same product or service. By placing enough opinions that lead to the same conclusion into a widely read forum, you may be able to set a trend that results in people believing lies. By making friends with people of different opinions, you may choose which identity to use when talking to each. False identities are good leaping off points for all sorts of crime. For example, in September of 1994, somebody used a false identity to threaten to kill the President of the United States via electronic mail. This was done using an identity provided on a FreeNet—a community-provided public service access point to the Internet.

Protection limit poking In most systems, information storage, retrieval, analysis, and communications services can be denied to one user by another. For example, many password protection schemes only allow a user to try to login a fixed number of times before they must see an administrator to have their user ID reinstated. An example of an attack would be to try to login to the other user's account using a wrong password. Once the limit is reached, the other user cannot access the system and is forced to go through an administrator to regain access. If the defense against password guessing is improperly implemented, incorrectly guessing the administrator's password can be used to prevent the administrator from logging in. If the administrator is the only one who can restore access and the administrator's access is disabled to stop further password guessing, the system may have to be shut down and manually modified in order to restore normal operation.

E-mail overflow In this attack, electronic mail (E-mail) is used to flood computer systems with information, thus reducing available resources for other purposes. In experimental attacks, this technique was shown to be very effective in denying services, [63] and several incidents since that time have demonstrated the same results with accidental causes. [222]

The experimental attacks consisted of sending electronic mail to computers throughout the U.S. military network from the Internet. In the first experiment, E-mail was sent to the 'root' user at each of 68 sites chosen from a (German) Chaos Computer Club listing. This was done to establish that mail sent to most of them would be received and stored in their computers. The following table describes the results:

Number	Response
40	got the mail—no response
10	refused the mail
1	no root user, identified self as 'TSO'
2	no such user ID, listed other user IDs
2	no user called 'root' on their system
7	not found by the mail system
6	got the mail—personal response

The second experiment consisted of sending mass quantities of mail into one site (done on an isolated computer designated for that purpose) to see how it affected operations. The first effect was a slight slowing of other processes on the system, presumably due to the disk output and processing required to process and store all of the mail. The second effect was consumption of all available disk space in the '/usr' partition of the disk. The target system had about 18 Mbytes of free space on that partition, and it took only 4.5 minutes to exhaust it, at which point the system started having severe problems because it could not create or add to files. The system console indicated that no disk space was available on that disk partition.

It typically takes about 30 minutes to find the specific problem in such an incident (in this case, the files consuming all of the disk space) once the systems administrator is able to login to the system. On some systems, the administrator cannot login properly without adequate disk space, but either way, the net effect is a half an hour or more of denial of services, corruption, and repudiation. The lack of disk space causes many programs to fail, and if you are unable to write a file to disk, it is hard to do much useful work. Files being written when there is no space left typically end up in an inconsistent state. Most programs dealing with files do not detect and properly handle these conditions, so the corruption goes unnoticed for the moment. Audit trails take disk space, and since there is none available, they cannot log the side effects of this disruption for later analysis. Depending on details of the implementation, the audit program may even stop operating entirely. After the problem is found, there is an even bigger problem. How does the administrator prevent this attack and still allow legitimate mail to pass? It turns out that this is not so simple in most modern computer mail systems.

After posting this information to the risks forum on the Internet, numerous replies asserted that this attack was not properly defended on existing systems. [181] One respondent pointed out that electronic fax and news transmissions had similar problems, and are not adequately addressed by many current systems. Some time after this experiment was published, an accidental disruption occurred when a law firm tried to advertise on the Internet and was flooded with hate mail. The service provider used by the law firm had to shut down because of the disruptive effect of all the e-mail.

Infrastructure interference By sending signals to a satellite or microwave dish, it's fairly easy to interfere with signals and disrupt these elements of the NII on a wide scale. One example was the Home Box Office (HBO) attack launched in the late 1980s where someone with a satellite dish sent his own signal to HBO listeners all over the United States. [166]

Infrastructure observation Radio signals are also fairly easy to observe. For example, the microwave dishes that used to carry many of the conversations into and out of Washington, D.C. passed their signals right over the Russian Embassy. It is widely believed that the mass of radio equipment in the embassy was used, at least partially, to listen to telephone conversations passing over this microwave link.

Sympathetic vibration Most modern communications protocols are designed to deal with common types of delay problems such as packets arriving too late to be of value. But the mechanisms used for retransmission are designed for reliability under random fault conditions and not under intentional attack. By creating packet feedback mechanisms, it is almost always possible to cause a network to overload with protocol packets, thus disrupting services. In some cases, this has even happened accidentally. [80] [156] Even modern electronic mail (e-mail) systems are susceptible to this sort of disruption. For example, there are many automatic mail responders on the Internet. These systems listen for incoming e-mail requesting standard information and respond by mailing the standard response back to the sender. By forging a sender identity, which is trivially done on the Internet, the response can be sent to another automatic mail responder. The two mail responders may then eternally send more and more mail back and forth in automatic response, flooding the Internet with junk mail and causing widespread havoc.

Human engineering This is a favorite of many attackers. The weakest links in many protection systems are the people, and the easiest way to exploit the weakness is by convincing the people you have a legitimate purpose. If you look and talk like a maintenance person, the receptionist will probably treat you like one. Several television shows have filmed and shown attacks where teenagers call into a company and act as if they are telephone repair people who lost the password to the maintenance computer or left their phone list at home. They then get the maintenance phone number and password from the operator and enter the telephone network as a privileged user from a pay phone free of charge. A skilled attacker can easily change billing information, make calls to anywhere in the world, and disrupt telephone service once such information is obtained.

Bribes In many cases, the worst paid employees are in the best position to attack information systems. For example, the night watchman is typically a low paid, transient worker. For $20, you can probably bribe the night watchman to use the telephone to call your brother in Iowa. Chances are you will be left alone to rummage through the facility if you use the technique right. For a bit more money, you can probably bribe maintenance people to let you take one of their shifts. After all, they get paid for doing nothing, and you get the run of the place. The net effect is a collapse of many of the physical security precautions that may have been in place, and with physical access, there is no limit to the potential techniques that can be used for leakage, denial, and corruption.

Get a job Bribes are quite limited. If you want to do a better job of attacking a system, why not apply for a job as a night janitor. The security check is probably minimal, and in many cases you will have unlimited access to the whole facility all night. Best of all, you get paid to launch the attack. It is also fairly easy to get a job as a computer operator or night operations manager if you forge the proper background. That might even get you authorized access to many of the information systems and make your attack far easier.

Password guessing The practice of guessing passwords has existed since ancient times. The reason that password guessing works so well is that people use easily guessed passwords, and the reason for this is inadequate training and inadequate use of technology. In an experiment I did in 1982, I successfully guessed more than 80 percent of the user passwords on a mainframe computer system trying only about 10 guesses per user. Similar experiments have been done by researchers for many years and, despite widespread dissemination of these results, the situation is much the same today.

Invalid values on calls In many computer systems, unanticipated requests for service (i.e., calls to the operating system with illegal or undocumented values) result in violations of protection. In DOS, where there is no protection in the operating system itself, many of the common activities such as spooling files to the printer require the use of undocumented operating system calls. This encourages abuse by outside vendors, and fosters incompatibility across versions of the operating system. In more advanced operating systems, protection is fairly effective except for implementation errors. One good example of an invalid call producing a negative result was in an early version of an IBM computer. In this system, there was an operating system call that shut down the computer by causing a physical mechanism to pull all of the boards out of the backplane. The call was not documented to users, and the people who implemented the operating system didn't protect the call from accidental or malicious use.

Computer viruses In every widely used operating system, protection is inadequate to limit the spread of computer viruses. Computer viruses are programs that reproduce. In the process, they may infect other programs which in turn infect other programs, and so they spread far and wide. There are now about 5,000 computer viruses known by researchers, and many more are created every day. The real threat of computer viruses is that they can act as vectors for spreading any other attack. With a computer virus, it is simple to corrupt data throughout an information network, to disrupt services on a wide scale, and to leak secrets from the best computer security systems available today. [44]

Data diddling Data diddling is a technique whereby data is illicitly modified. By illicitly modifying data, information systems may produce wrong results and, because few current information systems have integrity controls, these errors will likely remain undiscovered for a long time. Data diddling has been used to change salary rates, alter investment profiles, change patient records, and in all sorts of other ways. In most modern computer networks, data diddling can be done remotely without even entering the computer under attack by modifying information being sent through the network.

Packet insertion In most current networking environments, it is relatively easy to insert a packet forged to appear to be from a different source. There are even public domain programs that provide facilities to assist in this effort. Packet insertion has been used to replay financial transactions, gain entry into systems, bypass access controls, induce network control problems, and spoof file servers. In essence, anything that can be done from over a network legitimately can be done over the same network illegitimately. By inserting packets at the network level, all of the computer security in the computers that are connected to the network is defeated. [40]

Packet watching In most current networking environments, it is also relatively easy to observe packets flowing between networked computers. Some of the public domain software allows the listener to isolate traffic between particular sites and observe terminal sessions, including the entry of user identities and passwords. In one experiment at Queensland University of Technology, a graduate student under my direction implemented a simple program to analyze network traffic and produce terminal sessions between user and computer pairs. [42] [40] In a very similar effort detected in early 1994, thousands of user identities and passwords were stolen from computers attached to the Internet computer network. [5] The attackers have not yet been identified.

Van Eck bugging In the 1980s, a paper was published describing experiments that enabled a remote observer to use electromagnetic emanations from a video display to watch the display. [220] Since that time many people have shown that it is possible to electronically watch a typical video display from a location on the other side of a wall or from hundreds of meters away.

In one case, a British television station used this sort of equipment to show that Scotland Yard's computers could be observed from outside the building.

Conducted emanations over power lines can also be exploited to extract data from some computer systems. For a cost of only a few hundred dollars, anyone with the desire and knowledge to do so can observe information appearing on your video terminals in real-time, thus leaking information as it is created or used and gaining detailed knowledge of how it is used and by whom.

Electronic interference Normal air traffic control radar can cause interference and intermittent failures in computer equipment within a radius of several hundred meters. [13] Energy signals of sufficient strength can jam LAN cables, serial cables, keyboard connectors, mouse cables, and other electromagnetic devices. [27] In electrical power systems, it is fairly easy to induce noise characteristics that can cause computer failures as well. It is fairly common for electrical noise from rotating machines like electric saws and drills to do this. This can be used to cause random corruptions or denial of services.

Federal Aviation Administration (FAA) measurements of electromagnetic interference at one high-density U.S. airport peaked at 14,000 volts per meter from surveillance and satellite tracking radars. The FAA set a 200 volts/meter *no adverse effects* limit for one aircraft, partly due to rapid movement of both aircraft and radar beam. [13] Thus, the noise levels from our own infrastructure's safety equipment introduces adverse effects to our own aircraft.

PBX bugging Many modern telephone systems provide the capability to listen in on conversations, even when the telephone is hung up. The most common method is to set the *time till the on-hook condition causes the microphone to close* parameter in the PBX to an unexpected value. In many systems, this will leave the call engaged. The attacker then enables a conference call with that headset and listens in. This allows anyone with access to your PBX to listen in on private conversations in any office that uses the system without the people in the office either being aware of the interception or able to detect that the attack is underway. The next time you are in an important meeting in a room with a telephone, you should consider the possible consequences.

Open microphone listening Many current computers are shipped with microphones for voice input. Soon after the first of these systems was shipped, attackers found that they could listen to the voice input when the normal voice input programs were not functioning. This enables any-one with a minimal amount of access to listen to conversations without alerting the user. This technique can be used to record or listen to private conversations, to tell when people are or are not present, to listen to keyboard input and derive passwords, and in low noise environments, to listen to conversations in other rooms. Even after this technique was widely known, some of the major manufacturers of systems with this problem continued to produce systems with no mechanical microphone switch or activity light. [181]

Video viewing Some of the newest multimedia systems have video input capabilities to facilitate video conferencing. Just as microphones are com-monly left unprotected, video input devices commonly have no switch and are controlled by a computer which can be broken into over the network. Video viewing can be used to watch keystrokes, to see how people behave, to see who comes by and in offices, to see when people are in or out, to determine police and maintenance schedules, and to read plans and other documentation. When used in the home, private lifestyle information may also be attained. When used as a cable television inter-face device in a bedroom, the violation of privacy can be extreme. Again, the manufacturers have not responded, and in most current video input systems, attackers can watch and record what happens without alerting the user. [181]

Repair, replace, and remove information Some computer repair shops reuse old disks as replacements for a broken disk. Still others apparently extract data from disks before they reconfigure them. Under these con-ditions it is easy to take information from the disk and use or resell it. In one case I know of, a bank sold used computers without removing information from the disk drives. The result was a substantial amount of private information getting into a place it was not supposed to be.

Wire closet attacks Most buildings have wire closets that are used to connect information systems and power systems. It is often easier to gain access to these rooms than other parts of a facility. Once access is attained, wires can be tapped, cut, rerouted, wired together, or otherwise altered. Most facilities have poor documentation of how their wire rooms are configured. In a few hours, it is often possible to do enough damage in one wire closet in an office building to affect hundreds of workers over a period of a week or more. Consider how easily a telephone answering service could be damaged in this way.

Shoulder surfing This attack has been used since the earliest days of com-puting and is now commonly used by people who steal telephone access codes. The idea is to watch someone enter a password or PIN number and then to reuse it. In many environments, people are unaware of the possibility of shoulder surfing. For example, at the National Computer Security Center (NCSC) of the National Security Agency (NSA) in 1986, I was in the director's corner office, and noticed that the keyboard and video screen could easily be observed from outside the building.

Many people feel uncomfortable asking someone to look away while they type a password. This is a social custom that has to change if we are to continue using passwords as we do today. Once a password or PIN is attained, anything the original user could do can be done by the attacker, and the original user will likely be blamed for the results, at least for a little while.

Toll fraud networks In one modern version of shoulder surfing, people watch telephone credit card users enter their phone card information and quickly pass it to people throughout the U.S. via bulletin boards or other electronic media. In some cases, hundreds of thousands of dollars in telephone services have been stolen in a matter of hours. It is quite common for people to break into PBX systems with voice mail and use these systems to store telephone access codes for others to use. The average PBX-based toll fraud loss is more than $40,000.

Data aggregation Seemingly innocuous data can often be combined to get confidential information. [71] Perhaps one of the most impressive uses of information for tracking a person's movements was the use of credit card and other electronic records to track comedian John Belushi's movements in the last days of his life. In this case, an author wrote a book detailing exactly where he had been, what he had done, and who he had been with from minute to minute using electronic records.

Process bypassing A variety of semiautomatic processes are used in modern businesses. For example, a teller at a bank may make an entry indicating that you deposited $100 today. In this case, at the end of the day, the money in the cash drawers is added up, so an obvious fraud will be detected before too long. But in some of these processes, the checks are not as straightforward or well designed. In a typical case, a data entry clerk entered data indicating that a product had been returned when it had not. The result was that the system generated a check for a refund to the customer. Once the clerk noticed this flaw, she began to enter numerous returns that did not exist, and arranged for the checks to be forwarded to a friend. She took the money and ran. Whenever there is a process of this sort without adequate controls, such a fraud is possible.

Backup theft In cases where a lot of information is desired with a minimum of effort, it is commonly easier to take a backup tape than enter a system through the normal means. By borrowing a backup tape for a short period of time, it is usually possible to copy the contents and return the tape before it is missed. Security on backups is often far less stringent than on information systems. For example, many backups are transported to off-site storage facilities using common carriers. They may be left in piles at shipping docks for hours or days. In many cases, they are kept at the desk of a systems administrator whose office is not in the protected area of the computer room. Backup tapes often have all of the information on a system in plaintext form. By getting a copy of the backup tape, both the data and the programs become available for analysis. A serious attacker wanting to launch an attack against a live system may well decide to get a backup first, so that they can thoroughly test their attacks in a simulated environment before launching them for real.

Remote backups over local area networks are becoming increasingly popular, particularly for backing up large numbers of interconnected PCs. This means that an attacker can get a copy of a backup by watching LAN traffic. By forwarding that traffic through larger networks like the Internet, an attacker can watch backups from anywhere in the world.

Login spoofing When I was a professor at Lehigh University, I did an experiment where I logged into a timesharing computer system and ran a program that simulated the *login* screen. Whenever a user walked up to the screen, the program would simulate the login process, tell the user they had typed a bad password, terminate the program, and *logout*. When the user tried again, the login worked. Not one user noticed the attack and I was able to systematically gain user identity and password pairs, even from systems administrators. In the global networking environment, it is fairly simple to forge network identities. This can also be used for login spoofing.

Hangup hooking Modems don't always hang up the phone line instantly when the user hangs up the telephone. While I was still a professor at Lehigh University, I was demonstrating a login spoofing attack to the students in one of my information protection classes. I was logging into a remote computer, when much to everyone's surprise, another attack I had discussed previously was realized by accident. I had accidentally dialed into a remote computer and been attached to a previous user's account because the modem line they had been using didn't disconnect them before I dialed into the same phone line. If it can happen by accident, imagine how easy it must be to do intentionally.

Call forwarding fakery With modern telephone systems, it is common to use the caller-ID feature or dial-back capabilities to detect the source of an incoming call and route it appropriately. Attackers respond quickly to these sorts of technological defenses, and almost immediately came up with methods to use call forwarding to eliminate this defense. When a call-back modem is used, the attacker will forward calls from the call-back number to their location. When caller-ID is being used, they will forward the call through another number to break the link to their actual location. This is often done from telephone booths, so that eventually tracing back the call does not lead to the perpetrator without additional forensic evidence. Private Branch eXchanges (PBXs) can also be used as intermediaries to obscure the source of a call.

E-mail spoofing In one case, a computer operator erroneously took orders issued by his supervisor through electronic mail (e-mail). Since the electronic mail system was not secure at this installation, it was possible for any user to append data to the operator's incoming mail file. If the data was formatted correctly, there was no way to tell legitimate mail from a forgery. After several mysterious system crashes and file losses, the supervisor called the operator into his office to find out what was going on. The operator said that he was just following the supervisor's instructions, and that he could prove it! He logged into the system, and showed the surprised supervisor the forged messages.

> The vast majority of modern electronic mail systems allow forgeries to be made very simply, and many major corporations and government agencies use electronic mail as a major means of inter-office communication.

Input overflow In most implementations of higher-level computer languages, the most commonly used input routines do not check the length of input. Rather, they pack input characters into a finite-sized memory array starting at some memory location and continuing until an input terminating character is entered. If no bounds checking is done, it is easy for an attacker to create an input stream longer than the allocated area. The result is that the input data overwrites some other part of the computer's memory. Depending on what stored values the attacker overwrites, almost anything in the computer can be altered. This technique has been used in several attacks against electronic mail systems widely used in the Internet.

Illegal value insertion In many systems, illegal data values produce unpredicted behavior. For example, in some menu systems, entering a back-quote character (') followed by a command, followed by another back-quote may result in the command being executed outside of the menu system. Similarly, by using the '.sy' precursor to a line in a mail message in some mainframes, it is possible to gain control over the entire computer. I actually did this once as a demonstration on a production mainframe computer used by a major financial institution.

Induced stress failures Most systems can only sustain a certain level of stress before they begin to make mistakes. This may seem like a uniquely animal problem, but almost all current information systems have similar difficulties. The reason has to do with the fact that in order to keep costs low and allow flexibility, systems are almost always configured to allow one thing to be traded off against another. In the telephone system, for example, during very high call volume periods, calls don't always go through, you may get connected to a wrong number, or you may even get connected into an existing call. All of these things have happened to me. By intentionally seeking out or creating these situations, systems may be maliciously attacked.

False update disks An increasingly common way to enter a system is by sending a free update disk to a product. Such updates are commonly installed right away and without question, as long as they look legitimate. By placing a Trojan horse on a fake update disk, an attacker can place whatever programs are desired into a system. For example, an attacker could insert a program to search for desired data and use electronic mail to leak the information. In one case, thousands of disks were sent to computer users who were subscribers to a popular computing magazine. Literature claimed that the disks included a questionnaire to see if the user was likely to have contracted Acquired Immune Deficiency Syndrome (AIDS). It may seem hard to believe that anyone would use such a disk, but several thousand users did. As a side effect, these disks encrypted on-line information and told the user to send money to get the repair program. [44] Many less obvious spoofing attacks have been carried out, and it is very easy to send a legitimate looking update disk to an unsuspecting user.

Network services attacks In modern computer networks, the underlying protocols used to provide remote services are almost universally insecure. In fact, there are now several automated tools that systematically break into remote systems to test protection. [85] In many experiments, every host against which attacks are tried is taken over. For example, a widely published attack breaks into a significant percentage of all of the computers in the Internet by simply sending electronic mail. As a side effect, the mail program opens a terminal session for use by remote computers. The terminal session grants a high level of privilege to the attacker and does not produce the normal audit trails used to detect attacks.

Combined attacks Many attacks can be combined together to achieve an attacker's goals. For example, network packets can be forged in order to get access to a computer from which a password file is extracted, analyzed, and legitimate passwords are derived. With these passwords, on-line files can be modified to allow reentry at a later time, and this system can be used to launch attacks on other systems. This example may seem obvious, but there are a lot of far more subtle combined attacks that are far harder to defend against.

3.3 A CLASSIFICATION OF DISRUPTIONS

If anything should be clear from the examples provided in this chapter, it should be that a complete list of the things that can go wrong with information systems is impossible to create. People have tried to make comprehensive lists, and in some cases have produced encyclopedic volumes on the subject, but there are a potentially infinite number of different problems that can be encountered, so any list can only serve a limited purpose.

> A vital lesson to learn about information protection is that the assumptions made in the design, implementation, and use of systems dictate the protection attained. Any time decision-makers use an assumption to make a protection decision, they leave open the possibility that the assumption will be violated and that the resulting protection will therefore fail.

Benny Hill said it well: "When you *assume*, you make an *ass* of *u* and *me*." Having said that, I will now make some big assumptions.

The other side of the assumption coin is that when you make really good assumptions about protection, few, if any, avenues of attack are left open, and the cost of protection tends to be substantially lowered. In this book, I have taken the perspective that, regardless of the cause of a protection failure, there are three and only three sorts of things that can result:

1. Otherwise defect-free information can become corrupt,
2. Services that should be available can be denied, and/or
3. Information can get to places it should not go.

In the parlance of the information protection field, these are called corruption of information, denial of services, and leakage of information.

These terms are commonly shortened to corruption, denial, and leakage, respectively. Their opposites are called integrity, availability, and privacy (a.k.a. secrecy or confidentiality). For the purposes of this book, I will collectively call corruption, denial, and leakage *disruptions* and integrity, availability, and privacy, *protections*.

Corruption

Corruption is any illicit or unauthorized modification of information, whether by accident or intent. Since our use of the term information is broad, this is not limited to technological actions. For example, if a person enters unauthorized or incorrect information, this is a form of corruption.

Integrity is defined as soundness, purity, and completeness. [227] This would seem to be the opposite of corruption, and I will use the term in that way. In some cases, policy may state that integrity means that information correctly reflects an external reality in the model of reality used by the information system. Thus, integrity may go directly to the issue of information system design.

Denial

Denial of services is the failure to provide a service that should be provided as a matter of policy. Regardless of the cause, if service is denied when it should be provided, service is denied. Many policies have different levels of service and associated priorities, which is another way of saying that selective denial of services is acceptable under certain conditions.

The term availability has been narrowly defined in the field of fault-tolerant computing as the ratio of the mean time to failure (MTTF) divided by the mean time to repair (MTTR) plus the mean time to failure or, in simpler terms, the portion of time over the life-cycle of a system that it is operating correctly. I use the broader meaning of the term.

Leakage

Leakage of information sounds like the information is in a jar, and there are holes letting it out. And that's just right. When information gets to places it's not supposed to go, it fits into my meaning of the term leakage. For example, when someone accidentally sends company confidential information in electronic mail that goes over the Internet, this is a leak.

Privacy is one of three common terms used to describe the opposite of leakage. The other two are confidentiality and secrecy. These terms have essentially the same meaning, and yet they carry very different connotations in different communities. For example, privacy is thought to be a very important thing in universities, while secrecy is widely considered counter to the goal of a university. In military operations, privacy is not permitted to the individual, however, secrecy is vital to military success. Lawyers will all stand up for client confidentiality, but when it comes to privacy, they commonly debate the issue on a case-by-case basis. All of this notwithstanding, the terms will be used interchangeably throughout this document.

One more note on privacy is in order. Many people think of privacy as not allowing someone else to disturb them. Our use of the term is intended to include this meaning as well. In essence, this sort of privacy is preventing leakage of information from the outside to the inside, and as such, it is another side of the same coin. A hole that lets water out of a jar, can also let air in.

The Validity of This Classification Scheme

When I think about what I want information technology to provide me, I can sum it up in a few words:

> *Get the right information*
> *to the right place*
> *at the right time.*

This seems to me to require that information be unaltered, pure, and reflective of the reality it represents, that desired services are provided, and that information does not get to the wrong place or go at the wrong time—in other words, integrity, availability, and privacy. I am hard pressed to think of any other words I could add that would both add content and represent my desires more accurately.

As an exercise for the reader, and to make certain that my message is getting across, I would like you to go through all of the accidental and intentional events described earlier and classify each of them in terms of this classification scheme. Many things may fall into multiple categories, but is there anything that does not fall into at least one of them? If not, the classification scheme has worked, at least to some extent.

3.4   THE DISRUPTERS

In the realm of intentional attacks, there are always live agents lurking somewhere in the background, for only living creatures have what is commonly called intent. I have often been asked who attacks computers. Here is my response:

Insiders

> Many publications on computer security identify the most common source of intentional disruption as authorized individuals performing unauthorized activities.

Even the rather extensive clearance procedures used by the Department of Defense (DoD) have not proven effective in eliminating the insider threat. For example, in 1994, Aldrich Ames, a high-ranking official in the Central Intelligence Agency who was once responsible for Soviet counterintelligence, was found to be working for Russia. [29] It is prudent to take additional measures to prevent, detect, and respond to insider attacks.

Accidental disruption is also commonly caused by insiders acting imprudently, and it is sometimes very difficult to differentiate between accidental and intentional disruption in this context. This implies that more stringent techniques may have to be applied to observe insider behavior and reliably trace the specific actions of individuals in order to detect patterns indicative of intent.

The most costly sources of insider attack seem to be executives, people that predominantly use application programs, programmers, and other employees in that order. Executives often have authority to cause enormous transactions and do so. [54] People who use applications seem to accidentally find ways through systems, such as the illicit return of goods method described earlier. Temptation in conjunction with a lack of fear of being caught leads to reuse of the technique for personal gain. For example, I was at a national appliance store chain recently, and got bored while waiting a long time for the completion of a credit check. I was sitting at a computer terminal, so I decided to look up my transaction. It asked for an employee ID, and I typed 112. It then listed me as some employee and let me modify the price of the item I was purchasing. I put in a note that said *Great Guy*, set the price back to the correct value, and told the salesman what I had done. At the checkout counter, my bill said *Great Guy*. If I were even a little bit unscrupulous, I could easily have left the altered price and nobody would have probably even noticed. If they had, I could have simply claimed that I knew nothing of it.

Programmers have technical expertise and access, but they are typically watched more closely by management and administrators than others, and it is far easier to trace an intentional program alteration to a programmer than to trace the exploitation of a design fault in the overall system to a data entry clerk or executive.

One reason it is easier to catch programming changes is that a programming change can be seen as an alteration with obvious effects while other malicious activities are authorized by the design of the system. To see flaws that are the indirect result of design decisions requires the ability to step outside of the technical context of bits and bytes and understand the overall system view.

Private Detectives and Reporters

Modern private detectives use information systems extensively to trace people and events. Private detectives now advertise their use of computers to track down spouses who haven't paid child support after a divorce. With a social security number, it is simple to track down more than 90 percent of people in the United States in a matter of minutes. Getting a name, address, employer name, credit report, home and work telephones and addresses, and other similar information is easy. States are even putting information about their citizens on computers, and this means you can trace many activities through the department of motor vehicles, the court system, the taxation system, and more.

Getting much more information is also possible, but it usually takes a bribe, which is not as unusual as you might think. I heard one news director say on the air that if the reporter couldn't get the details of a sealed court decision within 24 hours, they would get another reporter. In the recent Tonya Harding case, where an olympic athlete was accused of plotting to assault an opponent, details of the plea bargain were known to the general public before the judge knew about them.

Consultants

Many companies use consultants in a wide variety of roles and, recently, *outsourcing* (the use of outside consultants to replace many of a company's employees) has become quite popular as a way to reduce the cost of information technology. These consultants, in most of their forms, provide part-time or short-term assistance. The problem is that there is no long-term motive for someone who knows they will be gone in a week or two to be protective of your technological resources.

Many documented cases have been reported where consultants have left time bombs or other potentially hazardous software in systems. A common theme is the claim that such measures are used to assure that their bill is paid. Of course, if someone does this, that person is breaking the law in most jurisdictions. It's called extortion. A far less obvious way consultants cause harm is by leaking details about internal operations.

Whistle Blowers

Whistle blowers may be good or bad depending on your point of view, but a common thread is their desire to get evidence of the things they believe to be wrong within an organization. In the process, some whistle blowers remove documents that are confidential, illicitly access information systems, or perform other functions that are not in keeping with the protection policy.

Hackers

Hackers (as opposed to crackers) are basically thrill seekers who use information technology rather than fast cars or bungee cords. They spend their time learning how systems work at a deep level and exploit this information to roam the information highways seeking out adventure. They have bulletin boards for sharing information, regular meetings, and perhaps the most famous of their efforts is the quarterly hacker magazine *2600*. In 1993, this magazine had the following table of contents: [1]

Title	Subject
A Guide to the 5ESS	Detailed operation of an AT&T telephone switch
British Credit Holes	How to subvert and take over a person's credit and identity
High School Hacking	Breaking into high school administrative files
Meeting Advice	Frustration of law enforcement activities at hacker meetings
. . .	. . .
AT&T Pages	Addresses of AT&T locations
Government bulletin boards	U.S. Government bulletin board phone numbers
Video Review	Critiques of security training videos
Toll Fraud Device	Plans for a 'red box' to make free calls from pay phones
2600 Meetings	Schedule of hacker meetings
ANSI Bomb	How to build a logic bomb for use on DOS machines

All of this information is widely known in the computer security community. For example, the risks forum, which is accessible via the Internet, had a far more extensive list of attack techniques and details than this magazine, and it is considered completely legitimate, while *2600* is viewed by many as an underground publication. [181]

Club Initiates

A recent trend in Europe has been the initiation of youngsters into computer clubs based on their ability and willingness to create computer viruses that aren't detected by popular computer virus detection programs. One of the side effects is the creation of a large number of fairly trivial variations on known computer viruses. Although many people in the antivirus market seem to fear these groups, any reasonably good virus defense can protect against these variations fairly simply.

I feel compelled to keep this in perspective. Gangs in the United States have initiations that, according to media reports, require youngsters to have unprotected sex with someone who has AIDS. This is the modern version of Russian roulette, a game wherein one bullet is placed in a six-shooter, the barrel is spun, and the player points the gun at their head and pulls the trigger. Other initiations include robbing a store, shooting a member of a rival gang, or illegally carrying drugs across a border. By comparison, the modification of a computer virus seems pretty mild.

Crackers

Whereas hackers are generally gentle in their illicit use of information systems, crackers are not. Crackers are professional thieves who steal through illegally accessing information. Safe crackers take valuable goods from physical safes, while computer crackers take valuable goods from or via information systems. As an example, in most large financial institutions, it is possible to transfer large amounts of money, stocks, bonds, or other fungibles by simply getting the attacker's information to the right place at the right time. Electronic funds transfer (EFT) fraud is usually for a high dollar value, occurs in well under one second, and is untraceable if done properly.

A few years ago, an information technology version of Charles Dickens' Fagin was arrested. In this case, a woman had been seducing young male crackers into performing theft by electronic means. She kept most of the money and kept the young men hooked by tempting them with a dream lifestyle.

Tiger Teams

A tiger team is the computer security parlance for a team of expert attackers who break into computer systems (usually) with the permission of the owner. Tiger teams are fairly widely used to test security systems, but as a rule, this is a waste of money. In almost every case, a decent tiger team can defeat the protective measures put in place. But this does not necessarily mean you should enhance protection. The real reason for tiger teams is to demonstrate weaknesses to upper management in a believable scenario. In this way, the information technology staff can scare managers into allocating more funds.

If all was right with the world, top-level managers would have a healthy respect for their dependency on information technology and its limitations, and it wouldn't be necessary to use these tactics. The dangers of this approach include offending top-level managers, providing attackers with knowledge on how to attack systems, and opening windows of opportunity for attackers to exploit.

The real problem with tiger teams is that if they don't find anything, it does not mean you are safe, only that they couldn't break in. None of the tiger teams used before the early 1980s ever tested a computer virus attack because viruses were unknown at that time. Today, few tiger teams test network attacks that will probably dominate the high quality attack technology over the next 10 years.

Competitors

Financial gain is one of the major motives for murder. If someone is willing to commit murder for tens of thousands of dollars, why would they hesitate to break into a computer for even more.

I was recently working on a proposal for a government contract that could be worth more than a billion dollars. I noticed that the information system they were using to do the proposal was a personal computer kept in a relatively insecure location, and networked over a relatively insecure network to other PCs throughout the United States. This seems to be fairly typical of big business, and it indicates a serious lack of concern that could substantially impact the outcome of government bids.

Examples of competitors launching attacks include the efforts by Hitachi to get IBM technical information in the 1980s and the French government's assistance of French companies in getting information from executives of other nations. [9]

Maintenance People

Many incidents of computer viruses seem to start when someone enters a facility to do maintenance of a network-based PC or printer. They may come from another site which had a virus. Instead of going through a cleaning process, they simply load their (newly infected) maintenance disks into your computer and do their maintenance tasks. But this is only the accidental path for maintenance.

It is now a common technique for attackers to dress and act as maintenance people in order to gain unrestricted access to a facility. This is so commonly known that it has been used almost universally in television shows and movies for more than 20 years, and yet, this technique still works in many organizations.

Professional Thieves

People who steal money for a living have recently started to learn how to use computers in their work. Willie Sutton (the famous bank robber) was once asked why he robbed banks. His answer: "That's where the money is." That's no longer true, of course. There is far more money transferred electronically now than was ever held in bank vaults. Just to give you a perspective, the average bank transfers its entire assets in electronic funds transfers between two and three times per week. In other words, if you could forge transactions over a two-day period, you could take all the money from the average bank.

Professional thieves are catching up to technology. It is now normal to read about tens of millions of dollars being taken in an EFT fraud. As an example, there are currently two unsolved EFT thefts from 1989 worth more than 150 million dollars each. [54] Information systems are clearly where the money is now.

A lot of people have suggested the use of information networks to allow remote home security systems to be enabled, to provide remote observation, and to allow remote activation of such things as coffee makers and ovens. But the same technology can potentially be exploited by people wishing to break into a home.

Professional thieves use a wide variety of indicators to determine when someone will be where and exploit these indicators to decide when to strike. To the extent that people place indicators of this information on networks, they provide thieves with the most important information needed to thrive.

Hoods

Hoodlums are more prone to extortion, kidnapping, beatings, and these sorts of things than the subtleties of electronic thievery. In order for them to keep up with the high-class thieves, they have to find newer and better ways to extort money. One of the ways is by controlling garbage disposal.

In one recent case, hundreds of millions of dollars worth of old bond certificates were improperly disposed of by a gang of hoods. The certificates were taken from New York to a New Jersey warehouse, and from there, they were distributed to sales people throughout Europe and sold to investment bankers. What's the information technology issue here? It turns out that old certificates are listed in information systems so they can be differentiated from new and valid certificates. But between the European Community and the United States, there is a significant delay, and the information systems are not used as much as they should be. Thus, the right information did not get to the right place at the right time to prevent the fraud from succeeding. This is also an example of how people can exploit timing problems in current information systems.

Vandals

Vandalism is a relatively simplistic activity carried out with the main purpose of causing arbitrary harm. In most cases, vandals don't have a clear understanding of the value of the things they are damaging when they do damage.

In one case I discussed with executives at a large company, the vandal was a union employee who repeatedly smashed video display terminals on the production floor with a hammer. He did it in plain sight during working hours, but the company could not invoke sanctions because the union supported the worker and the company couldn't afford a strike over a broken video terminal every week. Internet vandals regularly delete all of the files on systems they enter.

Activists

Activists have disrupted information systems to bring attention to causes. Although this has not happened as much recently, in the 1960s it was a widely used tactic by anti-war activists in the United States. [32]

Environmental groups, such as Greenpeace, have used physical means to prevent whaling and sit-ins to prevent opening of hazardous waste destruction facilities. It is certainly not beyond the realm of possibility that they would use computer networks to get their message across. For example, it would be a simple matter to cause messages to be displayed throughout the Internet or to dominate the computerized messages sent through *America OnLine* used on such television shows as CNN's *Talk Back Live*. This is an ideal venue for activists because they can get their message across while remaining essentially untrackable.

Crackers for Hire

Sometimes crackers are hired by other criminals to carry out jobs that involve special technical expertise. This represents a potent combination of high-powered talent and strong financial backing.

It is a good thing that most crackers aren't really as expert as they put themselves up to be. On the other hand, almost all current information protection is so weak that you don't have to be a real expert to get the job done.

Deranged People

Many people in society are deranged. Some of them use information systems to exercise their behavior. Widely publicized recent examples include computer stalkers, who use computer networks to locate, track, and stalk victims. In one case, a person seeking homosexual encounters with young boys used computers to entice them. In another case, a man stalked a woman and threatened to kill her over computer networks. The Internet is increasingly used by deranged people for this sort of activity, and it is very easy for them to do this anonymously.

Another area where computers have been used for a long time is in the area of pornography. If people are allowed to communicate without restriction and privately over computer networks, how does the state prevent pornographic information from being distributed in an electronic form? The balance between freedom of speech and the right of privacy also comes into play in light of recent cases where unauthorized pictures of women in toilets, dressing rooms, and tanning booths have been duplicated and sold in underground markets.

Organized Crime

When criminals organize, they become far more dangerous than when they are acting alone. They tend to have far more money, a wider diversity of talents, and a less risk-averse perspective. Organized criminals don't seem to have a problem with killing people that interfere with them, but they do have another big problem. The high overhead of organized crime makes it imperative that they generate a lot of regular income in order to sustain operations. This forces them to steal higher dollar values per crime or to commit more crimes per member than independent criminals. The former approach seems to be preferred because of the high risk and increased work load involved in increasing the per member crime rate.

In one recent report, it was found that organized crime is now paying about $10,000 per PC to have the PCs of top-level executives in large corporations stolen. Since the PC itself is worth far less than that much if purchased new, it is clear that the criminals are paying for the information and not the hardware. This is likely an attempt to make their crimes more profitable on a per crime basis.

Drug Cartels

Drug cartels are typically oriented toward a few specialty crimes: smuggling, drug sales, and homicide. Because of these limits on their activities, they tend to be far more protective of market share than many other criminals. Computers are increasingly being used by law enforcement to track cartels and store information on informers. Meanwhile, the cartels are increasingly using computers and high quality encryption technology to hide their activities. Information systems are also vital to the money-laundering activity required in order to turn drug profits into usable funds on a large scale.

Recent changes to international laws have been designed specifically to help trace the money-laundering activities of drug cartels. Whereas a few years ago, you could simply transfer funds through four or five countries before the process became untraceable, the process now requires that more countries get involved, and the number of countries that allow transactions to remain hidden from law enforcement is quickly reaching zero. The day may soon come when all financial transactions are directly reported to the government and analyzed by computers. This is already true of most transactions valued at more than a few thousand dollars.

Terrorists

Terrorists have historically gone after airliners, office buildings, and government offices because of their high profile and paralyzing effect. The great promise of info-terrorism lies in the large-scale impact, the minimal harm to people, the enormous financial effect, the ease of carrying out attacks with a small number of attackers, and the low risk of being caught.

One shot in the info-terrorist war was fired in New York when the World Trade Center was bombed, [97] but there are many other less widely reported incidents. For example, London has a lot of bombings directed against financial institution facilities which consist primarily of information systems. [151]

Spies

Spies have existed for at least as long as governments have existed, and their main purpose is—and has always been—to gather information from the enemy and provide it to the friendly, and to corrupt enemy information so as to confuse and misdirect their efforts.

> Spies exist at the corporate as well as the national level, with corporate spies being far less noticed and less pursued.

Among the numerous cases of electronic eavesdropping for leaking information, the case documented by Cliff Stoll in his best-selling book, *The Cukoo's Egg*, is one of the best known, [209] [208] but not one of the most severe. One of the most severe cases was discovered long after the six-month limit on storing audit trails made tracing the attack to its source impossible. In this case, many sites were entered with unlimited access. It is impossible to even assess the damage at this time. [28] [147]

In another recent case, Mr. Aldrich Ames, a top-level counterintelligence expert at the CIA, was found to be a spy for the former Soviet Union and, after the breakup of the Soviet Union, for the Russian government. According to recent reports, Mr. Ames may have sold information to the Russian government about secret key-escrow technology used in the *Clipper Chip* [185] touted by the U. S. government as a way to have secure communications within the United States while granting law enforcement the ability to tap into conversations when they have a warrant. Ames also accessed classified databases with information on undercover agents posing as businessmen in Europe. [224]

Police

Police powers to wiretap have been a controversial subject in the United States for a long time. A recent Supreme Court ruling indicated that listening to the radio signals of portable telephones without a warrant is legal. [223] Cellular telephones are not included in this ruling for now, but the Federal Bureau of Investigation (FBI) has been trying to illegalize encryption of telephone calls for a long time. [225] The court has also ruled that it is legal for the government to track telephone numbers of all telephone calls to determine who is calling who, and when. [150]

With these expanding police powers to search and seize otherwise private information, the right of privacy is rapidly waning. The way the law works today, you have a right to privacy if you have a reasonable expectation of privacy. Since you now know that your privacy in telephone conversations is limited, your expectation is lower, and as a result, you have less of a right.

Government Agencies

Government agencies are increasingly using intrusive means to access private information. The use of these techniques increases with the size of the agency, so that local governments virtually never use this sort of information, while the federal government has taken a quite intrusive position. For example, all international telephone calls can now be monitored, digital communications are commonly collected, and the government is pushing for regulations that would allow telephone taps to be instituted nearly instantaneously and without the telephone company being involved. In the cable networks, which are rapidly starting to provide bidirectional communication and computation services, the rules are unclear, but the government is pushing toward regulations that would permit unlimited eavesdropping on communications.

Among the possibilities for these media are the observation of video telephony, tapping of transactions going to and from bank accounts, tapping of contractual business transactions, and the use of audit trails to characterize peoples' behavior. The claim is that this is necessary in order to keep up with high-tech crime, and there are strong arguments on both sides. A possible scenario might help.

Suppose people start selling interactive videophone sessions with naked children. This would be considered pornography by many standards, and would presumably be subject to laws about obscene materials. But to tell if someone is doing this may require tapping of the line, which would presumably be a violation of privacy. Is it truly the right of the government to observe all communications in order to detect crimes? Suppose I call my wife over the videophone and we get naked and play some sexual game. What right does the government have to control or observe sexual behavior of a married couple? How can the government tell one sort of behavior from another and how can it assure privacy of one and observation of the other?

What if the government only tracks lists of services provided to each individual? Would such a database violate personal privacy? Suppose the tracking included lists of people who called doctors who primarily deal with the treatment and cure of sexually transmitted diseases. If the information got out, it could be quite embarrassing, but more importantly, it could be used to blackmail people. Even more importantly, it's nobody else's business. Perhaps in the information age, there will be no privacy of this sort anymore.

Infrastructure Warriors

In the information infrastructure, war takes on a different meaning. Infrastructure warriors seek to destroy infrastructure so as to disable the enemy's ability to sustain long-term military capabilities.

Some examples of infrastructure war include destroying the electrical power grid to cause electrical failures, destroying the water supply to kill or disable large segments of the population, elimination of telecommunications capabilities to make it impossible for the enemy to coordinate efforts, and destroying the highway system to make travel inefficient.

- In an extreme example, one patent describes a means and method for altering noise levels which is capable of disrupting atmospheric communications over vast areas of the Earth. Experiments have demonstrated the ability to disrupt all ground-based, airborne, and space-based communications using signals transmitted through the air. [77, 25, 15]
- An article in a recent *Wired* magazine names the "Top Ten" U.S. infrastructure targets, including the Culpeper telephone switch that

handles federal funds transfers and the WorldWide Military Command and Control System (WWMCCS). [230] [232]

- In a paper published in 1988, the authors suggest logistics attacks, and suggest that "software warfare holds promise of emerging as the first truly militarily effective form of economic warfare." [24]
- One paper presented to the Naval Postgraduate School in August of 1993 claims that with 20 people and $1 million the author can bring the U.S. to its knees. [206] Other expert claims range from $100,000 and 10 people for large-scale disruption over a period of weeks, to $30 million and 100 people for almost total information infrastructure disruption resulting in multi-year recovery time. [120]

The implication should be clear. Infrastructure must be protected because it is a highly vulnerable and highly critical element of the overall economic and military success of any nation.

Nation States and Economic Rivals

A number of countries have computer security groups and some of these are working to certify operating systems, hardware, and software. This demonstrates that these countries are working to discover flaws in existing products and that they are aware of specific techniques by which these systems can be disrupted. European participants in ITSEC (Information Technology Security Evaluation Criteria) include England, Netherlands, France, and Germany, [157, App E, p 283] with Italy beginning to join in. Russia, Japan, China, Australia, New Zealand, Singapore and South Africa are also countries with certification and/or active computer security interest.

A number of countries participate in the world market for telephone and data switching systems, and can be assumed to have the knowledge to disrupt telephone and data networks based on their design, manufacturing, and deployment expertise. Companies marketing Private Branch eXchange (PBX) or central office (CO) equipment include Hitachi, NEC (Nippon Electric Company) and Fujitsu (Japan), Ericsson (Sweden), Alcatel (France), and Siemens (Germany). [215] The United States depends on systems from these manufacturers for information assurance in telecommunications.

A talk by Wayne Madsen presented at IFIP SEC '90 (International Federation of Information Processing Societies annual Computer Security Conference) in 1990 provided a rating of various countries' ability to engage in computer "hacking," and the information that intelligence services were apparently becoming engaged in economic intelligence for business organizations. [164] More than 30 countries are given excellent ratings in computer-communications espionage, meaning they almost certainly have sufficient expertise to corrupt computer and network data and disrupt operations. Among these countries are India, Taiwan, Republic of Korea, China, Japan, and South Africa. [143]

Project Rehab, operated by Germany beginning in 1988, is a computer and network intrusion research effort which has accessed computer systems in the United States and other countries. The project depends on "hacker" techniques and other research, and has approximately 36 computer specialists and senior intelligence officials assigned. A primary focus is on cataloging network addresses and establishing pathways for later use. [164]

Military Organizations

> 95 percent of DoD telecommunications capability is provided by public networks owned and operated by common carriers. [184] These are the same networks that will be used in the NII. [155] This means that in wartime, information infrastructure attacks against military targets will necessarily cause disruption to civilian systems.

In military operations, the requirements for survivability are far more severe than in nonmilitary systems, and the losses when information systems fail are in terms of human lives and the future of nations.

One area where military efforts have paid off is in the use of electromagnetic pulses to destroy information processing equipment. In the most widely described scenario, the electromagnetic pulse caused by nuclear weapons travels over communications wires to destroy information systems for hundreds of miles around. The Ground Wave Emergency Network (GWEN) is the only U.S. strategic defense communications system hardened to survive a high-altitude electromagnetic pulse (HEMP). [12]

In a much less spectacular example, cars parked about 300 meters from an electromagnetic pulse (EMP) generator test had coils, alternators, and other controls disabled. The former Soviet Union developed an EMP weapon before its breakup, and nuclear EMP hardening has proven ineffective against this weapon. [92] In the United States, a Los Alamos EMP generator produced a 12 to 16 million amp pulse, with a rise time of 400 nanoseconds. Some 16 x 40-inch generators have produced about 30 million amps of current. [91] A generator of this sort could disable almost any current electronic information system at a substantial distance by damaging internal components.

There is some difficulty in deciding whether enough shielding has been used against electromagnetic interference (EMI). EMI was suspected in Army Blackhawk helicopter crashes, since the Navy version has more shielding and fewer crashes. [27]

One paper published in 1989 compares computer viruses to traditional electronic counter measures and states that computer viruses are uniquely qualified to disrupt tactical operations; that several recent trends in military electronic systems make them more vulnerable, including standard computers, software, and data links; and that protective measures must be initiated before viruses are used by an adversary. [55]

Limited direct evidence exists for associating virus discovery locations with virus origins (e.g., language particulars and programming styles) and there is a substantial body of indirect evidence in the form of discovery location statistics that suggests that disruption technology and expertise exist in many nations. One study associating virus discoveries with countries gave the following results:

Country	Virus Discoveries	Country	Virus Discoveries
Former USSR	76	Canada	23
United States	68	England	22
Bulgaria	61	Taiwan	16
Poland	38	Sweden	16
Germany	30	Israel	15
Netherlands	26	Spain	14
Italy	23	Australia	14

From 3 to 10 viruses were first discovered in Argentina, Austria, Finland, France, Greece, Hungary, India, Indonesia, Malaysia, New Zealand, Portugal, Republic of South Africa, Switzerland, and Turkey. [174]

Vendors of anti-virus software normally have detailed knowledge of computer operations and large collections of viruses to study. Anti-virus software vendors are in place in the U.S.(5), Israel(3), United Kingdom(3), New Zealand(3), Holland(3), Australia(3), Thailand, Iceland, Canada, Colombia, Sweden, and Ukraine. [200]

Another indicator is the countries of residence of speakers at the *International Computer Virus and Security Conference*, held in New York City each March. In 1992, technical talks were given by representatives from Germany(3), Bulgaria, Belgium, England(2), Iceland, Russia, Australia, Mexico, and Israel. [69] Authors of anti-virus hardware and software can also be found in China, India, Taiwan, Japan, Malasia, several CIS (the former Soviet Union) countries, and others.

It is clear from computer virus information alone, that many countries of security interest to the United States have knowledge and technology in the computer virus arena that could be directed specifically to disrupt the information infrastructure of the U.S. military.

Information Warriors

> Information warfare can be practiced by small private armies, terrorist organizations, drug lords, and even highly motivated individuals of modest means. This may represent a fundamental shift away from the notion that the hostile nation state is the major threat the United States has to be concerned with. [74] [213] [56] [214]

Five books on computer viruses, including two that are tutorials on writing viruses, discuss military use of viruses. [109] [135] [144] [30] [87] A recent popular novel has the central theme of crippling attacks on U.S. computers by means of viruses, computer terminal eavesdropping, high-energy radio frequency "guns," and electromagnetic pulses. The author's virus examples are not as subtle or malicious as a real attack by experts. [189] An interactive movie on CD-ROM, released in October 1993, illustrates information warfare against the U.S. It includes details about crippling and corrupting time standards, which affect precision weapon targeting and long distance telephone switches. [232]

The Chaos Computer Club in Germany maintains an annotated list of the Internet addresses of U.S. DoD command, control, supply, and logistics computers on one of their computer accounts in Germany. [198] Apparently selected from hundreds of publicly available military computer Internet addresses, listed systems are primarily Army, Navy, and Air Force logistics, computer, communications, and research sites. This listing is not kept in publicly available bulletin boards throughout the world, but access to it was attained via an international connection.

In order to detect attacks and test out defenses against them, military and commercial organizations have created tools to test for known defects. [85] Information warriors now have tools that automatically perform attacks against infrastructure targets. These tools are almost always successful in today's environment (in one test, the success rate was over 99.9 percent), and this is without human effort. With human effort and adequate resources, every current system is vulnerable.

3.5 MOTIVATION

We now know what sorts of things are done and who does them, but there is another issue of motive. Many people I have talked to have a hard time understanding why anyone would do such a thing, and ask me if I could explain what percentage of people do what for what reason. In response, I offer here some of the motives I have encountered, but

I caution you that there are no valid statistics on even the number of attacks underway today.

To some readers, this section may seem redundant, and to some extent it is, but motive is a very important and often overlooked issue in information protection. As any judge will tell you, motive, opportunity, and means are necessary components of proving criminal behavior. Without understanding motive, we may miss the opportunity to prevent and detect attack, and we will certainly miss a key component of understanding the challenge of information protection.

Money or Profit

Whether it is destroying another company's information systems to make them less efficient or taking money through electronic means, greed is one of the strongest motives seen. After all, people are willing to kill for far less than the average computer criminal takes in a funds transfer fraud.

Fun, Challenge, and Acceptance

Many hackers enjoy finding ways to get around restrictions. The ability to do something nobody else knows how to do is often used to show off, whether it is popping a wheelie or breaking into a computer. Some thrill seekers love the challenge of holding a global corporation at bay, and there is a certain sense of power and satisfaction in this sort of David and Goliath struggle. Still others use computer attacks as a way to be accepted into a hacker group in the same way as people use shooting other people as a way to get into an inner city gang. A good example is the hacker club in Germany that requires a unique virus be generated as a condition of membership.

Vengeance or Justice

Vengeance is often considered justice by the vengeful. It doesn't matter which way you view it, the important thing to understand is that people who feel justified may use any means to attain their ends, and certainly information system attack is widely considered justifiable. A good example is the case where two hacker groups in New York turned each other in because they each felt the other had insulted their honor.

Mental Illness

People who launch extremely malicious computer viruses are, in essence, randomly destroying other peoples' work. This sort of random destruction, if encountered in the context of shootings, would probably be associated with a mental illness or at least with some sadistic tendencies.

One of the most widely recognized areas where sadism seems to be the motive is in computer virus attacks where viruses are spread without specific targets and programmed to do mass destruction of data. [44]

Religious or Political Beliefs

Zealots who believe that God is on their side have been around since the concept of God was introduced. In their minds, almost anything can be justified if it is God's will or for a heavenly cause. The Crusades were one example of this. Another example is fanatics in the United States who believe they should murder doctors to prevent abortions.

A similarly powerful motivation for breaking the law is the *National Interest*. A good example is the Watergate case where Republicans working for the President broke into Democratic headquarters to get strategic planning details. The Iran-Contra affair is another example of this. It turns out that in the Iran-Contra affair, Oliver North was caught partially because, although he had deleted electronic mail that indicated possible guilt, the computer security system had backups that stored copies of that mail. [191]

Clearly, people who are willing to do these things will also be willing to exploit information systems to their advantage.

Self-Defense

When animals believe they have been backed into a corner, their fight or flight response is limited to fighting. Employees who feel they are about to be fired, companies in heavy competition, or any number of other situations may come to be viewed as a matter of self-defense, and this may result in abuse of information systems. A good example is the common use of time bombs by programmers as retribution for being fired.

Testing

Tiger teams exist to test protection systems. They are generally paid to demonstrate weaknesses. Similarly, researchers perform experiments on systems to test protection weaknesses. In these cases, the attacks are almost always legitimate and authorized.

Coercion

People can be coerced into action by all sorts of things. Their children can be kidnapped, their sex lives can be documented for possible release, and the list goes on and on. Under coercion, people may do whatever it takes to attack an information system.

Military or Economic Advantage

Nations commonly exploit information systems to their military and economic advantage. In the Gulf War, the United States destroyed Iraq's information infrastructure in order to win the war. [33] France sponsors eavesdropping as a national policy to help their corporations compete. [9]

Gathering or Destruction of Evidence

Whether it's the police, a whistle blower, or simply someone trying to get ahead in an organization, people commonly use information systems to get the evidence on others. On the other side, people who don't want evidence found have a tendency to try to destroy records in information systems. Again, the Oliver North incident comes to mind.

3.6   THE MAGNITUDE AND SCOPE OF THE PROBLEM

One quarterly report of large-scale disruption incidents for the fall of 1993 includes a Federal Aviation Administration (FAA) computer systems failure delaying regional traffic for 90 minutes (the cause is still unknown), an FAA weather computer system failure for 12 hours due to a time-activated logic bomb, a programming error in an X-ray system that resulted in wrong dosages to about 1,045 cancer patients, and a software error that crashed the Hamburg Integrated Services Digital Network (ISDN) telecommunications services for more than 11 hours. This is only one of several similar publications that report such incidents. [234]

Lapses in policies and procedures seem to be common for major software manufacturers. As an example, in 1992, Novell released a virus to thousands of customers when it noticed *after quality control was completed* that a key file was missing from the master distribution disks then being transported to the disk duplication facility. Instead of returning to the quality control process, the person transporting the disks for duplication loaded the file from the most convenient computer, which, by chance, contained a virus that was transferred to the floppy disk. The disk was sent to duplication, packaged, and shipped to customers. [70] The disks were apparently never tested at random after duplication for problems, the disks en route to the duplication facility were not sealed or permanently write-protected, the personnel were not properly trained, and the initial quality control process never detected that the correct file was not on the disk.

> AT&T reports that it knows of being *probed* more than once per day from the Internet. [19] Digital Equipment corporation provides similar data. [179]

Some consultants have suggested that companies interested in how often they will be attacked place a *honey pot*, a system put in place to be attacked, on the Internet and watch to see how often it is attacked. According to some people who have tried this, they are attacked more than once per day and usually the attacker cannot be traced. After a Sun employee described some relatively sophisticated network attacks against Unix-based computers, Sun had to shut down its internal network for a week because of outside penetrations they were unable to stop without isolating their internal networks from the rest of the world. [188]

In 1994, the Internet was attacked and passwords to about 100,000 systems were stolen by listening to network packets. At the same time, the DoD was under a concerted attack that persists through the time of this writing. In this case, compromised systems included those used for ballistic weapons research, aircraft and ship design, military payroll, personnel records, procurement, electronic mail, supercomputer modeling of battlefield research, and computer security research. [5] Although none of the released information was classified, information was apparently corrupted in unknown ways and services were denied at times. The attackers have not been caught yet, despite more than a year of ongoing attack after they were detected and some six months or more of attacks before they were detected.

Today's information-processing components consist largely of low-assurance computer systems. Every general-purpose DoD and civilian computer system tested so far has proven vulnerable to disruption. [44] Many existing DoD information-processing components don't even meet nominal business operational control requirements common throughout industry. For example, a recent GAO audit to determine if controls in large data centers were adequate to assure data integrity showed:

> "...that both [Cleveland and Indianapolis] DITSO Centers had serious deficiencies [that would] allow any knowledgeable user to gain access to pay data, and to add, modify, or destroy it, or accidentally or intentionally to enter erroneous data, without leaving an audit trail." [161]

A degree of assurance in existing DoD systems is provided by their physical isolation from an integrated network, but in most industries, communications is given priority over protection, and isolation is a rare exception, not the rule.

It is vital for decision-makers to understand that these newly connected systems are vulnerable to disruption of a wider variety from more sources and to make suitable investments in protection to offset the increased risk.

"Just how vulnerable our networks have become is illustrated by the experiences of 1988: There were three major switching center outages, a large fiber optic cable cut, and several widely reported invasions of information databases by so-called computer hackers." [157, p. 2] One outage in 1991 affected millions of customers and temporarily disrupted air traffic control centers in New York (which caused slowdowns in much of the northeastern United States and across the nation).

Protection of individual devices operating point-to-point is well within modern technology, but the overall end-to-end communication requirement is far more complex. Most commercial networks have little or no coverage against intentional disruption and commonly fail from software errors, mischievous, and malicious attacks. [80] [8] [157] [156]

Major concerns about network assurance come from several sources. Current network management information assurance standards are incomplete and have only addressed authentication requirements. [94] Current network assurance standards only address authentication. [154]

The Government Network Management Profile's (GNMP) primary goal is to develop interoperable products [94] to allow network managers to remotely monitor and control network resources residing on network components developed by different vendors. This interoperability goal makes the network management system vulnerable to disruption. From network management sites, the entire network could potentially be disrupted. A good example is that most of the major telephone networks have one or at most two network management sites that control all long-haul switching. A simple attack on three or four sites could disrupt the vast majority of communications in the United States for a substantial period of time.

The consolidation of the DISN network management into a hierarchical network management system was originally designed to make it possible for a network management center in one domain to "cut through," monitor, and directly control another domain. This could potentially be done without the authority or knowledge of any intervening network managers despite the authentication between sites. [141] Unless specifically addressed, this may allow a single attacker to disrupt the whole network. [162] The same situation currently exists in most telephone and cable company networks. More recent designs have moved toward a system of centralized monitoring and decentralized control via authenticated messaging to vendor-supplied data centers.

There is no current plan for creating a separate and different network management capability that can operate when the NII itself is not functioning. This lack of external control capability has historically proven inadequate, as the Internet virus of 1988 clearly demonstrated. [115] [114]

Current network management systems typically address known faults in known ways. [130] Some systems recover from high probability errors, [38] while others detect and recover from large numbers of burst errors, [36] but intentional attack is rarely treated in the available literature.

Local area networks (LANs) are highly vulnerable to attack from any point on the network, [40] as well as from outside networks connected through routers, gateways, or bridges. Some recent advances have provided costly and complex partial solutions to this problem, [19] [179] [34] but none of these solutions is comprehensive or feasible for use in an average computer facility.

Internet service providers commonly offer access to the Internet by providing leased lines between their local sites and public access points, computers that interface between user sites and the leased lines, and essentially no added protection. Thus, anyone who signs up with one of these service providers is leaving the protection to a service provider that profits from reduced cost more than anything else. In some rare instances, service providers offer protection services as a competitive advantage, but the market has not flocked to these service providers over others yet, and the protective services they offer are certainly not well designed for each client on a case-by-case basis.

Existing infrastructure components have well-known and easily exploited vulnerabilities to disruption, but even if these components were individually strengthened against disruption, they would not necessarily provide information assurance when networked together. The combination of otherwise assured systems in an assured network environment can lead to an overall system that is not assured. In one case, two systems that were independently safe against corruptions by a particular computer virus were both disrupted by that virus when they were networked together. The cause was a mismatch in the way integrity was implemented and the way peer-to-peer communications works in modern networks. [44] There is still no overall theory of how to safely connect network components, but in the limited cases where connection safety is understood, unsafe connections should be avoided. [49] [48]

> Simply bolting together a variety of information security features doesn't solve the protection problem.

To get synergistic benefits by combining information assurance features, they have to be properly combined, and this is not yet a well understood phenomenon. [44] In most cases, rather than enhancing protection by combining features, the entire system is only as strong as the weakest link.

The people who architect infrastructure must come to understand this issue and exploit that understanding to provide adequate information assurance.

3.7   ADDING IT ALL UP

It would take quite an effort to characterize all of the incidents listed in this book in terms of their financial impact, but a short table including relatively well-confirmed major losses cited earlier should serve as an indicator of the situation today.

Item	Annual Cost Estimate
Denial of services attacks	$4B
AT&T toll frauds	$2B
Other toll frauds (est)	$2B
FBI-reported computer crimes	$2B
Total	$10B

Less well documented losses include the 900 million break-in attempts per year over the Internet, unreported and undetected computer crimes, and all manner of other losses.

CHAPTER 4

Asleep at the Switch

I was recently on a consulting job where the company I was working for was providing my services to their client which needed an analysis of its information protection status. The single most critical flaw detected in the analysis was that the entire assets of the client could be electronically transferred to any desired recipient anywhere in the world. This could be done by thousands of different employees and it could happen accidentally or intentionally by simply telling the computer to make the transfer. If this was done, there would be no warning, no approval required, the incident would not be detected until checks started to bounce, and it could easily be made to appear that an innocent employee had made the transfer. When my report placed fixing this problem at the top of the list of issues to be addressed, the company I was working for decided to remove it because they thought the client wouldn't want to hear it. This is depressingly common in the information protection industry.

With this example in mind, *asleep at the switch* seems like an understatement. It's more like making sure that the switch doesn't work just in case someone is actually awake and might try to use it.

When I tell this sort of story to executives I know, they usually question my statements. The dialog might go something like this:

But an approval is required before the funds become available, right?
No.
Are you sure employees can really do that?
Yes.
Aren't you exaggerating just a little bit?
No.
How can you know for certain that this will really work?
A demonstration was used to prove it.

I find it hard to believe that this sort of thing could go unnoticed.
It was unnoticed until we did the study.

This may seem like it's a once in a lifetime situation, but in the information protection business, it is a daily occurrence. You may ask, *How can this be?* The answer is not so simple. In order to screw things up this badly, it takes a major lapse by a lot of people over a long period of time. And that's just what happened.

From the start, information protection has been bungled, and there's plenty of blame to go around. The military, intelligence, legislative, executive, legal, law enforcement, university, industrial, business, computer, and standards communities have all failed us. It's a rare circumstance when this many people screw up this badly. To understand what happened, the history of information protection has to be examined.

4.1   A HISTORY OF SECRECY

Information protection started as a field about four thousand years ago, when the Egyptians started using special hieroglyphics in the tombs of their pharaohs. [121] Over the next 3,950 years, most of the technical developments were in the area of cryptography, and almost all of the results were directed toward keeping information secret. The other developments were almost all related to personnel restrictions and physical security, and involved background checks, various wall and moat technologies, the design of safes and lock boxes, and other similar things. Accounting seems to be the rare exception where integrity was a vital and well-developed component of technology.

Up until the end of the nineteenth century, the dominant form of communication was via courier. There was no electronic data processing and the times involved in long distance communication were substantial. The dominant information protection technologies were designed to keep written information from being attained or understood by outsiders.

A Short History of Cryptography

Cryptography is the study of secret writing or, in other words, of transforming information into a form that obscures its meaning. In cases where release of information could cause harm, cryptography was a dominant technology for a long time.

> It is noteworthy that of all the cryptosystems developed in the last 4,000 years, only two systems in widespread use remain hard enough to break to be of real value.

One of them, the perfect cipher, takes too much space for most practical uses. The other, the RSA public key cryptosystem, is too slow for most practical uses. Both of them were developed in the last 50 years.

It was only after Shannon's information theory was published in 1948 [192] that reliable communications became systematically attainable in noisy environments. It was that breakthrough that led to the creation of coding theory, which in turn provided designers with the first systematic integrity and availability in communications systems.

A classification scheme for ciphers was given in 1978 by Gary Knight [126] in the first of a series of articles which posed ciphers to the reader. After a given period of time, Knight demonstrated reader solutions along with explanations of how they solved the ciphers. Versions of the solutions attained by the author were also given along with many mathematical techniques for "attacking the unknown cipher." In my mind, the most interesting thing about this series of articles was the way in which virtually every cryptosystem invented before the 1940s was systematically overcome by applying Shannon's information theory of secrecy systems, first published in 1949. [193] All of the systems had been broken piecemeal before that time, but for the first time, cryptanalysts had a general way to attack all imperfect cryptosystems.

Computer Security Kicks In

The first computer systems were just coming into being in the 1940s and they were first applied to two military applications. One application was to break cryptographic codes used by the Axis in World War II and the other was to compute firing tables for long-range artillery, also in World War II. [121] These systems were physically secured in secret facilities with guards and locked doors.

After the war, computers were applied to many other problems, but security remained essentially physical in nature until timesharing came into being in the late 1950s and early 1960s. In a *timesharing* system, two or more people can use the same system at the same time by literally sharing its time. With timesharing, it became necessary to separate the memory used by the users sharing the system in order to keep them from accidentally overwriting each others' programs and data. The scheme eventually settled on, and widely used even today, was to assign users unique identifying numbers and to associate storage with those numbers. You may not see those numbers being assigned and associated as a user of a system, but the underlying mechanism is still there.

Over time, there were developments such as the introduction of passwords used to keep users from accidentally using the wrong user number and access controls to prevent users from accidentally destroying data associated with other users. As more users began to use computers for a wider range of applications, some of those people became concerned about privacy issues (such as access to payroll data), the assignment of priorities to tasks (so that time-critical functions could be done before less vital functions), and other issues related to the scarcity of the computing resource. The scarcity resulted in hoarding, which resulted in people getting mad at each other, and in some cases, even attempts to violate the system security measures so as to get more of the limited resource. As the attackers got better, the defenders worked harder, and the battle raged.

It was only in the middle of the 1970s that people began to really model computer security in a meaningful way and use mathematics to try to systematize the field. In 1973, Lampson discovered a confinement problem with all computer systems that share information [128]. This demonstrated fundamental difficulties in confining information. Bell and LaPadula published a paper that modeled computer security after military secrecy methods [20], and secure operating systems were under widespread development following this model. Over the next several years, Biba published an integrity model for computing that was widely ignored when it came to implementation, [22] Harrison et al. published the first mathematical treatment of the overall protection problem and introduced the *subject/object* model of computer security that prevails today, Denning published an alternative *lattice* model of protection, [73] and many authors reported on computer security developments. [169, 99, 146]

By the early 1980s, summary papers [131] and books [71] brought the picture into clear view. The basic picture was that secrets could be kept by limiting the flow of information to go only from untrusted users to trusted users. It was at that time widely believed that the computer security problem had been nearly solved, and that in very short order, the military model of security which was based on secrecy would prove ideal for all applications. But then . . .

4.2   IGNORANCE IS NOT BLISS

Late in 1984, two very important things happened to the field of information protection. One was the first published results on computer viruses, [46] and the other was the official introduction of the *Trusted System Evaluation Criteria* (TCSEC). [124]

With the introduction of the issue of computer viruses in 1984, it was clearly and definitively demonstrated, both by theory and by experiment on existing military and commercial computer security systems, that the model of security based on secrecy had a fatal flaw.

> In essence, the vast majority of the work done over the past ten years in computer security had been demonstrated to be a house of cards that could be blown over by a programmer with nominal experience and only a few hours of effort.

No amount of adjustment of the computer security controls of the day could in any way reduce the impact of this result and there was no doubt about what it meant.

The computer security field had paid full attention to the issue of secrecy for almost ten years, and yet had completely ignored the issue of integrity. The result was seemingly devastating. All of the systems developed over years of painstaking effort could be overcome with almost no effort. Even worse, there was a federal criteria for computer security that had been developed over a number of years that was literally on the verge of being accepted as the official government and de facto global computer security standard, and there was nothing in that standard that could be used to help protect against computer viruses in the least. There were even systems waiting for the standard to be accepted so they could be certified for government use. There was a whole industry on the brink of starting a new era, and it turned out that they had missed a fatal flaw.

There was quite a stir and more than a few voices were raised, but in the end, momentum won out. The federal standard was accepted, the systems awaiting certification were certified, and the computer security world began a period of almost ten years of officially authorized insanity.

Insane: not mentally sound [227]

It seemed hard for me to believe at the time, but the momentum explanation makes sense of it. There was simply too much money and personal pride at stake for the government to change its direction, even though the direction was clearly flawed in the deepest way. But in information protection, ignorance is not bliss, it's suicide.

4.3   THE BIRTH OF THE PERSONAL COMPUTER

As if it weren't bad enough to have the military-industrial complex leading us down the primrose path, this was the dawning of the age of the personal computer, and it must have been a cloudy day, because the infant personal computing industry apparently couldn't see the forest for the trees.

The Multi-State Computer

I have already explained that since the beginning of timesharing in the late 1950s, computer designers knew how to provide limited protection in computers. What I haven't mentioned is the technical innovation that made this possible. This innovation was the *multi-state computer*. Now the technical people among you will probably get confused or upset by my terminology, but let me clarify before you call me names. All modern digital computers involve *finite state automata* wherein the machine uses its current *mental state* and current *inputs* to generate *outputs* and a *next state*. With such a machine and enough memory capacity, you can perform any *computation* that can ever be performed. [216] But this is not the innovation I am talking about. The multi-state computer was an innovation that provided two or more *master* states for a computer; one that is used by the *operating system* and one that is used by *user* programs.

- In the operating system state, the computer allows physical input and output to take place so that the disk can be read or written, any of the video displays can be changed, any keyboard can be read, and all of memory is accessible.
- In the user state, no physical input or output is allowed, only a limited part of the memory is accessible, and if any attempt to use an unauthorized capability is attempted, the state is changed to the operating system state, and the operating system program is run.

In this way, a user program can try to write to the disk, the operating system will intercept the attempt and act according to its programming. The operating system can be programmed to provide all sorts of services, such as making a physical disk appear as if it were a file system, providing separation of user files and memory space from each other, and supporting other information protection features.

A two-state computer can implement any protection scheme that any multi-state computer can implement, but with a one-state computer it is impossible to practically provide fully effective protection. For this reason, starting in the early 1960s, all widely used general-purpose computers were designed with multi-state capabilities. The one major exception was the microprocessor integrated circuit technology, which was primarily used to perform real-time control tasks. An example of a microprocessor application at that time was to control the video display terminals used to talk to timesharing computers. There was no reason for a real-time controller to have protection capabilities and, because it took space on the integrated circuit and the technology at that time wasn't advanced enough to put these features on the same integrated circuit as the rest of the computer, the multi-state machine was not implemented in those controllers.

The microprocessors at the heart of these control applications were very small and inexpensive. They could be placed on a single integrated circuit, and the control system manufacturers had made some standard control system printed circuit boards that exploited this technology by adding memory, input, and output to make control system design simpler and cheaper. When the fledgling personal computer industry grew up, there was little money to invest, and the companies had to go with the cheapest technology around. The result was a set of computer kits that allowed people to build a small computer from parts and implement programs by entering octal (i.e., base 8) or hex (i.e., base 16) codes of instructions into a set of switches. As these systems advanced, the microprocessors remained at their heart.

The One-State Computer Wins

The personal computer industry was miniscule compared to the large computer companies like IBM. For a while, IBM outwardly ignored PCs, but in time, the computer giant decided that if there was going to be a personal computing industry, IBM was going to be part of it. So they set off to enter the business quickly by having an internal contest. The contest was basically that the first group to come up with a working personal computer would have their product turned into the IBM product. The winner was an existing control system modified to meet the minimum requirements. The processor was an 8080 made by Intel, and IBM was in the market. [129]

At that time, the microprocessor was inexpensive, the design was workable from off-the-shelf components, and the project could be completed quickly. The relatively low cost in conjunction with the availability of a few tools and the CP-M operating system made the product a winner. To place protection into this architecture would have taken time and money, and nobody knew what would happen with computers over the next 20 years.

But the best intentions don't necessarily lead to the best long-term results. As it was said at that time (mostly by the well-dressed IBM representatives), "Nobody ever got fired for buying IBM," and indeed, customers bought IBM personal computers by the millions. The operating system became DOS, the 8086 was the microprocessor, and all was well with the world, except for one thing:

> When they created the PC, they forgot about protection.

I don't mean to slight Apple Computer in this discussion, and I will give them a dishonorable mention along the way. Apple chose the

6502 microprocessor as the basis for its early computer system designs, and as it moved to the 68000 and on up, Apple also ignored protection. As the only substantial competition for personal computer operating environments, they could have made protection into a market issue, but they did not. Instead, and perhaps rightly so from a business point of view, they emphasized ease of use and user interface as the differentiating factors for their products.

A Generation of PC Programmers

An entire generation of programmers was brought up on the PC and the Apple personal computer line. The result was devastating to much of the knowledge base gained from the first 20 years of widespread computing. Almost everything learned about timesharing, efficient allocation of resources, information protection, and other related fields was lost to the PC generation. Indeed, PCs have dominated the computing field now for more than half of its lifetime. Most 35-year-old programmers have never programmed anything else, and half the population of the world is under 35 years old. Most universities teach personal computers as the dominant technology, and if you look at the curriculum, you will find that information protection is not included.

Early personal computers had a big problem. The problem was communication, which they largely lacked. The modem was used for communicating to mainframes, terminal emulators allowed them to be used as terminals for mainframe computers, and the floppy disks were very useful for physically handing data from one person to another, but there was no really effective way to get personal computers to communicate until the local area network (LAN) came into widespread use. With the advent of the LAN, the protection problem reared its ugly head again.

With standalone PCs, protection is essentially a physical issue, just as it was in the early days of computing. If someone can gain physical access to the computer, they are in control. If they cannot, they have no way to access information. But in the LAN environment, like in timesharing environments, access to any entry point may provide access to everything. The LAN environment essentially extends the computer to a larger physical domain.

The larger the organization, the greater the need for widespread communication in order to attain the leverage of information technology, and so LANs were soon extended to the wide area network (WAN) technology already used by timesharing systems. Today, it is not unusual for a PC to be connected to millions of computers via the Internet. [158]

But the PC generation didn't know how to design and implement protection and the lessons of the first 20 years of computing were widely ignored. Even as the computing power increased in the early 1990s and the 80386 processor made the two-state machine available to the personal computer operating system designers, the designers simply didn't know what to do with the new capability. OS/2 and Windows came into popularity, but neither had any substantial protection capability because the PC generation hasn't been taught the lessons of the past. Even the file servers of the PC generation were not designed with good protection, and the result is a wide open, globally accessible environment.

> Today, protection is essentially nonexistent in more than 90 percent of the world's computers.

4.4   A SUPPRESSED TECHNOLOGY

But dropping all of the blame on market forces and a lack of vision only begins to address the underlying causes of today's problems. For, at the same time as these events were occurring, there was a systematic movement by the Government to suppress the information protection technology base of the United States.

Cryptography Leashed

The dilemma of cryptography has haunted governments throughout history. The people in governments want their cryptography to be very strong in order to keep their secrets secret, but they also want everyone else's cryptography to be very weak so they can read everyone else's secrets.

Nowhere was this made more clear than in World War II, where the United States and United Kingdom were successfully reading secret transmissions of Germany and Japan, and the Allied transmissions were not being read effectively by Germany or Japan. [121] The cryptographic advantage literally made the difference in the Battle of Britain, the Battle of Midway, and on many other decisive occasions. It also played a major supporting role in Patton's victories over the Africa Corps, the war in Europe, and throughout the South Pacific.

One of the results of the success of cryptography in World War II was that it came to be viewed as such a vital national military asset, that open research was suppressed. For example, cryptography is the only large class of information technology that is banned from export. Cryptographic results, as nuclear weapons results, are considered classified as soon as they are created. Research grant applications submitted to the National Science Foundation (NSF) in the areas of cryptography and computer security are required to be sent to the National Security Agency

(NSA) for review and, to date, the NSA has not rated any proposal high enough to get funding from the NSF.

When the RSA public key cryptosystem now used in so many commercial applications [182] was first published, there was an attempt by the U.S. government to suppress its widespread release. It ended up in Federal court, where the NSA refused to show any evidence, but told the judge that it would be against the national interest to allow the already published information to be further published. The court ruled against the NSA.

During the explosion of information technology, the government was trying rather hard to control the research in information protection by restricting research funding, bringing researchers who published results to court, and trying to discredit researchers. The problem with this strategy was that as our individual, corporate, and national dependency on information technology increased dramatically, our knowledge base in protecting that technology was suppressed. It's like suppressing the immune system of a person with a deadly disease. The person will eventually die.

But even with the national government's efforts to suppress the widespread development of information protection technology, at the height of the Cold War, some of its most precious secrets were being leaked to its worst enemies. As research was being suppressed at a national level, government employees were leaking information in exchange for cash, sex, and other reasons. *The Falcon and The Snowman* case [132], the Ames case, [3] and the Walker family case [145] are three widely published examples. So our enemies were learning the secrets of our protection, while our own people were being kept in the dark.

Law Enforcement Is Clueless

Recently, law enforcement has started to take computer crime seriously, but until the early 1990s, they were literally clueless. When Cliff Stoll called the FBI [208] to report the attack on his computer, the FBI asked how much was stolen. Cliff answered, "seventy-five cents" ($0.75). The FBI ignored all of the information about national laboratories being broken into via computer and concentrated on the known loss which was too small to be bothered with.

"But the times, they are a-changin'." The recent introduction of federal laws and an increased awareness by the FBI and other police organizations of the import of computers in crime has led to a lot more attention to this issue of late. Unfortunately, law enforcement personnel are not even close to expert in this field today, and by the time they are called, if they are called, it is rarely possible to catch an attacker.

Attacks Covered Up

You have no idea of how often computers are attacked.

> You are probably unaware that late in 1993, successful attacks were underway against large numbers of U.S. DoD computers throughout the world. In fact, even the DoD wasn't aware of this until early 1994.

Until you read this book, you were probably unaware that more than 100,000 computer system passwords had been gathered in recent attacks on the Internet and that those attacks are still underway at this time. If you are unaware of attacks against hundreds of thousands of computers at one time where those attacks are announced in the media, you are almost certainly unaware of the many more attacks that happen every day and are covered up.

An example of a coverup from my personal experience might be helpful in understanding the issue. I was asked in to do some consulting for a large company I have worked with before and was given no particular details ahead of time. This may seem unusual, but in the information protection business, it's fairly common for people under attack to give no unnecessary details over the telephone. In this particular meeting I went to, I was told that about $100 million had been stolen and that nobody had been told about it because the company was afraid their customers would lose confidence. By the time they called me, it was apparently too late to recover the money because the incident had happened more than six months earlier. I was later told that the theft was eventually written off as a one-time loss due to restructuring (or some such thing) and the stockholders were never told the truth.

Now I must say that there probably are not very many cases of $100 million losses due to computer fraud per year. For example, the FBI claims to know of only two such cases still unsolved from 1989. [54] But, of course, the example I just described was not reported to the FBI, so these numbers are at least a little bit low. How low are they?

It is impossible to tell you how low the official figures on losses due to computer crime are. One reason is that there is no uniform way to evaluate such losses. For example, the Internet Virus in 1988 resulted in estimated losses ranging from a few million dollars to tens of millions of dollars, but in court, the official losses in the criminal charges were placed at or about $50,000. This difference is in part because the legal requirements for the crime Morris (the admitted and convicted perpetrator) was charged with were only $5,000 in damage, so it was unnecessary to try to elevate the figures above that. But the real value of a loss of this sort should include lost time for all of the users, damage to the reputation of the affected companies, the cost of replacing lost or corrupted data, incidental damages created by the downtime, and a whole host of other factors. [113]

Another factor is that only a portion of actual computer crimes are ever detected and, of those, only a portion are ever reported. I obviously don't know what portion of the crimes are detected, since I would have to detect all the undetected crimes in order to know that, but you may legitimately ask how I know that all of the crimes are not detected. It is not because I am a criminal who hasn't been caught. I have three types of evidence that convince me that this is the case.

1. I have spoken to a number of computer criminals that have never been caught.
2. I have performed tests to demonstrate weaknesses that show that certain types of crimes are undetectable in certain environments.
3. When computer criminals are caught, they sometimes admit to crimes that were not detected.

Even when computer crimes are detected, they are not always reported. For example, in one recent study I did for a large company, about 20 incidents were detected by employees over the last year, but only two of those were reported to the police. One reason the police were not called was that the employees detecting the incidents had no official mandate or mechanism for reporting incidents to management. Top-level decision makers never had the choice of reporting or not. The executives only found out about the incidents in the course of the study.

Another reason many incidents are not reported is because they involve information that the company does not want released. In papers published by American Telephone and Telegraph (AT&T) [34, 18] and Digital Equipment Corporation (DEC), [179] computer crimes are described and their frequency is given, but if these published papers are accurate, few, if any, of these incidents were reported to the police. For some reason, these criminal acts were eventually disclosed to the public, but they were apparently never reported to the police.

Perhaps the best way to measure actual incidents is to look at how many attacks have been detected in your organization and how many of those have been reported to the police. Assume that everyone else acts about the same way, and you should have an idea of the level of crime today.

4.5 THE UNIVERSITIES FAIL US

While you would expect universities to be in the forefront of information technology, they certainly are lagging in information protection, at least in the United States. The story here begins with the late 1970s. At that point, there was a growing interest in information protection in the university community as reflected by the increased number of journal articles from universities at about that time. [44] But three things happened to prevent the further growth. One part of the problem was the suppression by the government of sponsored research into information protection described earlier. Another part has to do with the general lack of funding for university research in the 1980s. The third part has to do with inbreeding.

The general lack of research funding started in about 1980 when Ronald Reagan became President of the United States. In his first year in office, the budget for unclassified research and development went from 4 percent of the federal budget to under 2 percent. The effect was devastating to the universities because they had depended on the government for research funding to such a large extent that many programs were eliminated. Many of those that survived did so by converting to low-cost development programs for local industry. In the following years, most businesses followed the government's lead and reduced research and development spending, and those reductions also affected the universities.

> As spending is cut, research programs tend to move from looking far into the future toward solving today's most pressing problems. Thus, research becomes a reactive effort rather than a proactive effort, and advances in fields like information protection tend to fall by the wayside.

The inbreeding problem is caused by the tendency for research in universities to follow the same lines as previous research in those universities. In the 1960s and 1970s, the computer science community was fairly young, and widely associated with the hippies of that era. The whole idea of secrecy was in violent opposition to the goals of open research, and the computer science community was one small and happy family. The result was that a large portion of the best known researchers in the field and most of their students took a perspective of ignoring information protection except in a few areas where it made computing easier. They didn't teach their students about protection, the subject was poorly covered in even the best of textbooks, and the curriculum lacked in this area to the point where the average graduate had only about 15 minutes of exposure to the field. [44] The best of these students commonly became graduate students, and eventually, after being weeded out by professors with little or no interest in information protection, some of them became the new generation of professors. Thus, the inbreeding caused a neglected field to be further neglected until it was almost forgotten.

4.6   AN INDUSTRY OF CHARLATANS

If the universities failed us, it was unintentional, but the computer security industry had a much different agenda. Their goal was to promote ignorance and fear so they could sell more low-quality products with lower development cost. If you know this business, you know that there are many legitimate companies that have good products, but there are also a lot of companies that think they are legitimate, but lack in the underlying knowledge needed to qualify them to do good work in this field.

One class of good examples are the products on the market today that provide PC security in the form of a program to associate a password with each file. Now I don't want to make the blanket claim that there is no application in which this technique is workable. But I think I should point out just a few of the problems with this scheme that you should be aware of before you buy.

- Effective password protection requires hard-to-guess passwords and a secure channel from the user to the computer. Most of these schemes don't provide adequate protection against easily guessed passwords or provide a secure channel.
- The use of multiple passwords leads to forgetfulness, while the repeated use of the same password is a waste of time and effort. If you want one password to protect your files, you should have a different sort of protection scheme.
- Implementations tend to be flawed in that they are easily attacked. For example, most such schemes don't prevent widely used commercial utilities such as Norton Utilities from accessing files unhindered.
- Forgotten passwords lead to easy breaking schemes or lost files. In the former case, the providers of the protection provide a utility program used to break the scheme or another vendor will provide it for a fee. For example, WordPerfect's encryption was trivially broken by researchers at Queensland University of Technology, and hundreds of people requested copies of the code-breaking program so they could recover files they lost when someone forgot a password. Lost files are often more of a risk than the risk of their contents being released.
- Repeated password entry is inconvenient. Most users prefer to enter a password when they begin use and have access to whatever they are authorized to do from that point forward.
- Trojan horses easily bypass this protection. For example, it is simple to record keystrokes without the user knowing it by using an inexpensive off-the-shelf product. By recording the passwords as they are entered, access can be gained.
- In many of these schemes, booting the computer from a floppy disk allows protection to be ignored.
- This scheme ignores human factors, integrity requirements, availability requirements, and the history of protection.

Most importantly, this scheme is, at best, only a small part of an overall protection effort. It has to fit into the rest of the protection effort in order to be effective. Most products don't fit well into an overall protection scheme unless they are made to operate in that scheme. That means that regardless of how low the purchase price of this scheme may be, it is likely to cost a lot more to use than it's worth.

By far, the vast majority of the current protection products have similar problems. They are, at best, quick fixes to one problem applied to a different problem without ample consideration of the real issues.

One of the prepublication readers of this book commented that ignorance is not malice and neither is doing something cheaply for a profit motive. I must strongly disagree. When a company presents itself or its products as anything other than what they are, this is intentional and therefore malicious. I would not find fault if companies like this presented a product as a cheap and only mildly secure solution to a common problem, but when a company presents itself as expert in the field of information protection and it is not, this is no different than a group of medical technicians presenting themselves as doctors.

4.7 INFORMATION ASSURANCE IGNORED

One of the major side effects of widespread leakage has been an undue concentration of the information protection field on the issue of keeping secrets from being leaked. Of that effort, the vast majority of the work assumes a model based on military classification methods in use since before electronic information technology existed. The net effect is a set of protection technologies that are almost entirely aimed at addressing only one of the three areas of protection of vital concern today, and the least important one at that.

Information Assurance is Vital

Information assurance is assuring the availability and integrity of information over the entire range of potential disruptions from accidental to malicious. This is the most vital issue in information protection today and is widely misunderstood and ignored, especially by the people who practice computer security. [63]

The information assurance problem seems to stem from a desire for efficiency that overrides all other considerations. Many people have heard the term *optimal* used to describe the most efficient method for doing a particular thing, and there seems to be an almost religious vigor for pursuing optimal solutions. What a lot of people miss is that the term *optimal* only has meaning in a context. That context inherently limits the scope of what optimality implies.

The most common context for seeking optimality in information technology today is minimizing computer time or minimizing computer storage space. But minimum time leaves no slack room to check the propriety of results, and minimum space leaves no spares to be used in case of failure. The combination leaves no redundancy that can be used to assure integrity or availability, and the result is that any fault, no matter how minor, delivers a wrong result, delivers a result to the wrong place, or delivers it at the wrong time.

A good example of efficiency replacing effectiveness is in the way compilers are commonly used. When programs are written and tested, programmers commonly use *debugging* options and *bounds checking* on *arrays*. The debugging option allows program elements to be traced as the program is executed, so that the programmer can find errors and determine their origin. Bounds checking on arrays performs tests every time memory is accessed to make certain that only the proper portion of memory is being used. If the program is perfect, debugging and bounds checking perform no useful function, but programs of substantial size are almost never perfect, even after substantial testing. The problem comes when the program is ready to be delivered to the customer. In order to make the program as small and fast as possible, software manufacturers commonly turn off debugging and bounds checking, recompile the programs, and ship them out. But this means that errors not detected during testing may go unnoticed during operation. Users may simply get wrong results, and since there is no error detection in place, they may never know about the errors or be able to trace them back to the computer program.

The cost and effciency advantages brought about by implementing the NII will increase the nation's dependency on it. If elements of the NII are not available, information is inaccurate, or the NII does not properly provide required functional or information transfer capabilities, time will be lost and overall effectiveness will be diminished. It is precisely the standards designers use to make technology efficient that make it easy to attack. [57, pp316–320]

Secrecy Standards DO NOT Address Information Assurance

It is critical in understanding the information assurance challenge to understand the difference between *information assurance issues* which *relate to all information* and information systems, and *secrecy issues* which *relate to confidential data*. Confidential data is almost always controlled based on its **content**, and is controlled because knowledge of it might be useful in ways that could adversely affect the owner's interests or actions, because release could be a violation of laws, or because release could result in the assumption of financial risk. Information assurance requirements apply to *all information*, and are based on **use** rather than content.

Existing policies and standards that guide protection of data sensitivity are not adequate for addressing information assurance. [37, 63] The strongest evidence is that no computer security system designed to protect sensitive data from release is effective against malicious computer viruses. The reason is that malicious viruses corrupt information and sometimes deny services, while secrecy systems protect against information leakage, and not corruption or denial of services.

Fault-tolerant Computing Standards DO NOT Address Information Assurance

It would be natural to assume that information assurance is already provided by existing fault-tolerant computing standards and practices such as protection against random noise, [14] [152] lightning, [140] RF noise, [177] loss of packets, [111] and other transient factors that cause disruptions in information systems. Unfortunately, intentional attackers are not accurately modeled by the statistical models of faults used to develop existing reliability standards.

Let's look at what a typical text says on the subject: "The noise analysis of communications systems is customarily based on an idealized form of noise called 'white noise', the power spectral density of which is independent of the operating frequency. The adjective 'white' is used in the sense that white light contains equal amounts of all frequencies within the visible band of electromagnetic radiation. . . . " [104] The reason cited for the random noise models is the ease of analysis, [148] but ease and adequacy of analysis are not always compatible.

One of the most common techniques for detecting corruption in memory and transmission is the use of a "parity" bit associated with each byte. The parity bit is set to 1 or 0 to make the total number of "1s" even or odd, depending on whether the even or odd parity convention is being used. This technique detects all single bit errors, which is quite effective against particular sorts of random noise that cause transient faults. It is not effective against an intentional attacker who can change sets of bits collectively while maintaining parity, thus corrupting the information and avoiding detection.

On disk storage, in LAN packets, and in some satellite transmission, cyclical redundancy check (CRC) codes are used to detect classes of faults that result in errors to linear sequences of bits of, at most, some predefined length. [111] Again, these codes are ineffective against an intentional attacker, because it is easy to determine the constant coefficients of the coding equations by watching packets, and from this it is easy to forge packets at will undetected. [44]

"Most communication channels incorporate some facilities designed to ensure availability, but most do so only under the assumptions of benign error, not in the context of malicious attack." [157, note 6, p. 160]

Perfect Systems Are Infeasible

The field of *high assurance* computing addresses information systems for the most critical applications (e.g., life support systems, flight controls, nuclear warhead detonation). Unfortunately, building perfect systems is far too costly and resource-intensive for the wide variety of systems and networks found in the NII, and only adequately addresses certain types of very well-defined control applications.

Substantial work is oriented toward designing a perfect system wherein all inputs, states, outputs, and state transitions are specified in full detail and mathematical proofs are provided to show that the design is properly implemented. [101, 134] Although this type of solution may be applicable to certain limited control problems in embedded systems, these sorts of solutions are computationally infeasible for any large system, cover only sufficiency and not necessity [47], only cover limited function systems against disruption, [44] and are beyond current and anticipated capabilities over the next 20 years for the sorts of systems desired in the NII.

An alternative path to a similar solution is the use of programs to generate programs. In this technology, a small number of programs are designed to automatically write the rest of the programs. Designers spend a great deal of time and effort in perfecting the design automation system which, in turn, designs other systems. [196] This technology is far from perfected, and even if it were perfected, it leaves the problem of writing perfect specifications, which is at least as hard as writing perfect programs.

In the hardware realm, design automation has been highly successful, but this does not imply that it will be as successful in the software realm. There are substantial differences between hardware and software. For example, the complexity of current software is many orders of magnitude higher than the most complex designs now done by automated systems, the physical properties of hardware are abstracted out of most software design, and software is designed based on a finite but unbounded, randomly accessible space, while hardware is designed based on a relatively small, finite, and bounded space with only local access as provided by explicitly created wires. Furthermore, hardware design automation takes substantial amounts of computer time, still leaves design flaws such as data dependencies that have resulted in disruption, and is based on specifications that are susceptible to errors.

Another alternative is the use of extremely intensive testing to detect the presence of errors and correct them. The problem with this approach is that testing for 100 percent coverage is as complex as perfect design. Imperfect testing leaves systems that fail when *rare* events occur. The problem with the recent Intel Pentium microprocessor is a good example of how testing fails.

In one study, the combination of two events characterized as low probability caused 50 percent of systematically designed, well-tested, small control programs to fail. [106] If this is the current state of the art for low probability events in small programs, extremes in testing are not likely to be successful against intentional attacks on large, globally networked infrastructures.

For the sorts of general-purpose systems in the NII, there are classes of attacks that cannot be perfectly defended against. Two well-known examples are computer viruses [47] and exploitation of covert channels. [128] If people spend their resources trying to implement perfect solutions to these problems, they will surely fail and go bankrupt in the process. But as individuals and as a nation, we cannot simply ignore these and other similar problems, because they present a real and identifiable threat to our economic and national security and directly affect all aspects of our society.

Feasible solutions will not be perfect. Rather, they should responsibly trade cost with protection.

Poor Assumptions Lead to Disruptions

Well-trained intentional attackers understand the common assumptions made by designers of information and secrecy systems, and explicitly design attacks to exploit the weaknesses resulting from these assumptions. Protective techniques that work against statistically characterized events are rarely effective against directed attack, and techniques designed to provide secrecy are rarely effective against disruption. One relatively limited study of the impact of malicious node destruction using a structure that works very well against random destruction found that preventing intentional attacks with standard fault-tolerant computing techniques may require an order of magnitude increase in costs. [148] Studies and demonstrations of computer viruses in secrecy systems approved for government use have demonstrated that these systems are ineffective against disruption. [44]

Current system reliability estimates do not account for deliberate software corruption. [157, p55] Telecommunication networks can fail from software malfunction, failures can propagate in operations or control systems, [84, p32] and system availability estimates seem to overlook this cascading effect. One company advertises that if its 800 service fails, restoration is guaranteed in under one hour, and telephone networks are supposedly designed for something like five minutes of downtime per year. [102] Yet, in a single incident in 1990, the American Telephone and Telegraph (AT&T) 800 network was unavailable for more than four hours, [84] which seems to imply that this failure covers expected outages over the next 48 years! (5 minutes per year = 4 hours per 48 years)

> Considering that a similar failure brought down telephones in several major cities for several days in 1991, [81] there appears to have been a flaw in this availability analysis.

Gateways, terminal servers, and routers are commonly used to control traffic in networked environments, and they are quite effective against random or accidental misrouting of information, but in a hostile environment, they commonly fall prey to disruptive attacks. General-purpose computers used as gateways are easily overwhelmed and corrupted. Terminal servers are commonly accessible by users logged into any computer in the network and can be altered to remove usage restrictions, connect users to wrong systems, or even lock out legitimate terminal server administrators. [51] Routers designed to control network traffic and prevent overloading in large networks are also easily bypassed by using the administrative mechanisms which permit remote control of the router or forgery of machine identities with authorized access. [42]

The public telecommunications networks are a critical part of the NII, but they lack the information assurance features required for critical operations. Service assurance features are designed into these systems at every level, [84] and yet they still fail to meet even the challenge of accidental errors and omissions. As an example, in 1991 there was a major failure in telephone switches in several large U.S. cities that lasted for several days. It was finally traced to a 3-bit error (a 'D' instead of a '6') in one byte of a software upgrade. [81] This is the simple sort of mistake that even minimal software change control detects. The change was apparently never tested at all, was put into widespread use, and caused widespread disruption.

In many cases, telecommunications disruption must be resolved in very short time frames. For example, some telephone switching systems must be repaired within 1.5 seconds or the circuit failure errors passing through the network will cause a propagating positive feedback which may deadlock more of the network, [165] eventually cascading into a major problem. An attacker only needs to disrupt two sites for 1.5 seconds to cause such a cascading effect.

According to a National Research Council (NRC) report: "As computer systems become more prevalent, sophisticated, embedded in physical processes, and interconnected, society becomes more vulnerable to poor systems design, accidents that disable systems, and attacks on computer systems. Without more responsible design, implementation, testing, and use, system disruptions will increase, with harmful consequences for society. They will also result in lost opportunities from the failure to put computer and communications systems to their best use." (The opening paragraph of [157].)

Information Assurance Standards Are Inadequate

It is enlightening to examine the current U.S. Government standards base upon which open systems are now being acquired. [163] The DoD standards document begins with a list of protection service standards, including some that seem to be information assurance standards needed to fulfill requirements of the NII. Unfortunately, almost none of the list of service standards is currently specified (see following table):

Service Standard	Status
Authentication	Not Available—In Process
Access Control	Not Available—In Process
Non-Repudiation	Not Available—In Process
Confidentiality	Not Available—In Process
Integrity	Not Available—In Process
Auditing	Not Available—In Process
Key Management	Not Available—In Process

Most of the "Not Available—In Process" items are specified as, "This work is still in the early stages and is not yet of practical use. It should not be referenced in a procurement." Further, there is no clear migration path from current designs to designs with these services, so there is no defined way for the designers of the NII to even plan for future assurance. Notice that *availability of service* is not even on the list of standards to be developed.

By way of reference, the International Standards Organization (ISO) standard upon which this list was based was in approximately the same incomplete state about 10 years ago, when the protection addendum to the ISO standard was newly created. [112] To date, no significant progress has been made in these areas and no current open system products provide substantial coverage of these areas.

Risk analysis for many other areas is fundamentally different than the techniques that apply to malicious disruption. Specifically, if an attacker knows how to disrupt a system, success in an attack is virtually certain. The probabilistic approach to analyzing defenses and attacks may not be appropriate for considering human agents with malicious intent. That's why 50 years worth of theoretical downtime can be exhausted in a single incident. [84] Obviously, the standards for risk assessment used to derive infrastructure availability figures are not up to the information assurance task.

Another place where information assurance standards are lacking relates to common mode failures and correlated events. [160] Common mode failures are failures wherein the same mechanism affects several different components. Several major incidents per year involving common mode failure in redundant systems now occur and there seems to be a strong correlation between these events and inadequate standards or capabilities for redundancy. The White Plains telephone cable incident in December of 1986 involved seven redundant circuit connections for the Advanced Research Projects Agency Network (ARPAnet) intended to assure that no single (or multiple up to 6) failure could disable the network connection. Unfortunately, the telephone company ended up routing all seven connections through the same optical fiber and, when that cable was cut, all seven redundant connections were disrupted.

In many cases where redundant input is required, it isn't exploited for error detection and correction, which is the worst of both worlds. An example may help clarify this point. In the United States, postal zip codes directly imply the state. Why then ask for the state? For efficiency reasons, systems should not. On the other hand, by asking for the state and zip code, systems could detect inconsistency and act to correct the error before it creates a larger problem (e.g., sending a paycheck to the wrong place).

> In most current systems, we have the worst of both worlds. Systems ask for both zip code and state, but never compare them to find errors. Such systems have both extra data entry and inadequate coverage of errors. [50]

4.8 CURRENT DISRUPTION DEFENSES DEPEND ON PEOPLE

Current defenses against disruption depend almost entirely on human prevention, detection, differentiation, warning, response, and recovery. Detection of most disruption attacks comes only when people notice something is going wrong. In many cases, detection never occurs, while in other cases, detection takes several months. Differentiating natural, accidental, mischievous, and malicious disruption is a manual process, and the root cause is often undetermined or misidentified as accidental. Warning has to be properly controlled to prevent false positives and false negatives, and depends on forensic analysis. Response commonly takes from hours to days and is almost entirely manual. Recovery too is almost always a manual process, takes from hours to days, and is often performed improperly.

> In many cases, attacks are not detected at all. For example, in more than 100 legitimate computer virus experiments, no user has ever noticed the presence of a computer virus. [44]

The vast majority of known information system attacks are first detected by attentive users noticing unusual behavior. This is widely known in the computer security community and is supported by virtually every source that discusses the issue. For example, more than 5,000 computer viruses have been detected in the last three years and almost all of them were detected by users noticing anomalies. The Internet virus of 1988 was detected when users noticed dramatic network slowdowns. [115, 114] Hundreds of other failures in national telecommunications networks and individual systems are first detected by user complaints. [80, 157, 156] In major bank frauds involving electronic funds transfers, it is common for the first detection to be at the next bank audit, typically several months later.

Indirection between cause and effect dramatically increases the time required to track an attack to the source. Whereas total denial of services to a system or infrastructure is widely noticed almost immediately, business disruption caused by subtle denial of services or corruptions may be far harder to detect and associate with a cause. For example, suppose a disruption caused orders placed for certain replacement parts to be ignored by the output routines in the order fulfillment subsystem of a supply and logistics system. Orders would be placed and the computer would indicate that the orders had been processed and shipped, but no shipments would arrive. Similarly, disruption in the form of subtle corruption could transform airplane engine part numbers into similar part numbers indicating different components, perhaps toothpicks. The order would be processed, but the resulting shipment would contain the wrong parts. It would probably be blamed on a data entry error and, if it only happened 10 percent of the time, the cause might go unnoticed for a long time, while the efficiency loss could be quite substantial. Another subtle disruption approach is to slowly increase the level of denial of services over time so that the operators become acclimated to the slower and slower pace over a long period.

Differentiating natural disaster from other causes is generally not too difficult because natural disasters are easily detected on a wide scale. Differentiating accident from mischief from malice is yet another problem.

The Internet Virus was apparently an accident, and yet clearly many believe it was mischief and a few still believe it was malicious.

> Many disruptions are treated as accidental to avoid investigation. Almost no current organization has a way to tell one sort of disruption from another.

Limiting damage often takes too long to be effective. In the case of the IBM Christmas Card Virus of 1987, several days after the attack was launched, it was widely noticed, and over the next several days, IBM staff members tried unsuccessfully to disconnect their internal networks from the global networks. [110, 44] A defense against the Internet Virus was only devised after more than a full day of effort by people nationwide, and implementation of the workaround took several days. [115, 114]

Recovery is sometimes impossible, while in other cases it takes from days to weeks. For example, a company in Germany was the subject of extortion from a hacker (1988–89), who showed them a few lines of program code which would have caused the gradual corruption of all inventory records. They did not find the altered code for several weeks. [96] The Chicago telephone center fire in 1989 took months to recover from, and tens of thousands of customers were without service for extended periods. [157]

If the recovery process is improperly performed, many other problems can result. Audit trails may be lost, thus preventing accurate determination of cause. The *recovered* system may be more vulnerable to disruption than the original. The recovery process may itself cause disruptions.

Human attack detection has several problems in addition to the limited response time and large numbers of false negatives. Perhaps the most important problem is the expectation of breakage and the inability to differentiate properly between breakage and malicious attack. Another problem is the tendency to detect fewer faults over time in an environment where faults are commonplace. [149] This can be exploited by the attack wherein the number of disruptions are slowly increased, while the human operator becomes increasingly insensitive to them. Enhanced training improves performance, but humans are clearly still limited, particularly when it comes to detecting subtle attacks characterized by the coordination of numerous seemingly different and dispersed events and attacks designed to exploit the reflexive control aspects of human behavior. [95]

Automated tools for detecting misuse in computer systems and local area networks are currently emerging and this technology is rapidly

approaching commercial viability. [72] The most advanced misuse detection systems include localized responses to statistical anomalies and
rule-based response to known attack patterns. [176, 175, 136, 137, 138, 203]

Based on observations made during one recent study, [63] some authors believed that response to attacks is characterized by thresholds of
detection and response capacity. By lowering thresholds of detection, the
defender is likely to detect more attacks, but the number and likelihood
of false positives will also increase, and so will the cost of responding to
the relatively minor incidents. By increasing the threshold of detection,
response resources may be concentrated on the most important incidents,
but a small incident with widespread impact may not be noticed until
the damage becomes severe.

This leads to the issue of attack and defense. Given the option of a
directed attack against a specific target or a more general attack which
increases the overall noise level, the threshold scheme employed for defense has a substantial effect on the optimal attack decision. It is always
possible for an attacker to remain below the threshold of detection for
any imperfect detection system, so a fixed threshold system leaves the
defender open to noise-based attack. Similarly, a substantial directed attack will sound off any capable detection system and generate a response,
but it may also be possible to create the appearance of substantial attack
in order to force the defender to respond more strongly than necessary,
thus creating an environment where the defender constantly *cries wolf*.
In either situation, a fixed response level is easily exploited, so a flexible
and adaptive response is necessary in order to be effective.

In addition to detection thresholds, there is a response capacity inherently limited by the available response resources. In a human-based
response system such as the one currently in place in the NII, response
time lags further and further behind as the number of incidents increase,
eventually leading to a situation where important attacks are not noticed
for a substantial amount of time. Increasing human resources is quite
expensive and is only effective when the level of attack warrants the
number of respondents. It takes a long time to train experts in this field,
and there are relatively few experts available and woefully few places
where new experts can be trained.

An attacker can alternatively create and not create attacks so as to
force a defender to waste resources with an overblown defensive capability or an attacker can use attacks to determine response characteristics
and work out ways to overwhelm the defense. This area is particularly
amenable to analysis based on reflexive control. To form a strong defense,
the flexibility must be designed so as to prevent this sort of analysis. [95]

Clearance processes do not detect people who change sides after
they are cleared, people who have breakdowns, and people subjected to
extortion. Many sources claim that the majority of computer crimes come

as a result of an authorized person using that authority inappropriately. Although sufficient evidence is not available to support this contention, there is clearly a potential for *soft-kill* harm from an insider that is greater than from an outsider, because the insider has fewer barriers to bypass in order to succeed.

> The current NII design assumes that insiders act properly to a large extent. A proper infrastructure design should not make such an assumption or depend on it for meeting design criteria.

4.9 THE REST OF THE WORLD RESPONDS

There are a small number of research groups around the world that have been working on the information assurance problem for a number of years. Known foreign research locations include The People's Republic of China, Russia, Germany, Israel, Australia, Denmark, England, and Japan.

The People's Republic of China has a group headed by Yue-Jiang Huang that has produced both internal and international hardware enhancements to personal computers for protecting against many forms of disruption. This group is also doing substantial work in the use of nonlinear feedback shift registers for both secrecy and integrity applications.

In Russia, there is at least one group working on disruption prevention, detection, and response systems. This Moscow-based group at the Central Research Institute *Center* in Moscow is working on new hardware architectures that provide enhanced integrity protection and limited availability against general classes of malicious threats. They seem to have an emphasis on computer viruses, but far more general application can be made of their architecture. [212]

Research groups in Israel regularly publish results on their research in international journals and several groups have started work on protection of information systems against general classes of malicious corruption. [98, 190, 178]

An Australian research group directed by Bill Caelli and centered at Queensland University of Technology is concentrating a substantial amount of effort in the design of high-integrity networks capable of withstanding malicious disruption. They also have people working on cryptographic integrity techniques and key management systems with revocation for use in systems similar to the NII.

At least one Canadian author has published work on limits of testing and coding spaces against malicious disruption attacks. [123]

A German research team at the University of Hamburg has gone a step further than most groups in this area by forming a database of parts of computer viruses. They essentially break the thousands of known viruses into component parts (i.e., self-encryption, find file, hide in memory, attach to victim, etc.) and store the partial programs in a database. Many known viruses have common components, but there are on the order of several hundred of each different component part. This gives them both the capability to detect and automatically analyze many viruses in very short time frames, and the capability to generate on the order of 10^{20} different viruses automatically by mixing techniques together. [90]

Several other countries have started to publish papers in the information assurance areas and, although there is no apparent evidence of massive efforts, it seems that the international interest in this field has increased substantially since the Gulf War.

Yet, with all of this international attention to this problem, the United States doesn't even support adequate response to widely publicized ongoing attacks throughout the DoD.

CHAPTER 5

Protecting Your Information Assets

Information protection is a multifaceted discipline encompassing a wide range of management and technical specialties, and affecting every aspect of modern life. In the space available, it is impossible to adequately cover even a small portion of the information protection field in great depth. Instead, protection issues will be covered from several different perspectives to present a broad view of the overall problems and solutions.

It may seem strange at first not to address protection by simply detailing how to protect against each attack. This well-known process of elimination seems logically sound at first glance. It is commonly used in many fields, and it is one of the fundamental processes of rational problem-solving.

The problem with the process of elimination in this particular field is that potentially infinite numbers of different attacks exist. [44, 47, 216] As the world famous philosopher of science Karl Popper so rightly pointed out, [170] you cannot prove the truth of a universal statement (e.g., we are protected) about an infinite set (e.g., against all attacks), with a finite number of examples (e.g., by this list of defenses). It only takes one falsification (e.g., one successful attack) to prove the statement false.

> When defenders try to answer each attack with a defense, they spend a lot of money on defenses and end up with an expensive and poorly coordinated defensive program that may only work against yesterday's attacks. This is what I call a reactive protection posture.

A good example of a reactive protection posture is the way most people defend against computer viruses today. Until they experience a virus, most people will do nothing. During their first experience, they buy products until they find one that detects and removes the computer virus they encountered. They may then use that product sporadically for some time. If they get hit again, they may find that their current product doesn't work on this new virus, and they will purchase a new version that does handle it. If one of these viruses destroyed all of the information on their disk, they will suffer the consequences, but very few people, even those who have lost a lot of work, have gone to a proactive approach. They wait till they see an obvious symptom, and then they react by looking for a cure.

The technical aspects of this field are deeply interesting to many information technologists, but a common mistake is to forget that technology only exists in a human environment. The quality of protection and its cost and effectiveness are determined by the quality of the judgments made by those who design and implement it.

Technology experts have a tendency to use their knowledge as a lever to get to what they feel is the right solution. In the computing field in general, and in the information protection field in particular, technical people who don't understand people solutions seem to leap to technical solutions and stand behind them as if they were the only solution with any hope of working. To managers, it may seem like they are getting a snow job, but it's usually not intentional. The friction between the manager and the technologist causes frustration which makes for more friction, and on it goes. The net effect is that the technical and management people don't work well together, and protection ends up being ineffective.

The solution I offer when I encounter this problem is that the technologist should learn about the broader issues at stake and the manager should learn enough about the technical field to keep from being snowed. That's one of the main goals of this chapter. For those with a narrow focus and a lot of technical knowledge, I hope to demonstrate that the solutions to protection problems are not purely technical and that no technical solution will ever completely solve the problem. For those with a broad focus but little technical knowledge, I hope to provide the ammunition required to defend against technobabble. For those with both a broad perspective and a strong technical background, I hope to increase both breadth and depth of understanding of the information protection issue.

5.1   INFORMATION PROTECTION

Information is defined as "symbolic representation in its most general sense." Protection is defined as "keeping from harm." Since the concept of harm does not apply to inanimate objects (you can damage them but not harm them), the field of information protection is *preventing harm caused by symbolic representations.*

- Protection products rarely keep you safe. The sales pitch for security products is basically that there are dangers in the world and that the product being sold will keep you safe from those dangers. Like the safety features in automobiles, people will drag out charts comparing the performance of their product against those of competitors to convince you that they have the safer product. It is a somewhat misleading way of selling protection because by far the most important elements in automobile safety are how, when, where, and how much you drive.

> Antilock brakes only rarely save a life, and they won't keep you alive very long if you drive drunk. You may feel safer with them, but you may not be much safer unless you practice the other elements of safe driving. Information protection works the same way.

- Information protection does not always protect information systems from harm. Designers may decide to shred paper, burn electronic media, or even blow up computers. Shredding paper prevents leakage of potentially harmful information in paper form, burning used floppy disks prevents their contents from being read and exploited, and blowing up electronic devices is used in smart bombs as a cost-effective way to keep the information technology used to guide the bomb from getting into enemy hands.
- Information protection is a form of self-defense. What is helpful to one person may be harmful to another. In the art of self-defense, it may be necessary to harm an attacker in order to defend yourself. In some cases, the techniques used in information protection may harm other people inadvertently. For example, monitoring user activities may create an atmosphere of fear among workers. This particular problem can be easily cured by proper protection strategy. It represents a tradeoff between strategic and tactical response to protection issues, and handily brings up my next point.
- Information protection has been, is, and will likely always be a study in tradeoffs. Designers trade costs against potential harm, long term for short term, people solutions with technical solutions, integrity with availability with privacy, and one person's harm for another person's benefit.

- Information protection is broad in its coverage. For example, toll fraud prevention is part of information protection. So are the elements of physical security that could lead to someone changing the contents of physical file cabinets. Information protection has a lot to do with hiring and firing policies too. In the case of organizations connected to the NII, information protection may include deciding which vendor to use in supplying services and how to route information sent through the NII. Information protection extends well beyond the information technology department's normal influence.

> Most people probably want to feel that their computers are safe, and many people in the computer security business try to get money for helping them feel that way, but frankly, a good psychologist might be less expensive. Relatively few organizations or individuals behave as if they really want to be kept from harm, especially if it costs them something or if they haven't just been harmed.

- In many organizations, effective information protection requires cultural change. This is one of the hardest sorts of change for most people to make because it requires that they find new ways of thinking about issues, that they gain a new level of awareness about things around them, and that they act based on this awareness. The feedback mechanisms in most organizations are not oriented toward rewards for loss prevention, and are often quite brutal toward the person who finds a problem. The "kill the messenger" theme seems popular.
- Information protection can't be left to someone else. This doesn't work, no matter who you are in an organization. In the information age, information protection is everyone's problem. From the highest ranked officer in the largest organization to the lowest paid office clerk in a Ma and Pa shop, everyone has responsibility for information protection, and protection will not be fully effective until everyone assumes their responsibility.

As I have said before, my basic perspective is that information protection is something you do, and not something you buy. The most effective efforts at information protection are proactive in nature, customized to the organization, and at least 50 percent people solutions.

5.2   INFRASTRUCTURES ARE DIFFERENT THAN OTHER SYSTEMS

There are substantial differences between designing a typical information system and designing a good information infrastructure, and the techniques normally used in information system design are often less than ideal in infrastructure design. One of the most glaring examples of these differences is in the tradeoffs between efficiency and effectiveness.

> In designing typical information systems, good designers almost always choose to do things for efficiency, while good infrastructure designers almost always choose to do things for long-term effectiveness.

- A typical system designer will choose to perfect a hardware device or interface rather than use one that has flaws. An infrastructure has to support all manners of devices and interfaces, whether operating perfectly or with flaws, and regardless of design mismatches. These devices will change over time, and a good infrastructure should support the range of changes over the expected lifetime by being designed to be changed.
- A typical system designer will choose to use components with almost identical electrical characteristics, matched timing limits, and equal reliability. An infrastructure is composed of components with a wide range of electrical characteristics, timing limits, reliability traits, and other design constraints. Over a period of decades, almost everything in an infrastructure will change, but the infrastructure as a whole should be designed to continue operating.
- A typical system designer will assume in the design of each component that all of the other components work properly, and repair faulty component designs until this is true over the testing period. An infrastructure should be designed to operate properly when SOME of the components operate properly, not only when they ALL operate properly. A faulty component should not have a significant effect on overall operations, and components should be designed to operate on the assumption that other components work improperly. Infrastructures regularly have components changed, upgraded, removed, or added, and should operate without substantial problems regardless of these changes.
- A typical system designer will implement central control mechanisms, synchronized clocks, duplexed bus usage, and other techniques that share resources for efficiency. An infrastructure should not have a central control, an off switch, or a lot of dependency between components. Highly efficient resource sharing should not be critical for infrastructure operations; it's not that efficiency should be ignored, but rather that it should not be depended upon. Economics move us toward removing redundancy from data entry in order to increase efficiency. This economic policy itself may be flawed from

an infrastructure standpoint, even though each application using the infrastructure may have this as a design goal.

- A typical system designer will use top-down design to break large problems into smaller, more manageable parts. This reduces design complexity [199] and allows design challenges to be addressed by subgroups. The problem is that technical expertise tends to be grouped near the bottom of the design structure while management tends to be grouped near the top. In infrastructure design, the best designers should be concentrated at the top, because there is a need to design an overall infrastructure that operates regardless of the components that are eventually attached to it, and that requires central technical design standards.
- In a typical system design, the designer is provided with a description of the range of uses of the system before starting the design process, and designs the system specifically for the purpose. In an information infrastructure design, the designer is faced with designing an infrastructure that will support an unknown mix of current and future applications. A good infrastructure designer must design the infrastructure to be adapted over time to optimize performance for changing needs, and must not limit the utility of the design by making it too specific or too inflexible.

> Unlike the automotive highway systems developed under the WPA, our information infrastructure was and is being developed by commercial vendors for the purpose of making a profit. That's one reason cable television is rarely found in rural areas, while the highway system extends throughout the country.

If commercial vendors were building toll roads, they probably wouldn't put them where they are now. They would probably have a hub and spoke system like the airlines have, and freight would be handled very efficiently by a few large freight companies through their selected hubs. Eventually, high-speed trains would replace much of the highway system because they can carry freight far more cost-effectively and faster than highways.

The tradeoffs between social goals, such as equal access and survivability, and financial goals, such as cost and performance, are being made by corporations today. Without making a value judgment about which is better, it is important to understand that efficiency under normal operating conditions almost never equates to efficiency or effectiveness under exceptional conditions. For this reason, any system designed purely for financial efficiency under normal operating conditions is highly susceptible to intentional disruption.

The infrastructure design issues of the NII are not ⏐
dressed effectively and the implications on long-term infc
ance may be significant. Most organizations that build th
mation infrastructures face these same issues.

5.3   A PIECEMEAL APPROACH

With this overall perspective in mind, I will now give examples of piecemeal protective techniques that are effective to some extent against each
of the elements of attack described earlier. The list of defenses for each
attack is by no means exhaustive or even close to it, just as the list of
attacks is not exhaustive, but this should give you some idea of the different ways in which attacks and defenses are approached on a piecemeal
basis.

As I have discussed earlier, piecemeal approaches are not cost-effective
and leave numerous weaknesses. On the other hand, many people who
actually defend against systems still use them. This description of piecemeal approaches should give you some idea of why they fail. All you
have to do to understand this is to contemplate implementing all of these
techniques in your organization in order to provide a reasonable level of
protection. Clearly, you will run out of time, patience, and money before
you are done.

Eliminating Attackers

Attackers can be eliminated from the pool of threats by a wide variety of
different techniques and policy decisions. Someone once said that if you
are worried about people throwing stones, don't live in a glass house.
It is much the same way with information systems attackers. We can
eliminate tiger teams by simply not inviting them in. Many hackers can
be stopped by placing adequate notice on system entry to convince them
that they are not welcome. Outsiders launching over-the-wire attacks
can be eliminated by separating the externally networked portion of
the information environment from the internal network components. So
much for the easy ones.

Terrorists tend to be reasonably well funded, but they aim at disrupting infrastructure, are particularly oriented toward the financial industries, and want to generate high-profile incidents. Terrorists can be
reduced as a threat by locating information systems in places they are
not likely to attack.

> Clearly, large high-profile buildings in the middle of large finan-
> cial centers are prime targets.

Many studies in the 1960s and 1970s relating to anti-war activists indicated that locating computer installations in particular sorts of buildings decreased the chance of attack. The bottom floors of low-profile buildings seem to be relatively safe. Buildings that are not marked or otherwise promoted to indicate the fact that they house major information centers are also less likely to be attacked. Physical distribution of resources also reduces the effect of any single incident and thus reduces the value of attack for terrorists.

Insiders are commonly cited as a major source of attack. Eliminating the insider threat is a complex issue, but some aspects include good pre-employment employee screening practices, good internal employee grievance practices and procedures, high organizational morale, and good personal support services for employees under stress. For example, in one company I used to run, we had a policy of doing whatever we could to help employees who got in trouble. One employee ended up arrested for driving while intoxicated. We helped get him into a half-way house, drove him to and from work, and helped him get counselling. Over the years that followed, he was one of our most loyal, trustworthy, and hard-working employees. Although the American corporation no longer provides lifelong job security, there is a lot of benefit to maintaining good working relationships.

Private detectives and reporters are pretty hard to stop once they decide to try to get some information about an organization, but there are some things that work well once you are aware that they are trying to attack your information systems. One thing to do is get an expert in surveillance to sweep for outside attackers. Although this is cost-prohibitive for many small businesses, for large organizations, the $20,000 or so that it costs to locate obvious problems may be very effective. Legal means are also quite effective in limiting these sorts of attacks because these attackers are generally anxious to stay out of jail and retain their licenses or jobs.

Effective methods against potentially hostile consultants include strong contractual requirements, very high-profile public prosecution of consultants caught violating protection, and refusal to hire ex-computer-criminals as computer consultants. This last point is one of the most daunting of all to me. As one of the many hard-working legitimate experts in this field, I often find it unbelievable that a computer criminal is hired over a legitimate consultant. Most computer criminals know far less about protecting information systems than legitimate expert consultants. They usually only know a few tricks that the consultants are also aware of.

By paying ex-criminals in this way, you discourage honest experts and encourage crime.

Whistle blowers are best stopped by not doing anything that someone may feel they have to blow a whistle about. Most whistle blowers have at least a semi-legitimate complaint to air. If your organization has a legitimate means to air that complaint and give it a legitimate hearing, you will eliminate the vast majority of these problems. A further step might be to provide the means for the whistle blower to get to the legitimate authority through legitimate means without getting the press or other parties involved. It is far better to provide the information through the legal process than to have it show up on the front page of the *New York Times* when you don't know it's coming.

Club initiates are a very minor threat to anyone with a strong program of information protection. As a rule, they take the path of least resistance, and as long as you don't provide that, they will get frustrated with trying to attack your systems and attack someone else.

Crackers tend to be far more determined than hackers or club initiates. They also tend to have a much better set of tools, are more willing to take risks, and are less afraid of the implications of being caught. In other words, they are fairly serious attackers. But they don't have the large financial resources or motivation to launch the extremely high-profile attacks that more serious criminals have the capability to launch. Except for producing high-profile cases against crackers, it is very hard to prevent cracker attacks by discouraging them.

> A broad range of defenses are likely to prevent most crackers, but these defenses don't necessarily need to be very deep in order to be effective.

Competitors may be very hard to stop. This problem is significantly worsened by the fact that competitors probably know more about how your operation works than noncompetitors, they probably know how to do subtle damage that is hard to detect, and they may well have several of your ex-employees available to intentionally or accidentally help them in gaining intelligence. The thing that usually stops competitors is the fear of being caught, and this is commonly increased by projecting the impression of a good comprehensive protection program. Please note that impressions are not always reflective of reality.

Maintenance people are hard to defend against by piecemeal methods. By their nature, they have access to a lot of facilities, they are in those facilities when other people tend not to be, and they are relatively low paid. This makes them high risks. The normal defense is a combination of good personnel practices, procedural techniques such as sign-in, sign-out, and good inventory controls, and physical security such as locked doors and alarms for information system sites. Unfortunately, in today's distributed computing environment, the computing power and information is widely distributed throughout the organization, and only special pieces of equipment like file servers and PBX systems can really be protected against maintenance people by physical means for reasonable cost.

Professional thieves tend to look more deeply into attacks than some of the other attackers we have considered here. This means that it is that much harder to keep them out. They also tend to be more willing to learn about technology than other attackers. They will often pick locks or enter through windows in order to get high-valued items. Part of the saving grace here is that they also tend to steal things of high value and small size and they work for money so they tend not to cause denial of services attacks unless it facilitates a theft. The best defense is a strong overall information protection program, since they might use any combination of attacks in order to achieve their goal. Piecemeal approaches will not be of any real value here.

Unlike professional thieves, hoods tend to use brute force over stealth, which makes them susceptible to physical security precautions. Strong doors, well-trained guards, good alarm systems, and similar things tend to be most effective here.

Vandals are a major problem in a lot of inner cities, especially during riots or periods of social unrest. South Central Los Angeles is one of the worst areas in the United States for vandalism, and yet the University of Southern California is right in the middle of that community and suffers relatively little in the way of vandalism. This is because of a combination of a reasonably good system of gates and walls, a university police force oriented toward reducing vandalism, and very good relationship with the surrounding community.

> A good public image may be the most important part of their strategy because by keeping the surrounding community supportive of the University, they greatly reduce the pool of attackers and bring social pressures to bear against would-be vandals.

Activists tend to be most interested in denial of services and leaking information that demonstrates the validity of their cause. The best defenses against activists tend to be strong public relations, legal proceedings, portraying them as criminals, and of course not having a high-profile or widespread reputation for doing things they tend to protest against. During the Vietnam War, protests tended to concentrate against schools with reserve officer training corps (ROTC) programs, while the environmental movement leads people to protest against oil companies, fisheries, and other similar targets.

Crackers for hire are really dangerous, except that they tend to be less expert and less willing to research than the professional thief. The most effective defenses will be the same for the cracker for hire as the cracker not for hire, except that the motivation may be higher and thus more assurance is necessary in order to provide effective defense.

Mentally-ill people seem fairly random by their nature and might even be treated in the same way as a natural disaster. They may do anything depending on their particular illness and they tend to be hard to predict. Today, they are using information systems to find out personal information about people as a part of stalking or attempts to locate and seduce victims, but they may turn to other things as time passes. In this case, keeping information confidential is a vital component to protection, and this relies on a wide variety of techniques ranging from controlling information flow in the organization to personnel policies and procedures, to awareness, and on and on.

Organized crime has money, attacks with strong financial motive, and is willing to do great bodily harm in order to steal money. They are willing to bribe people, extort money, and place employees in organizations, which makes them very difficult to defend against without a comprehensive protection program. No piecemeal defense will work against this sort of attacker.

Drug cartels tend to have money and use violence to get what they want, but they appear to be less involved in attacking corporations than law enforcement agencies. Their strongest desire seems to be finding the identities of drug enforcement agents, undercover police, and other people they are at odds with. They are willing to spend a lot of money, bribe people, place employees in key organizations, extort cooperation, and otherwise do whatever they feel necessary in order to protect their interests. Protection against these attacks requires a strong overall information protection program. No piecemeal defense will work against this sort of attacker.

Spies tend to be well funded, are provided with very good technical information, have a long time to penetrate an organization before carrying out attacks, are well trained, are cautious, and tend to behave as a malicious insider. The most effective methods for detecting spies historically have been auditing and analysis of audit trails, particularly of personal financial data.

Police armed with search warrants are almost impossible to stop legally. The only real defense against the state is the proper application of lawyers. The same is basically true for government agencies.

Infrastructure warriors are very hard to stop in a free society. The problem is that in order to prevent attacks against infrastructure, you have to either prevent the free movement of people, or use some form of detection to locate attackers before they carry out their attacks. This often calls for an aggressive strategy in which you actively seek out potential attackers and try to track and observe them so as to catch them before they carry out disruption. It is helpful if you can use borders to keep them out, but in the United States, borders are, for all intents and purposes, open to any serious attacker wishing to enter. For example, the border between the United States and Mexico is crossed by hundreds of illegal entrants each day. Passing the Canadian border usually only requires a driver's license which is not well-verified at the border.

Nation states and economic rivals can only be successfully defended against by a nationwide effort at every level of government. More details of this sort of defense are described in a case study. Military organizations and information warriors are also covered to a large extent in case studies later in the text.

> Finally, geographic location has a great deal to do with attacks on information systems. By placing data centers in the Midwest, for example, organizations can eliminate many of the serious attackers from the list.

Eliminating Motives

Many things motivate people to attack information systems, and it is important to remain flexible in considering protection alternatives. For example, during one study, I heard a very brief description of the new set-top boxes proposed for the next generation of cable television. I began to ask about colors and shapes, and was loudly rebuffed by a manager on my team who thought it was a ridiculous question to ask and could not possibly be related to the protection issue we were examining. I explained that we had all seen hundreds of intentionally damaged set-top boxes in the repair room earlier that day. Since the set-top boxes used in this cable system were black metallic boxes and since there are many studies that have shown that people react differently to different colors and shapes, I thought it might be worth looking into letting people choose from different colors and shapes.

> It turns out that this seemingly unimportant change can save as much as a few thousand dollars per day in reduced damage to information systems in each of several hundred cable systems which are part of this cable corporation. The total savings could exceed $100 million per year.

There are two important points here. One is that seemingly small and unimportant changes may have dramatic financial implications. Limiting the scope of investigation limits its value. The second one is the reason this example is provided under the heading of eliminating motives. This change is designed to change the average person's perception of the set-top box. It uses color and shape to make people feel better about the information system in their environment. This reduces their desire to damage systems and provides protection against many attackers who could not be stopped by many other more expensive techniques.

Naturally, color and shape are only some of the things that can be used to reduce peoples' motives to launch attacks. The motives that relate to any particular organization differ with the sort of things they do. For example, very few political motives exist for extracting confidential information from cardboard box manufacturers in rural America. In order to address motive, it is important to get a handle on who might be motivated to launch attacks against your organization. Armed with this list, you can try to find ways to reduce or eliminate their motives.

One of the most important motives has historically been revenge. Revenge typically comes from disgruntled employees and ex-employees, customers, business contacts, and others that may have a reason to believe that they have been harmed by an organization or one or more of its employees. Reducing this motive is strongly tied to the way people believe they are treated. Public relations is a very important aspect of controlling motives because it addresses general perceptions that people have of the organization. An abusive employment screening and interview process is commonly cited as a cause of disgruntled people. The way customers and business contacts are treated is another very important aspect of eliminating the motives for possible future attackers.

Another important motive for attack is money. One of the ways this motive can be reduced or eliminated is by creating the perception that there is no financial gain in attacking your information systems. Just as it is risky to announce that this weekend you will have a record amount of cash in your bank vault, there is a risk in publicizing the fact that very valuable information has been placed in your information systems.

Fun, challenge, and acceptance motives can be easily countered in one of two ways. One way is to put up enough of a barrier to entry that it isn't very fun or affordable to disrupt information systems. The other tactic is to make it so easy to disrupt systems that it is no fun or challenge to do so. The latter strategy was taken by MIT when students were using creative methods to deny services on computers during the school year. They installed a *crash* program that would deny services to all users by simply typing a command. The system would go down safely and automatically return to service an hour or so later. At the beginning of every semester, there were *crash* commands entered for a few days, but once the novelty wore off, nobody bothered to launch an attack.

Self-defense is a powerful motive. The only way to stop people from defending themselves is to not back them into a corner. Similarly, religious or political beliefs are typically unchangeable, however, you can often avoid their consequences by proper use of public relations.

Coercion is hard to eliminate as a motive since, under the right circumstances, almost anyone can be coerced into almost anything.

Military or economic advantage will likely always exist as a motive as long as people live in a competitive society with geopolitical inequities. Gathering or destruction of evidence is another motive that is unlikely to be eliminated without eliminating all crime.

> One thing seems clear. An organization can often reduce motivation by controlling the perceptions that people have and the way they treat and interact with people. This involves ergonomics, psychology, public relations, personnel, marketing, and many other elements.

Eliminating Techniques

For any specific attack, there are a host of technical defenses. Technical defenses against specific attacks are often classified in terms of their ability to prevent, detect, and correct attacks and their side effects. Defenders can try to eliminate attack techniques by addressing them one-at-a-time, but by the time all of the attacks we have discussed are eliminated in this way, the cost of implementing and operating defenses will be so high that the solution will be impractical.

Most Trojan horses can be prevented and detected by a strong program of change control in which every change is independently examined before being put into use. Sound change control increases programming costs by about a factor of 2. Detection of the damage caused by a Trojan horse would require a comprehensive and generic detection capability, since a Trojan horse can cause arbitrary damage. The cure once a Trojan horse is identified is to remove it, try to find all of the damage it has done, and correct that damage. Time bombs and use or condition bombs are similar to Trojan horses in terms of defenses.

Dumpster diving can be avoided by using a high-quality data destruction process on a regular basis. This should include paper shredding and electrical disruption of data on electronic media for all information being abandoned. Detecting dumpster diving can be done by relatively inexpensive surveillance (a camera or two and a few motion sensors), at least until the point where the trash is picked up by the disposal company. When dumpster diving is detected, it is important to determine what information could have been attained and how it could be used, and then to make changes so that attempts to use the information will be useless.

False identities can be detected to a large extent by thorough background checks, but even the United States government cannot prevent all fictitious people from getting into highly sensitive positions. Once a fictitious person has been detected, effective countermeasures include getting law enforcement involved, determining what sort of damage might have been done by that person to date, and preventing further damage by changing responsibilities or having the person arrested. In an intelligence operation, it may also be worth providing the person with fictitious information so that they feed the enemy false or misleading data which will waste enemy resources.

Protection limit poking can only be prevented effectively by a mandatory access control policy. Systems using such a policy are available today, but they are rarely used because most organizations are not willing to take the time and effort to understand them and decide how to use them effectively. Simplistic detection of anomalous protection settings can be done by using automated checking programs that detect changes or incorrect protection settings, but these are far less effective and more resource-consumptive than a mandatory access control policy. Naturally, they are far more widely used.

E-mail overflow can be countered by designing an electronic mail system that works properly. Specifically, it should detect space restrictions and react by automatically replying that the mail should be resent later. A priority system should be used to allow lower priority mail to be blocked sooner than higher priority mail. Most organizations don't have a desire to redesign the software they use as a part of their protection program. Other alternatives include using mail gateways that limit the impact of overflow, administering systems so that mail overflow doesn't adversely affect other operations, and detecting potential overflow before it affects systems, then using human intervention to counter the situation.

Infrastructure interference is impossible to prevent without good physical security throughout the infrastructure and sufficient redundancy and automated usage of that redundancy in the infrastructure to force disruption of more infrastructure elements than the attacker is capable of destroying in a given time period. Detection of subtle interference involves integrity checking systems, while less subtle disruption (such as bombs) often reveal themselves too late.

Infrastructure observation is impossible to prevent in today's environment, however, the use of strong cryptographic systems can make the observed information very expensive to extract value from and thus useless to all but the most serious attackers.

Sympathetic vibration exists in any underdamped feedback system. The defense is to make the network protocols overdamped so that at any frequency at which it is possible to launch attacks, the feedback mechanisms prevent this problem. Each node in a network should also have provisions for temporarily ignoring neighboring nodes that are acting out of the normal operating range and rechecking them at later times for restored service.

Human engineering can only be effectively prevented by training and awareness programs that keep employees from being taken in by potential attackers. This is most effective in combination with policies and procedures that reroute potential attacks to people specially trained in dealing with these problems. For example, some telephone companies hand off calls to a specialist with the right facilities and skills. If something illegal is done, the caller can be traced and law enforcement authorities can be brought into the case. False information can also be provided to give access to a system designed to track attacks, gather information on attack techniques, and get enough evidence for a conviction.

Bribery is prevented by raising children with strong moral values, providing adequate compensation to employees, keeping them aware of the potential penalties of breaking the rules, keeping them aware of moral responsibilities, instilling a good sense of right and wrong, good background checks for financial difficulties, and other personnel techniques.

Getting a job and using that position to attack information systems can only be prevented by good hiring practices.

> Proper protection will also limit the effect that an individual can have on the overall information system, so that in a large organization, no individual can cause more than a limited amount of harm. This involves access controls, separation of function, redundancy, and other similar techniques.

Password guessing can be prevented by requiring hard-to-guess passwords, by using additional authentication devices or techniques, by restricting access once authentication has succeeded, by restricting the locations from which access can be attained to each account, and by using usage times, patterns, or other indicators of abuse to restrict usage.

Invalid values on calls can be prevented by properly designing hardware and software systems. Unfortunately, there is often little choice about this, so detection through auditing and analysis of audit trails, redundancy, and other techniques are commonly used to augment protection. A good testing program can also be used to detect these inadequacies before they are exploited by attackers, so that other protective measures can be used to cover the inadequacies of these system components.

Computer virus defenses tend to be very poor today. They are expensive to use, ineffective over time, and ineffective against serious attackers.

The virus scanning technology in widespread use is only good against viruses that have been reported to virus defense companies, which means that if someone writes a virus to attack a specific organization, it will not be detected by these techniques.

> The only strong techniques are a comprehensive change control program, integrity checking with cryptographic checksums in integrity shells, and isolation to limit the spread of viruses. This, in turn, implies proper management of changes in information systems.

Data diddling is normally prevented by limiting access to data and limiting the methods that can be used to perform modification. This, in turn, requires strong access controls, effective management of changes, and integrity checking for both software and data. Redundancy can often be used to facilitate integrity. Rapid detection is mandatory if data diddling protection is to be effective. Trying to correct data diddling is usually very expensive, while the cost of incorrect data may increase dramatically over time.

Packet insertion is feasible any time control over the hardware level of any system on a network is attained. To prevent insertion, it must be impossible to gain hardware control. Packet insertion can also be done by placing a radio tranceiver or other hardware device on the network. This can only be prevented by physical security of the network hardware. An alternative to preventing insertion is to make inserted packets less harmful by encrypting network traffic, but then the encryption hardware and software will almost certainly be available to anyone with physical access. One means of detection includes using hardware identification information to authenticate packet sources, but this fails when traffic passes through routers and gateway machines. Another technique of detecting illegal equipment is the use of a time domain reflectometer that detects every physical connection and provides distance information. A very high degree of configuration control is required in order to use this technique since any change in wiring will set off an alarm.

Packet watching can be done with the same technology as packet insertion. To prevent theft of passwords, they should be encrypted. The same is true for other valuable information sent over networks. If network-based backups are used, cryptographic or physical protection is required to prevent an attacker from getting a complete copy of all information on the network in only a few hours. Prevention and detection are the same for packet watching as packet insertion except that the packet watcher plays no active role, so techniques like associating hardware identities with packets don't work.

Van Eck bugging can only be prevented by reducing emanations, increasing the distance to the perimeter, or the introduction of noise. Noise generators that are able to effectively mask Van Eck bugging tend to be in violation of Federal Communications Commission (FCC) transmitter standards, and may interfere with radio and television signals, cellular telephones, and other electronic equipment. Increasing perimeter distance can be quite expensive since the necessary distance to prevent observation of video display emanations is on the order of 200 meters. Any receiver and retransmitter in that perimeter can be used to extend the distance. Finally, reducing emanations increases costs of displays by about 25 percent. It is fairly common for organizations with serious concerns about emanations to make entire facilities into Faraday boxes because of the increased convenience and reduced overall cost of protection. By doing this well, it is also possible to eliminate some other forms of bugging and electronic interference.

PBX bugging defenses are almost always dependent on getting an expert to examine the configuration of the PBX system and correct known deficiencies. With the addition of voice mail systems and the use of multiple PBX systems, this becomes a far more difficult problem. For example, a common technique is to restrict access to outbound trunk lines from anyone attached to an incoming trunk line. But with a dual PBX configuration, an attacker can go from one PBX to the other. Most current PBX systems will then lose the information about the incoming call source. The attacker then uses the outbound trunk lines of the second PBX to make an outbound call. Thus, all of the problems of networked computers may come into play in a complex telephone system, and protection techniques may involve a great deal of expertise, possible alteration of existing PBX software, audit trail generation and real-time analysis, and other similar techniques. Similarly, it is often necessary to disconnect maintenance lines when they are not being used for maintenance, to enforce strict rules on passwords used in voice mail systems, and to implement training and awareness programs.

Open microphone listening can be prevented by physical switches on telephone lines, but in most digital systems, this is expensive and causes the system to lose function. In one telephone system, some of the more expensive terminal devices have a handset/headset switch which disables the speaker phone and handset features. By combining this with a physical switch in the headset, protection may be afforded. In other systems, a thorough audit can be used to detect some attacks underway at the time of the audit, but even once attacks are detected, it may be hard to track down the attacker. Even with the knowledge of how to launch this attack, it may be hard to prevent its repetition without a comprehensive approach to protection.

Video viewing can often be stopped by adding physical switches on video and audio devices and a pair of lights, one that is hardware-activated whenever the device is in use, and the other that is hardware-activated when the device is not in use. The pair of indicators covers attacks that involve broken lights. Another way to limit this attack is by using a secure operating system environment, but for this particular attack, most current systems do not provide very high assurance.

> Repair and maintenance functions, by their nature, may require physical access to equipment. Thus, any physical security is likely to be ineffective against attack by maintenance people.

For a high level of assurance, one or more trusted individuals will have to supervise every action of the repair team, only certified and physically secured components can be used in any installation or repair process, and the inventory and distribution processes must be carefully controlled. To limit exposure, information can be stored in an encrypted form with the encryption keys and hardware physically separated from other components, such as disks and backup devices. Preventing corruption during maintenance requires that maintenance procedures have the same quality of controls as normal operating procedures.

Wire closet attacks are usually preventable by simply locking wire closets. For higher valued installations, alarms can be added to provide detection. Physical security and good personnel policies also help reduce this threat.

Shoulder surfing has been around ever since passwords were used in computers. A little bit of education and awareness can almost completely eliminate this problem. A proper social environment should also help in eliminating any embarrassment caused by asking someone to step aside while a password is typed. Some of the other mechanisms used to eliminate password guessing also apply to shoulder surfing. Toll fraud networks may be avoided by the same techniques that are used against shoulder surfing. It is also helpful for service providers to have real-time fraud detection in this sort of defense. For example, the same caller cannot realistically make several calls at one time from several different phones in the same airport, nor can they make calls from San Francisco five minutes after making calls from Los Angeles.

Data aggregation is very hard to stop except by preventing the data from getting to the attacker. Thus, access controls and other techniques are effective against outside attackers, but authorized users performing unauthorized functions require tighter and tighter real-time audit trail analysis.

Process bypassing is most often prevented by separation of function. For example, two people that don't know each other are unlikely to cooperate in a fraud, so by splitting the process into two parts and requiring a double authentication before sending a check, this sort of fraud is usually eliminated. The down side is that this makes systems seem less efficient, and in some cases may cost more than the loss from frauds. An alternative is a strong audit policy and random checks to assure that legitimate claims are fulfilled and few illegitimate claims are made. Audit trails also help catch the people responsible for these attacks.

> Backup theft really results from organizations treating backup information differently than live information. In effect, the same sorts of precautions must be taken with all copies of information in order to provide effective protection.

Login spoofing is defended against by providing a secure channel between the user and the system. For example, a hardware reset button on a personal computer can be very effective in removing some sorts of spoofing attacks. Login spoofing in networks is far more complex because when a network resource crashes or become inaccessible for one reason or another, it is simple to forge the identity of that computer and allow logins to proceed on the forged machine. Cryptographic authentication can increase assurance, but this depends on properly functioning information systems.

Hangup hooking can often be eliminated by purchasing the right hardware and configuring the operating system to enforce disconnection properly. Hardware hangup is detectable on many modems if properly configured. To a large extent, this depends on using the proper hardware handshaking, which in turn relies on using a full modem connection rather than a two or three wire connection as used to be common in external modems. Unfortunately, over many modern networks, this hardware solution does not work. Instead, remote users must explicitly logout or a forger can continue a session after the originating party disconnects or reboots their computer. In this case, encryption or authentication of network traffic may be required in order to effectively address the problem.

Call-forwarding fakery can often be blocked by restricting functions of PBX systems or requiring entry of forwarding information from the telephone wire being forwarded from. This limits attacks to those who can modify the PBX, those who can physically access the telephone wires, and telephone instruments using nontrivial telephone equipment. An example of how nontrivial telephone equipment can be exploited is an attack based on the dial-out capability of some modern fax machines. For example, the Brother 780-MC fax machine allows faxes to be recorded and forwarded to another telephone number. If you can guess the 3-digit password, remote access can be used to dial call-forwarding information into the telephone company, which in turn reroutes the line. To counter this, it is necessary to disable these features either at the telephone company or at the fax machine. Either one restricts legitimate access to restrict attacks.

> E-mail spoofing can be prevented by using authentication in electronic mail systems. For example, the public domain software package PGP provides very good authentication and reasonable confidentiality.

Input overflow attacks can be avoided by proper program design, but unfortunately, most programmers are not properly trained in this aspect of program design and most programming aids don't provide adequate automation to prevent this sort of disruption. In this environment, the best we can do is prevent these errors from adversely affecting the rest of the environment by providing integrity checking and using access controls and other similar techniques to limit the effects of these design flaws.

Illegal value insertion can easily be kept from causing harm through the use of integrity checking on all data entry. Unfortunately, many programs do a poor job of this, but fortunately, many of the newer program development systems provide stronger input validation, and this helps reduce the problem in many cases.

Induced stress failures exist in many cases because systems are inadequately tested and debugged before being fielded and because the designs don't use conservative estimates or strong verification mechanisms. One of the contributing factors to this problem is the rush to market for new products and the rapid product replacement cycle, particularly in the PC environment. This may be very good for the companies that sell these products, but it is not good for their customers. The solution is a more conservative approach to purchasing and a thorough testing and evaluation process.

The damage from false update disks can be prevented by having strong policies, procedures, training, and education. In order to be effective, this must be backed up by a good testing and configuration control program that is uniformly and universally enforced. Other techniques for defending against this threat are strong on-line integrity facilities and comprehensive access controls.

Network services attacks are usually countered by removing network services, concealing them within other services so that additional authentication is required, the creation of secure versions of these services, and the creation of traps so that when attackers try to use services, they can be traced. This is essentially the issue addressed by the network firewalls now becoming widely popular.

Combined attacks raise the bar far higher. For example, suppose sample software is provided for your testing program by transmission over a large network such as the Internet. The program must first be decompressed before it can be placed on a floppy disk for transfer to the testing system because it uses a decompression program for Unix that doesn't run on the DOS system used to test this product. In the decompression process, it creates a network control file that is rarely used. This control file causes the computer on your network to get instructions from the attacker about what to try on your system and returns results via electronic mail to the attacker.

> The firewalls on current network gateways to the Internet won't stop this program from looking for its instructions at a remote site, because the firewall is designed to prevent outsiders from getting in, not insiders from getting out. It won't stop electronic mail either, since that is what these firewalls are usually designed to allow to pass.

Your change control system probably won't detect the introduction of a new and legitimate program into your file space on your Unix account, and the files transferred to the test site won't include the file used for the attack.

So the attack works even though each of the elements individually might have been covered by a defense. For example, you may have used strong change control to protect the on-line Unix system from getting in-house software without approval, strong testing to prevent that software from being used before test, a trusted decompression program to decompress the incoming files, a secure operating environment to prevent the decompression program from placing files in another user's area, a firewall to prevent over-the-wire attacks, reduced network services to prevent attackers from entering from over the network, and awareness to prevent this attack from being launched by sending a floppy disk directly to the user. Yet, despite all of these precautions, this attack can succeed because it uses synergistic effects and piecemeal defenses don't provide synergistic defense. In order for piecemeal defenses to be effective against synergistic attacks like this, each combination of attacks must be explicitly covered.

Eliminating Accidental Events

Unlike intentional events, accidental events can almost always be characterized by stochastic processes and thus yield to statistical analysis. There are three major ways people reduce risk from accidental events. They avoid them, they use redundancy to reduce the impact of the event, and/or they buy insurance against the event. Avoidance typically involves designing systems to survive events and placing systems where events don't tend to occur. Redundancy involves determining how much to spend to reduce likelihoods of events in a cost-effective way. Insurance is a way of letting the insurance company determine the odds and paying them to assume the risks.

Errors and omissions happen in all systems and processes. For example, the Internal Revenue Service (IRS) reports about 20 percent data entry error rates, and they enter more data than almost any other organization on Earth. Better results come from the U.S. Postal Service (USPS) which enters zip codes from hundreds of millions of letters every day. Protection against errors and omissions requires redundancy of one form or another. If the redundancy costs more than the damage from the errors and omissions, it is not cost-effective to protect against them.

Power failure occurs quite often. Even disruptions that don't turn off the lights, such as voltage spikes and low voltage periods, may interfere with information systems. Some power problems may not cause an information system to stop operating, but may induce transient errors that are not detected by most modern systems. Protection against power disruption includes surge protection, uninterruptable power supplies, motor generators, and redundant power sources. Power failures of substantial duration are more likely on the East coast and the West coast of the United States than in the central states.

Cable cuts can be avoided by increased use of the cable location system. This system provides a telephone number to call before digging holes. When you call and identify where you are planning to dig, they provide you with information on the cables in that area so you can avoid hitting them. Organizations can try to protect themselves by using redundant service connections, but it is vital to be certain that these connections are actually redundant. At an infrastructure level, we currently have no way to track cable redundancy, and this is a necessary change if we are to provide high availability against this sort of incident.

Fire has many causes, ranging from electrical wiring failures to smoking in airliner bathrooms. Fire also tends to disrupt electrical power, lighting, and other elements often required for information system operation. Automatic fire suppression equipment is commonly used in large data centers, while smaller offices use hand-held fire extinguishers or alarm systems. Fire resistant safes are vital to assuring the integrity of backup tapes and other magnetic and paper media during a fire. Small fire-rated safes can be purchased for less than a few hundred dollars. Off-site backups are also commonly used for protection of vital information against loss in a fire.

Floods almost always occur in low-lying areas or next to creeks, rivers, or other bodies of water. The best protection against floods is proper location of facilities. Computer centers should not be placed in basements or flood plains, except in rare cases. The use of raised floors helps reduce the threat of water damage.

Earth movement tends to happen near fault lines and where mine subsidence causes sinkholes and other similar phenomena. Again, location is a vital consideration in reducing this risk.

Solar flares increase background radiation which in turn introduces noise into communications and data storage devices. Effective redundancy in communications and storage includes the use of cyclic redundancy check (CRC) codes, parity check codes, and other similar protection. Satellite communication is most affected, followed by radio, overground wiring, and underground wiring.

Volcanos are almost always at known locations. The further away you are, the safer you are. They also damage infrastructure when they erupt and infrastructure dependencies should be examined for enough redundancy to cover such eruptions. There is no effective physical protection against a volcano at this time.

Severe weather, static electricity, air conditioning loss, and that whole class of scenarios cannot be completely avoided by geographic location, however, some places seem to encounter more severe weather than others, and some tend to have infrastructure that withstands these incidents better than others. Analysis of infrastructure reliability is appropriate to finding proper locations.

> Moving computers should include a pre-move backup and a post-move verification of system and file integrity.

This implies a method for integrity checking. Most PC-based systems don't have substantial storage integrity mechanisms, however, systems like Unix and VMS do have built-in facilities for this purpose. Computers are relatively fragile, and as they age, wires become brittle, connections of boards to backplanes become corroded, and component connections become less flexible. For this reason, mechanical movement should be followed by a thorough diagnostic check of all system elements.

System maintenance sometimes causes downtime, but as a rule, the downtime is worthwhile because the result is, more often than not, beneficial. In cases where downtime is unacceptable, systems that use redundancy to continue to operate during maintenance are appropriate. Inadequate maintenance is generally far worse than downtime caused during maintenance because flaws that might be prevented, detected, or corrected during maintenance occur during normal operation instead.

Testing often uses rarely used and poorly tested features of an information system, and as a result, it is more likely to induce failures on a step-by-step basis than normal operations. Many systems now have built-in self-test capabilities, and these sorts of systems are usually designed to be tested during operation or under well-defined conditions. Testing should be carried out under well-defined conditions, both because this makes the results of the test more meaningful in relation to other comparable tests, and because it provides procedural mechanisms for assuring that tests don't cause harm.

Humidity, smoke, gasses, fumes, dust, heat, and cleaning chemicals can best be prevented from affecting information systems by environmental controls such as air filters, temperature controls, humidifiers and dehumidifiers, and other similar technologies. In circumstances where these factors are present, controls should be used. It is also helpful to avoid this sort of circumstance by locating information facilities as far as possible from the sources of these factors.

Temperature cycling normally results from turning systems off and on and from differences in day and night temperatures. The solution is a temperature-controlled environment and continuous operation 24 hours a day, 7 days a week. In most systems, this extends the life.

Electronic interference can be avoided by not locating equipment in areas with interfering signals, by using power conditioners and other similar equipment, and by enclosing equipment in a Faraday box.

Vibration is primarily a problem in mobile systems such as cars, aircraft, and space vehicles. When conditions warrant, there are systems specifically designed to withstand vibrations.

Corrosion is normally a problem in unprotected environments. The best protection against corrosion is to provide special environments for computer equipment. It is also prudent to locate information systems away from potentially corrosive materials.

> Geographic location has a great deal to do with natural disasters. In the United States, the West coast has volcanos and earthquakes, the East coast has hurricanes and winter storms, and the central states have flooding in low-lying areas. By placing data centers in the Midwest, organizations can eliminate most of the natural disasters.

Eliminating Effects

Corruption is most commonly prevented by the use of redundancy. In order to be effective against intentional attack, the redundancy must be designed so that it cannot be forged, removed, or otherwise bypassed without high cost.

Denial of services is also most commonly prevented by the use of redundancy, and it has the same restrictions when dealing with intentional attack as corruption.

Leakage is most commonly prevented by making information inaccessible or hard to understand once accessed illicitly. This involved access controls and cryptography.

5.4   AN ORGANIZATIONAL PERSPECTIVE

It should now be apparent that if organizations try to provide information protection on a piecemeal basis, they will spend a great deal of money and get very little in the way of overall long-term protection.

> This is what the vast majority of organizations do today and, as a result, they get fairly poor protection, pay too much for what they get, and encounter an ongoing series of difficulties that they have to deal with on a case-by-case basis.

There is of course a far better way of dealing with the protection challenge. The basic concept is that organizations must deal with the information protection issue from many organizational perspectives. By combining these perspectives, the net effect is a comprehensive protection program with built-in assurance. The overall cost is lower because optimization is done at an organizational level instead of a piecemeal level.

To appreciate this, it might be helpful to think about the many types of protection described in the last section. I think you will find that every aspect is covered from the organizational perspective, but even more importantly, many scenarios that have not been called out in this book are also covered.

There is one other point to be made before going on. Any organization that takes the organizational approach to protection will almost certainly have to go through a cultural change in order for the approach to work. This approach is designed to create a culture in which information protection is effective.

Protection Management

Protection management is the management part of the process by which protection is implemented and maintained. In order for protection to work, adequate resources must be applied in an appropriate fashion. Protection management works toward optimizing the use of resources to make protection as effective as possible at or below budgeted cost levels. In most large commercial organizations today, the highest-level information protection management personnel report directly to corporate officers. Protection management typically takes place at all levels of the organization. It is fairly common for lower-level technical information protection management to be carried out by relatively untrained systems and network administrators who also have nonprotection roles in maintaining the operation of information systems. Top-level information protection managers are usually dedicated to the information protection task.

> Proper protection management affects all elements of the protection process and improper management makes effective protection almost impossible to attain.

Two of the most critical functions of protection management are in budgeting and leadership.

Without adequate and properly allocated funding, protection becomes very difficult to attain. For example, it is common to spend a lot of money on people who are partially involved in the protection task while spending far too little on those who are fully dedicated to the task and on the support systems to facilitate protection. This is in large part because the hidden costs of information protection are amortized across the entire organization. For example, every systems administrator spends time in protection functions but this time is not commonly differentiated from other time. The effect is that from a budget standpoint it appears to be more cost-effective to have the administrators spend their time on protection than to have more protection specialists. In fact, a protection specialist is usually far more effective in resolving issues quickly, has much greater knowledge and far better tools, and is much more likely to come up with better and more cost-effective, long-term solutions.

The leadership issue usually comes to a head when the top-level managers in an organization are subjected to the same protection standards as everyone else. It is commonplace for these top-level managers to simply refuse to be subjected to these standards. The net effect is that a privileged class comes into being. The rest of the organization then enters into a seemingly eternal power struggle to get the same privileges as the top-level executive and, over time, more and more people choose to ignore protection as a symbol of their status. It doesn't have to be this way. Perhaps one of the best examples of leadership is what happened some years ago when AT&T changed its policies.

Basically, AT&T implemented a system where internal auditors would go from area to area identifying protection issues to be addressed. Line managers would be given a form which they could either sign on one side to agree to pay for the protection improvements out of their operating budgets or sign on the other side to refuse to pay for the improvements and take responsibility for the results. Failure to sign the form results in sending the form to the next higher-level manager. The first such form was not signed, sent up the ladder, and in a short period of time, reached the CEO. The CEO could have done many things, but his leadership changed the corporate culture in short order. He called the next manager down the line who had refused to make the decision and told him to have one side or the other signed by the end of the day, or start looking for a new job. By the end of the day, the effect had rippled all the way down the ladder, and the lowest-level line manager had signed one side or the other. That was the last time the decision was ever passed up the ladder. The result is an organization where people at every level take responsibility for information protection very seriously. The effect has been a high degree of information assurance.

Protection Policy

Protection policy forms the basis upon which protection decisions are made. Typical policy areas include but are not limited to:

- Guiding principles and motivations behind the policy
- Specific requirements for integrity, availability, and confidentiality of various sorts of information and the basis for differentiating them
- Policies regarding hiring, performance, and firing of information workers
- Statements of the responsibility of the organization and workers

> Protection policy is normally the responsibility of the board of directors and operating officers of a company and has the same stature as any other official statement of corporate policy.

I keep talking about a protection policy as the basis for considering integrity, availability, and privacy. The reason policy is so important is that it is impossible to achieve a goal unless you know what the goal is.

The first and most vital step in achieving protection in any environment is to define the protection policy. This is something that should be done very carefully. For example, suppose I just use my earlier goal (*i.e., get the right information to the right place at the right time*) as the policy. If this is the only guiding force behind decisions, the policy may put me out of business very quickly. I will never achieve my real goal, which should be a balance between cost and protection.

Policies can range from the very simple (such as the AT&T policy of having auditors indicate appropriate requirements and managers make decisions about implementation) to the very complicated (such as the DoD policy which consumes several encyclopedic volumes on each sort of information system). There are many books filled with protection policies.

Protection policy defines the set of circumstances that protection is supposed to cover and how the tradeoffs work between cost and assurance. To the extent that policy doesn't explain these things, it leaves holes that will be filled or left open at the discretion of those who try to implement policy. The result of poor policy is lack of control, and lack of control in information protection has the potential to lead to disaster. At the same time, policy should not over-specify things that require lower-level decisions, or it will tie the hands of those who implement protection to the point where they may be forced to act foolishly.

One way to think of policy is in terms of what it does and does not say to those who have to implement protection. It should specify that all of the components of protection need to be addressed in an ongoing fashion and that everyone in the organization should participate in the effort at some level. It should not specify standards and procedures, specific documents, audit techniques, safeguards, or other elements of protection in detail. It should state goals and specify that certain tradeoffs need to be addressed, but it should not specify what to do or how to do it at a detailed level. It should specify top-level elements of personnel structure and minimum levels of involvement of top people, but it should not be tied to personalities or special capabilities of people in particular positions. It should be designed for the long term and thus change rarely, but it must be able to adapt without dramatic change in order to retain stability in the organization.

Standards and Procedures

Standards and procedures are used to implement policy at an operational level. It is not unusual to have employees who are unaware of or ignore standards, and procedural compliance is rarely adequate to effectively implement the desired protection. In assessing standards and procedures, it is important to determine that they are adequate to meet operational requirements, and that they are adequate in light of the level of compliance, training, and expertise of the people implementing them. Standards and procedures apply at all levels of the personnel structure, from the janitor to the board members.

> Standards provide goals to be achieved, while procedures provide approved means of reaching those goals.

We may have a standard that dictates that all job and duty changes should be reflected in changes in authorization to information systems within 48 hours of the change of status, except in the case of termination or demotion, in which case changes to authorization must be made by the time the employee is notified of the change. The standard may seem pretty reasonable, and a lot of companies have a standard of this sort, but many of the companies with this standard lack the procedures to carry the standard out. The procedures that go with this standard must include, but not be limited to, the mechanisms by which employee job and duty changes get reported and to whom, who is responsible for making changes, how the current status of employee authorization and the authorizations associated with each job are specified and maintained, what to do in the event that the person normally responsible for this activity is on vacation, how to protect the information on employee authorizations, how to change authorization information reliably, and what to do with information created and/or maintained by the employee when job changes take place.

To a large extent, standards and procedures dictate the degree of assurance attained in the protection effort. If the standards miss something or the procedures that implement them are poor, the level of assurance will almost certainly be low. If the standards are well done and comprehensive and the procedures implement those standards efficiently and reliably, assurance will be high and protection will work well within the rest of the organization.

Documentation

Documentation is the expression of policy, standards, and procedures in a usable form. The utility of documentation is a key component of the success of protection. Protection documentation is intended to be used by specific people performing specific job functions, and as such should be appropriately tailored. Documentation should be periodically updated to reflect the changing information environment. These changes should be reviewed as they occur by all involved parties. Documentation is normally in place at every level of a corporation, from the document that expresses the corporate protection policy to the help cards that tell information workers how to respond to protection-related situations.

Documentation essentially increases assurance by providing a way to access the procedures in written form when necessary. Many modern organizations are moving toward on-line documentation, but they often ignore the requirement for documentation in a form that is usable when their computers are not operational. If the documentation required to make the computer usable is not available when the computer breaks, it is not of any value.

> On-line documentation is not likely to be very useful in recovering from an attack that deleted all of the on-line information or in recovering from a widespread power failure.

Documentation cannot realistically cover every situation that can come up in full detail, but good documentation provides a range of information including immediate responses to a select number of critical problems, more in-depth material that explains how and why things are done the way they are, and even the detailed technical information used to create the information technology in the first place.

In order to be effective, documentation also has to be properly located and considered as a part and parcel of the information systems themselves. Detailed design documents are rarely helpful to the end user of today's information technology, while most help cards must be instantly accessible if they are to have utility. Documentation also has to be tracked and updated to prevent having the wrong information used when problems occur. In today's environment, there are commonly many versions of a particular software package. It is common to have incompatibilities from version to version. Having an improperly matched manual can waste a lot of time and effort.

Most modern computer hardware and software manuals do not place protection prominently and, in some cases, they don't mention protection issues at all, even though they greatly affect product operation. For example, manuals almost never tell users what protection settings should be used for different files under different conditions. Products rarely provide protection options in their user interfaces. When they do, there is almost never a way to automate the proper protection decision. This means that in order for these programs to operate properly, the user has to become aware of the protection implications on their own, make good protection decisions without adequate supporting material, and manually set protection to the proper values. Protection documentation should address these concerns explicitly so that the user can do the right thing without having to be a protection expert.

Documentation should also be created by information workers as they work. A simple credo may help: The work isn't done till the documentation is finished.

Protection Audit

Protection audit is vital to assuring that protection is properly in place and in detecting incidents not detected by other operating protection techniques. Audit is also important to fulfilling the fiduciary duty of corporate officers for due diligence, detecting unauthorized behavior by authorized individuals, and assuring that other protective measures are properly operating. Audit is normally carried out by internal auditors, and verified by independent outside personnel with special knowledge in the fields of inquiry, who work for and report to corporate officers, and who have unlimited access to examine, but not modify, information.

Protection audit is used to test and verify coverage. In the process, it increases assurance and identifies vulnerabilities. Audit is normally a redundant function used to provide increased integrity, but in some organizations, it is used as a primary means of detection and response. For example, in accounting, most cases of fraud and embezzlement are detected during the audit process.

Automated audit generation and analysis techniques have also been implemented in order to provide near real-time detection of events. For example, in most timesharing computer systems, real-time log files are generated to record protection-relevant events. These audit trails can then be analyzed by real-time analysis programs to detect known attack patterns and deviations from normal behavior.

Technical Safeguards

Technical safeguards are commonly used to provide a high degree of compliance in addressing specific, known classes of vulnerabilities. For example, cryptography, access controls, and password systems are all technical safeguards.

Technical safeguards must not only meet the requirements of addressing the vulnerabilities they are intended to mitigate, but must also be properly implemented, installed, operated, and maintained. They are also subject to abuse in cases where they are inadequate to the actual threats or where they create undue burdens on users. Technical safeguards are typically implemented by systems administrators based on guidance from protection managers.

Technical safeguards are designed to cover attacks. They cover such a broad range and have been the subject of so much work that many books and thousands of scientific articles on the subject have been published. Technical safeguards range from special-purpose techniques that detect a specific attack to generic techniques that cover large classes of accidental and intentional disruptions. Technical safeguards also range from well-thought-out, well-designed, carefully implemented customized solutions to poorly conceived, poorly designed, and poorly implemented off-the-shelf products.

> Unfortunately, most technical safeguards have not been designed to be easily and effectively managed by an average person. In fact, most of them cannot be effectively managed even by a well-trained protection specialist without special training and custom made tools.

The lack of adequate protection management tools in support of technical safeguards is slowly being addressed, and over time, operational management of technical safeguards may reach a level where average users can protect themselves. But for now, this is a major shortcoming of technical safeguards that limits their effectiveness.

Incident Response

Incident response is required whenever a protection-related incident is detected. The process of response is predicated on detection of a protection-related event, and thus detection is a key element in any response plan. The response plan should include all necessary people, procedures, and tools required in order to effectively limit the damage and mitigate any harm done to as large an extent as is possible and appropriate to the incident. In many situations, time is of the essence in incident response. Therefore, all of the elements of the response should be in place and operating properly before an incident occurs. This makes planning and testing very important. Incident response is normally managed by specially trained central response teams with a local presence and cooperation of all affected users.

Incident response is, by definition, reactive in nature. That is, it covers incidents that are not covered proactively. Incident response also implies incident detection, which opens a whole new set of issues. Specifically, if it can be detected, why can't it be corrected or prevented automatically? If it cannot be detected, how can incident response help, since no incident can be responded to unless it can be detected. The ultimate goal of incident response is to identify and implement protection enhancements.

Then there are the issues of what to respond to at what level. If the incident response team overreacts every time an incident is detected, it may cost a lot and make true emergencies less likely to get the desired level of attention. If the incident response team underreacts, it could be very costly. This means that incident response must be measured according to the seriousness of the incident, but this then places still more emphasis on the detection system. Response teams must be able to properly differentiate between incidents of different levels of severity in order to provide the proper measured response. The more we know about differentiating incidents, the better we are able to defend against them in a proactive way.

Next, we have the issue of reflexive control as applied to the incident response team.

> A serious attacker may stress the incident response capability to detect weaknesses or may hide a serious incident in the guise of an incident that has low response priority.

The resources available for incident response tend to be limited. A clever attacker may stress the response team by forcing them to use more and more resources. This then forces the incident response system to increase the threshold of detection in order to continue to meet cost constraints. By raising the level high enough, an attacker can force the incident response team to ignore the real attack in favor of diversions.

The solution is a well-qualified response team. Incident response almost invariably involves people. To be effective, these people must be well-trained and experienced in the field of information protection. A good incident response system also involves all members of the organization to the extent that they often must act in conjunction with the response team in order for response to operate effectively.

Testing

Any system that is expected to work properly must be adequately tested. The testing requirement applies to human as well as automated systems, and to the protection plan itself. It is common to implement new or modified computer hardware or software without adequately testing the interaction of new systems with existing systems. This often leads to downtime and corruptions. Similarly, disaster recovery plans are often untested until an actual disaster, at which point it's too late to improve the plan. Testing is normally carried out by those who have operational responsibility for functional areas.

Testing increases assurance by providing verification that systems operate as they are supposed to. It is commonplace for inadequately tested systems to fail and affect other connected systems. This commonly results in denial and corruption. The response to denial and corruption, in turn, often leads to leakage. Testing extends far beyond any special system components provided for protection. It also includes all components of information systems including, but not limited to, people, procedures, documentation, hardware, software, and systems.

Many large organizations have configuration control that involves testing each new component in a special test environment to increase the assurance that the new component will operate properly within the existing environment. This commonly delays the introduction of new software into a PC-based environment by several months. Many mainframe environments stress change control which uses testing as a key component to assuring that changes operate properly on test cases as well as samples extracted from real data. Most other environments seem to be poorly controlled from a testing standpoint today, and the effect on availability and integrity is sometimes severe.

> Testing is almost never perfect. Performing a test of every possible interaction between two fairly small programs operating in a PC-based environment would probably take more time than the expected lifetime of the universe.

On the other hand, almost no system of any substantial complexity works perfectly the first time it is tested. As a rule, the cost-effectiveness of testing goes down as more testing is done on the particular configuration. For this reason, most testing efforts concentrate on the interaction between a recent change and its environment. A good testing program will be designed so that it tests for high-probability events first and gets high coverage quickly. Testing should be terminated when the likelihood of finding new errors becomes so small that the cost of testing exceeds the likely loss from remaining errors. Most companies stop testing well before this point.

Physical Protection

There is no effective information protection without physical protection of information assets and the systems that store and handle those assets. Physical protection is expensive, and thus must be applied judiciously to remain cost-effective. There is a strong interaction between the design of systems and their physical protection requirements. Physical protection is typically implemented and maintained in conjunction with operations personnel who are responsible for other aspects of the physical plant. It sometimes involves an internal security force of one form or another. Physical protection covers disruptions and increases assurance provided by other protective measures by making it more difficult to modify the way systems operate.

> Almost no hacker is willing to deal with guards holding rifles, and even some pretty serious criminals are unwilling to risk assault and battery charges to enter a facility.

Some of the key decisions in physical security lie in deciding who the protection system is designed to keep away from what and what natural events are to be defended against. Natural events are normally dictated by physical location. For example, flood protection on the top of a mountain is rarely appropriate, while any vital site in California had better have adequate earthquake protection. Mischievous attacks from disgruntled ex-employees should probably be defended by almost any organization, but terrorist protection is rarely necessary for small firms unless they are located very close to major targets, because terrorists don't get as much press coverage or cause as much damage by blowing up a small company as a big one.

Personnel Issues

Information systems are tools used by people. At the heart of effective protection is a team of trustworthy, diligent, well-trained people. Although there are no sure indicators of what people will do, individuals who have responsibilities involving unusually high exposures are commonly checked for known criminal behavior, financial stability, susceptibility to bribery, and other factors that may tend to lead to inappropriate behavior. Although most people provide references when submitting a resume, many companies don't thoroughly check references or consider the effects of job changes over time. Personnel security considers these issues and tries to address them to reduce the likelihood of incidents involving intentional abuse.

In most corporations, there is a personnel department that is supposed to handle personnel security issues, but it is common to have communications breakdowns between personnel and technical protection management which results in poor procedural safeguards and unnecessary exposures.

In order for protection to be effective, the linkage between the personnel department and the information technology department must work well and be supported by standards and procedures.

Personnel department protection efforts concentrate on enhancing assurance, eliminating insider attacks, and reducing motives for attack. Motives are reduced by properly selecting employees who are less likely to be motivated to launch attacks and more likely to participate willingly and actively in the protection effort. Insider attacks are reduced by proper compensation, hiring, firing, and change of position procedures. Proper investigative procedures also greatly decrease the chances of insider attack, but it is important to differentiate between the things that make people unique and indicators of malice. Different isn't always bad. Many companies have hiring policies that tend to exclude the very people who might best serve them.

Legal Considerations

Legal requirements for information protection vary from state to state and country to country. For example, British law is very explicit in stating the responsibility to report computer crimes, while U.S. laws do not punish executives who fail to report incidents. Software piracy laws, privacy laws, Federal Trade Commission (FTC) regulations, recent federal statutes, contracts with other businesses, health and safety regulations, worker monitoring laws, intellectual property laws, and many other factors affect the proper implementation of information protection.

Legal matters are normally handled in conjunction with corporate legal staff and involve all levels of the organization.

Protection Awareness

Protection awareness is often cited as the best indicator of how effective an information protection program is. Despite the many technological breakthroughs in information protection over the last several years, it is still alert and aware employees that first detect most protection problems. This is especially important for systems administrators and people in key positions.

The main role of protection awareness is to increase assurance and, as such, awareness programs should be directed toward the specific goals of the overall protection effort. For example, if terrorists are not of particular concern, the awareness program shouldn't emphasize them, but it is generally beneficial for people to be aware of their existence, what they tend to do, and why they are or are not of great concern in this particular organization.

Awareness programs normally extend to all employees and consume anywhere from a few hours to a few days per year. This time is commonly divided into regularly scheduled events such as a computer security day, a quarterly training session, or a monthly newsletter. Posters are commonly used to increase awareness and discussions of current events provide a way to bring the issues home.

Training and Education

Training has consistently been demonstrated to have a positive effect on performance, especially under emergency conditions. For that reason, training programs are a vital component in the overall protection posture of an organization.

> It is common for people who once helped the systems administrator by doing backups to become the new systems administrators based on attrition, and end up in charge of information protection by accident. The net effect is an environment which relies on undertrained and ill-prepared people who are often unable to adequately cope with situations as they arise. The need for training increases with the amount of responsibility for protection.

Training and education increase assurance in much the same way as protection awareness does, except that in an awareness program, the goal is to remain alert, whereas in an education and training program, the goal is to impart the deep knowledge required to enhance the entire protection program and to create a responsive environment in which actions reflect policy.

Every employee with protection as a substantial concern should have at least a few hours per quarter of training and education, while those who are responsible for protection should attend regular and rigorous professional education programs.

The lack of information protection education in universities places a special burden on other organizations to provide the core knowledge that is lacking, while the rapidly changing nature of information technology makes it necessary to keep up-to-date on protection issues on a regular basis.

Education in information protection commonly takes one of two forms. For organizations with a relatively small number of people with protection responsibilities in any given geographical area, training courses are offered by short-course companies in cities around the world. These courses tend to use well-qualified specialists to address a wide variety of subjects at appropriate levels of depth. For organizations having at least 10 employees with protection responsibility located in physical proximity, in-house short courses are often preferred.

The main advantage of in-house courses is that they are specialized to the organization's requirements, they allow confidential questions to be asked in an appropriate venue, and the cost is far lower than the cost of sending the same number of employees to an outside short course. Good short courses in this field typically cost about $500 per person per day, not including transportation or housing. For less than $5,000 a very well-qualified expert can fly in from anywhere in the United States, stay over night, provide a full day of semi-customized education, include a great deal of supporting material, and return home.

Many of the best experts in the information protection field do this sort of educational program for companies on a regular basis as a part of their consulting practice. The long-term relationship built up by this practice is very beneficial to both parties.

Organizational Suitability

Information protection spans the organizational community. It crosses departmental and hierarchical levels, and affects every aspect of operations. This implies that the information protection manager be able to communicate and work well with people throughout the organization.

> To be effective, the mandate for information protection must come from the board of directors and operating officers.

The organizational culture is very important to the success of information protection. A proper culture reinforces cost-effective, high-assurance coverage of the protection issue. A culture that punishes those who report protection problems, that gives no rewards for good protection or punishment for poor protection, and that doesn't provide the power base from which protection gets priority over less important issues, makes effective protection almost impossible to attain.

Other Perspectives

There are clearly other ways of organizing protection issues, and this one is not particularly better than any others except in that it seems to provide broad coverage from a perspective that has proven useful to many organizations. I sometimes get comments like, *it doesn't include x*, where *x* is *disaster recovery* or *access control* or some such thing. Like the pasta sauce commercial, my response is: *It's in there.* Here are some examples:

- Disaster recovery is normally covered under incident response. The disaster is the incident and the recovery is a proper response.
- Access control can come in many forms. Physical access control is a combination of physical protection, technical safeguards, personnel, policy, and procedures. Logical (i.e., operating system) access control is normally handled under technical protection.
- Worker monitoring is a combination of legal considerations, technical safeguards, policy and procedures, and audit.

5.5   SOME SAMPLE SCENARIOS

These two examples serve to demonstrate the difference between the organizational and piecemeal approaches to protection.

HERF Attack

In the near future, your organization is attacked by a deranged individual who uses a high-energy radiation field (HERF) gun to destroy information systems from a range of about 20 meters. This individual has decided that your organization is the devil incarnate and will continue to do this until caught.

Suppose you have decided on a piecemeal defense based on the list of attacks and defenses described earlier. Now this new attack comes up. You are not prepared and your organizational response is unpredictable. Typically, the failure of several information system components in close physical proximity will be viewed by the local administrator as a result of a power fluctuation, a lightning strike, or some such thing. Replacements will be purchased, and nothing else will be said. This may happen once a week in a large organization and, since each administrator is acting on their own, the overall picture may never become clear. The problems may simply persist indefinitely. I have seen this happen in many large organizations (although none of them have been due to a HERF gun yet).

> The cost will be shared across the organization, and it will reflect in inefficiency and poor overall financial performance. It may never be traced back to the attack.

Perhaps a few administrators chatting in the hall will eventually describe a common incident and the alarm will go out, but even then, the response will be piecemeal.

Now suppose we have an overall organizational protection system set up. The first attack will probably work in much the same way, except that it will be reported to the incident response team, and they will assist in resolving the problem. When the second attack takes place, the response team will again be notified, and now they will begin to suspect a correlation. As the symptoms become clear, they will probably contact a real expert in the field to tell them what could have caused such a thing and how to defend against it. Within a few days, they will know that this attack was caused by a HERF gun, and they will probably contact the FBI (for interstate) or local law enforcement to help them solve the problem. The resources that will be applied will probably allow rapid detection of this attack as it is underway, and the perpetrator will be hotly pursued. Everyone in the organization will be made aware of the situation, and special precautions will be put in place to limit the lost time and information until the attacker is found.

Learned Shared Attack

Over the last several weeks, a network-based attacker has probed your technical defenses against over-the-wire attack and has finally found an attack that works. The attacker has shared this attack with thousands of other attackers who are now running rampant through your information systems during the evening hours. The attackers may be denying services, leaking confidential information, or corrupting information throughout the organization's information systems. One of the first things they do is modify the security systems to allow reentry once the shared attack is defended against.

With a piecemeal defense, someone may eventually notice that people are logged in at unusual hours, or that performance is slow at night, or some such thing. Then, if this is a systems administrator, they may try to track the source down using whatever tools they have. If they are really good at what they do, they will eventually figure out that a serious attack is underway and then call in help from the rest of the organization or describe it to the systems administrators' group at the next regular meeting, if there is such a thing. Eventually, this problem will be tracked down to the specific attack being used and this hole will be filled, but by that time the attackers will have introduced several other holes through which they can regularly enter, and the battle may rage indefinitely. Something similar happened at AT&T in the 1980s several months after attackers had been regularly entering systems all around the United States used for routing telephone calls. The AT&T incident continued for more than a year after it was first detected.

As I write this book, I know of another similar attack pattern against U.S. military systems that, by my accounting, has been underway for more than a year. This attack was not detected until at least six months after it began.

> The military attack just described cannot be effectively countered at this time because there are no funds allocated for calling in external experts or implementing more effective defenses, and many of the organizations under attack don't want to take responsibility for the defense because of political issues. A small team of specialists have been trying to keep up with the attacks for the last year, but frankly, they are overwhelmed.

With an overall organizational protection system in place, detection is far more rapid because people throughout the organization know to notice suspicious things and report them. The awareness combined with training and education of the incident response team should dramatically reduce the time before the attack is detected. Once detected, experts can be brought in to analyze and counter the specific attack, and then organizational resources can be applied to provide improved protection against this entire class of attacks for the future.

5.6   STRATEGY AND TACTICS

Two critical planning perspectives for information protection are usually not addressed or even differentiated: strategic planning and tactical planning. An important reason to explicitly look at these two perspectives is that they reveal a lot about how money is spent and how planning interacts with operations.

The difference between strategy and tactics is commonly described in terms of time frames. Strategic planning is planning for the long run, while tactical planning is planning for the short run. Strategic planning concentrates on determining what resources to have available and what goals an organization should try to achieve under different circumstances, while tactical planning concentrates on how to apply the available resources to achieving those goals in a particular circumstance.

In the planning process, so many things should be considered that I cannot even list them all here. They tend to vary from organization to organization and person to person, and they involve too many variables to draw general conclusions without sufficient facts. I have collected what I consider to be the major issues in planning and done some initial analysis to help in your planning, but these efforts cannot possibly substitute for expert analysis based on technical and organizational knowledge of your requirements.

General Principles

> First and foremost, planning a defense is a study in tradeoffs. No single defense is safest for all situations, and no combination of defenses is cost effective in all environments. This underscores the basic protection principle. *Protection is something you do, not something you buy.*

General strategic needs

- The organizing principle is a clear statement of protection policy that establishes the strategic goals and philosophical background for protection.
- At the core of any strategy is the team of people who develop it and carry it out, both in the long run and in tactical situations. The first and most important thing you should do is gather a good team of people to help develop and implement strategy.
- Any strategy that is going to work requires resources, both over the long run and during tactical situations. I commonly see strategies which fail because of insufficient resources, resources poorly applied, a lack of consideration of the difference between strategic and tactical needs, and insufficient attention to detail.
- In order to assure that strategies will work in times of need, it is necessary to test tactical components ahead of time. The most common problem I encounter in tactical situations is events that were not anticipated during strategic planning and not discovered during testing. The effect is almost always a very substantial added expense.

General tactical needs

- Efficient response in tactical situations normally calls for the complete attention of some number of trained experts carrying out well-defined roles. In addition, it commonly requires that a substantial number of nonexperts act in concert at the direction of those trained experts.
- Tactical situations require that sufficient resources be on hand to deal with the situation. If sufficient resources are not present, the cost of attaining those resources on an emergency basis tends to be very high, the delays caused by the acquisition process may be even more costly, and the inexperience with the newly attained resources may

cause further problems. In many cases, the human component of these resources is partially fulfilled by an outside consultant.

- A small amount of resources properly applied almost always beats a large amount of resources poorly applied. You don't necessarily need to spend a lot to have a strong defense, but you have to spend wisely and react quickly.

Some Widely Applicable Results

Even though there are a vast array of different environments, there are some strategies and tactics that seem to be almost universally beneficial.

- **Consider Highest Exposures First:** In planning a strategy for defense, it is important to consider the potential harm when assessing what to do. Specifically, the highest exposures should receive the most attention and should be addressed with the highest priority.
- **Use the Strongest Defenses Feasible:** All other things being equal, it is better to use a stronger defense than a weaker one. As a rule, sound prevention is better than detection and cure, and general purpose detection and cure is better than special-purpose detection and cure, but a false sense of security is worse than any of them.
- **Proactive Defense Is Critical:** *Be Prepared*—it's the Boy Scout slogan— and it applies in information protection more than most places. In every comparison I have done or seen, people that take proactive action get away with lower cost, smaller incidents, and faster recovery than those who simply wait for a problem and then react.
- **Rapid Central Reporting and Response Works:** Epidemiological results are clear in showing that rapid centralized reporting and response reduces incident size, incident duration, and organizational impact.
- **Incident Response Teams Work:** In order for protection to be effective, you need a team that receives incident reports and responds to them on an emergency basis. This team is virtually always the same team that helps determine proper proactive strategy, implements tactical response, and performs analysis after incidents to improve future performance.
- **Keep Good Records and Analyze Them:** Record keeping is one of the most valuable aids to improving tactical and strategic response. When properly analyzed, records of incidents allow planners to devise more cost-effective tactical responses, which, in turn, provide more accurate information for strategic planning to reduce costs while improving response.
- **Don't Punish Victims:** One of the most common strategic mistakes is punishing those who report incidents or accidentally become a vector for attack. Punishment may be direct or indirect and may include

such subtleties as requiring the victim to do extra paperwork or such abusive treatment as getting a lecture on following written policies. When you punish victims, you increase response time because others become hesitant to report incidents. Statistics support the improved response of organizations with policies not to punish.

- **Procedural Methods Fail:** Many organizations make the mistake of relying on procedure as a preventative defense. The fact is, people are not perfect. When they make mistakes, assessing blame is not an effective response. You should plan on procedural failures and plan a response that considers people as they really are.
- **Training and Education Works:** You have to train your users to use your tactical capabilities or they will be ineffective in live situations, and you have to educate your experts in order to develop an effective plan and carry out the plan effectively in emergencies.
- **Defense-in-depth Works:** The synergistic effects of multiple defenses make defense-in-depth the most effective solution available to date.

5.7 THE COST OF PROTECTION

Organizations don't like to spend money on information protection if they can avoid it, because it is not profitable in the normal sense of the word. If you have better information protection, you don't lower costs and you don't increase sales or profit margins. All you do is prevent loss. In that sense, information protection is like insurance, a necessary cost of doing business, but not one that most organizations are anxious to emphasize.

Another major problem in analyzing the cost of protection is that, without good statistics, it is impossible to quantify the actual benefit associated with the cost. Good statistics aren't widely available because reporting is inadequate and mechanisms for compiling reported statistics don't exist.

I am not going to solve either of these problems here. But I do want to address another perspective on the cost of protection. Rather than address how much should be spent, I want to address the question of when to spend in order to be cost-effective.

Cost Increases Dramatically with Life-cycle Phase

There is a great deal of historical data that strongly supports the contention that organizations should spend money on information protection now rather than waiting until the NII is widely implemented and operational. Many experts in information protection indicate that after-the-fact protection is much less effective, much more expensive, rarely adequate, and hard to manage. The data from several significant studies indicates that the costs associated with addressing information assurance now may be as much as several orders of magnitude less than addressing it once the integrated NII is widely operating. According to numerous studies on the cost of making changes to information systems as a function of when the change is introduced in the life cycle, cost increases exponentially with life-cycle phase.

According to one study, compared to finding and correcting problems in the analysis phase, the average cost of a change (i.e., correcting a software fault), is increased by a factor of 2.5 in design, 5 in testing, and 36 in system integration. [231] In another study of large high-assurance software designs with high-quality specifications and extensive testing, the cost of a change after a system is in operation is calculated to be 100 times the cost of a change during the specification phase. [23] The same study showed that the larger the system, the more cost advantage there was to making changes earlier.

According to one software engineering text (that may be less reliable than the previous two extensive studies), the cost of fixing an error rises as more work is built upon that error before it is found and fixed. "The cost to catch a mistake and make a change at the time of writing the requirements specifications may be $10, and during the design $300. While the product is being built, the error may cost $3000; after the product has been delivered, the mistake could cost as much as $15,000 to fix, and possibly much more in losses to the client because the product didn't work." [207] The costs of extensive testing alone can double the overall system costs [231] while producing little advantage against malicious attacks. The following figure illustrates the cost of changes.

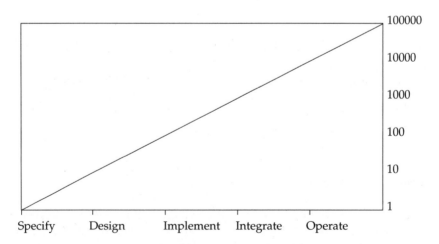

The cost of changes versus design phase.

Covering intentional disruption is a more stringent requirement than covering random events, but the costs of added coverage are not always substantial. The study of node destruction in a uniformly connected network demonstrated that 10 times more links were required in some circumstances to withstand intentional attack than random destruction. [148] On the other end of the spectrum, cost-analysis of fairly strong proactive integrity protection techniques proved 50 times more cost effective over the lifecycle of a system than defenses based on a reactive approach to attacks. [45]

It appears from the historical data that several orders of magnitude in reduced cost may be attained by making proper information assurance decisions early in the design process. Perhaps more realistically, organizations cannot afford adequate protection unless it is designed into systems from the start.

Procurement Is Only Part of Lifecycle Cost

Another issue in cost analysis that must be considered is the difference between lifecycle costs and procurement costs. Perhaps no area demonstrates the lack of attention to this difference more clearly today than the area of computer virus defenses. Many organizations have purchased virus scanning programs as a defense against computer viruses on the basis that the cost per system is only about a dollar. Unfortunately, this is only the purchase cost and not the usage cost. The factor of 50 cost increase previously described represents the difference between using a virus scanner every day and using a more cost-effective protection technique. [45] The cost of the scanner may be only $1, but the two or more minutes per day consumed by performing scans at system startup brings the lost time to more than 600 minutes (10 hours) per system per year. Even at only $10 per hour of downtime, the costs of using the scanner are 100 times more than the cost of purchase in this example. Other factors in virus scanners make them far more expensive to use than alternative technologies, and more recent analytical results show that using imperfect scanners (which all current scanners are) may lead to the spread of harder to detect viruses, just as the use of antibiotics have led to the so called "superbugs" which resist antibiotics. [44]

According to industry sources about 20 percent employee overhead is required for systems administration of integrity protection in a typical banking operation. [44] In some industries, the overhead is substantially lower, but any organization with serious intentions to implement information protection should budget at least 5 to 10 percent of the information technology budget for information protection. This budget normally consists of at least 90 percent ongoing costs and at most 10 percent acquisition costs. Because of the wide range of requirements involved in implementing a comprehensive information protection program, lifecycle costs of technical safeguards had better be a very small budget item.

Cost Increases with Immediacy

To perform an emergency upgrade of all current systems to implement all of the protection requirements described in this book would require an enormous amount of money. This would be impossible to do by the end of today no matter how much money was available for the task. The cost of implementing protection is far lower if it is well planned and carried out over a reasonable amount of time. This is shown in the following figure.

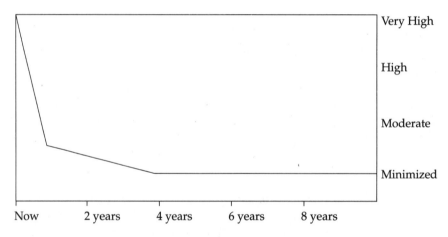

The cost of protection versus when it is achieved.

For most modern information systems, the replacement cycle is on the order of 2 to 4 years. This is closely related to the replacement cycle for PCs because they constitute more than 80 percent of the computers in the world and they have a very short replacement cycle.

The situation is quite different for infrastructure elements such as cables and satellites, where investments are intended to pay for themselves over time frames of 10, 20, or even more years. In these cases, the time frames have to be adjusted appropriately. The same is true for physical protection of buildings, where replacement cycles are on the order of 40 to 80 years.

Cost of Incidents Increase with Time

The longer you wait before providing protection, the more losses you suffer from incidents. The cost of these incidents will eventually exceed the cost of providing protection. In addition, reported incidents have increased rather dramatically over the last several years and the number of potential attackers increases dramatically as computers are interconnected. It is a reasonable expectation that, all other things being equal, the number of network-based attacks increase with the number of computers to which your computers are attached. If this is true, then the number of network-based attacks on the Internet should double every 8 to 10 months over the next 5 to 10 years and then level off as market saturation is reached in the United States. Worldwide, this increase could realistically continue for another 15 years, but not much longer. This is shown in the following figure.

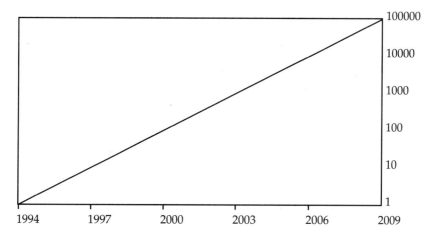

Network-based attacks per day over time.

Given the AT&T and DEC figures of more than one network-based entry attempt per day as of early 1994, we would expect that by the end of a 10-year period, there would be about 1,000 entry attempts per day. This is a little less than one every minute.

This exponential growth in attacks provides substantial support to implementing protection sooner rather than later. Of course, exponential growth in attacks by a finite population of people can only go on for so long. Eventually, the curve will level off. On the other hand, automated attacks are becoming more common, and as computer performance increases, so does the rate and sophistication level of these attacks.

Cost Increases with Coverage and Assurance

Increased coverage and assurance are generally attained by spending more on protection, but people commonly use this fact as an excuse to limit coverage and follow fads in spending money on protection. In fact, the cost of protection can be greatly reduced by making well-thought-out decisions. One analysis described in a case study in Chapter 6 produced a savings of almost 50 percent over a previous design.

The most common analysis of protection is based on statistical analysis and assumes random events with given probabilities. This risk analysis technique asserts that you can assess an expected loss from each of a set of attacks by multiplying the loss for each attack by the number of times that attack will be experienced in a given time interval. Risk can then be reduced by implementing protection that has known cost and reduces the probability of loss or the amount of loss. If the reduction in expected loss exceeds the cost of the defense, then the defense is cost-effective. The standard advice is then to implement the most cost-effective protective technique first and continue implementing cost-effective techniques until none are left to implement.

This standard form of risk analysis, in my opinion, is utterly ridiculous. I say this with some trepidation because if you ask 100 experts in this field about it, probably 98 will agree with the standard risk analysis, at least until they read my explanation. So here it is. The problem with this sort of risk analysis is that it makes assumptions that do not reflect reality. Specifically, it assumes that attacks are statistically random events, that they are independent of each other, that available statistics are valid, that protective measures are independent of each other, that expected loss reduction can be accurately assessed, and that the only costs involved in protection are the costs of the protective techniques. All of these are untrue and each is a very significant defect that independently could invalidate the analysis. In combination, they completely invalidate standard risk analysis:

- Attacks are not statistically random and are not independent of each other. If they were, we would not see the phenomena where one successful attack is rapidly followed by thousands of follow-ons. Examples include toll fraud against PBX systems, network attacks following the disclosure of over-the-wire attack techniques, and computer virus attacks. Furthermore, attacks gain and lose popularity with time so frequently that an analysis done today will be invalid in a few months. In today's environment, any assumed statistics used to develop a protection strategy will probably be invalid before the strategy is fully implemented.

- Current statistics are not valid. The most important reasons for this are that there is no standard reporting, many detected incidents are not reported, and many incidents that occur are never detected.
- Protective measures are not independent of each other. For example, integrity controls are not effective without access controls and access controls are not effective without integrity controls, but in combination, they are quite effective. Many of the most effective protection strategies rely on synergistic effects between protective measures. This means that there is a nonlinear relationship between the amount of protection and the money spent, with relatively little protection gained by piecemeal spending and most of the coverage and assurance provided as the final pieces of the protection scheme are put into place.
- Expected loss reduction cannot be accurately assessed. In fact, there is no standard method for even assessing actual loss from an incident after it takes place. It is not unusual for differences of several orders of magnitude to exist between different estimates of loss from the same incident. And that is when the analysis is performed after the incident takes place.

> If experts can't accurately determine loss from a known incident after it takes place, how can they be expected to accurately predict expected loss from large classes of incidents before the fact? They cannot and they do not. Instead, they use an estimate without any real basis such as the worst case they could think of, or a wild guess. And that is only for the expected loss. When it comes to reduction in expected loss, the hand-waving really begins.

- Protective techniques that reduce the risk of specific attacks are only a small component of the cost of effective protection. For example, how do you assess the reduction in expected loss from Trojan horses in commercially purchased software through the use of improved documentation? Documentation is critical to effective protection, and yet there is no way to assess a specific risk reduction related to a specific attack through improved documentation.

Combined Cost Factors

When we combine all of these cost factors together, we get an interesting picture of the overall cost of protection. Without using any specific numbers for any specific situation, the picture generally looks like the following figure.

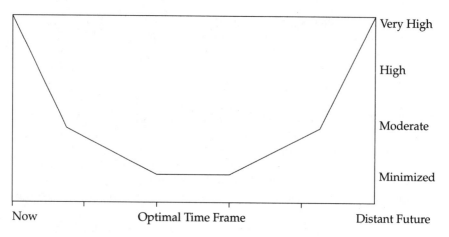

Very High

High

Moderate

Minimized

Now   Optimal Time Frame   Distant Future

Overall protection cost versus when protection is in place.

In words, the most cost-effective way to implement protection is to spend a reasonable amount of money over a reasonable period of time.

> Don't be in such a rush that you waste money, but don't wait so long that you lose more from disruption than prudent protection would have cost.

The problem in analysis is to determine the region of the curve with minimum cost. Naturally, nobody has ever performed enough analysis to be able to provide a closed-form solution to this problem, so everyone who tries to do this analysis is left with highly speculative estimates. My speculative estimate is that the most cost-effective time frame for protection is closely related to the replacement cycle of equipment when that time frame is less than three years. In every other case I have seen, budgetary constraints limit the time frame for effective protection.

Without careful analysis, it would be easy to bankrupt any organization in an attempt to "armor-plate" information systems with ad hoc, after-the-fact enhancements. Organizations should undertake a careful analysis to determine the cost-effectiveness of information protection techniques on a class-by-class basis. This effort should be undertaken at the earliest possible time in order to afford the greatest cost savings.

For obsolescent systems, the cost of injecting protection may be astronomical, so a different approach should be considered. A time frame should be established for replacement or enhancement of these systems, and planners should plan on requiring appropriate information protection features in replacement systems over that time frame. Based on normal replacement cycles, this process should be completed over 3 to 7 years for most organizations, and 7 to 12 years for high capital investment systems such as national infrastructure elements.

History shows that the cost of incremental improvement increases as perfection is approached. Rather than strive for perfect protection, risks should be managed in a reasonable way that balances cost with the protection it provides.

Based on these factors, the most cost-effective overall approach to providing protection is to immediately incorporate protection requirements into design standards, and to provide network-based tools and techniques to detect and respond to disruptions of current systems. Information assurance features are phased in over time based on normal system replacement cycles. Substantial immediate improvement is attained by implementing network-based protection features and training information workers. Over the long term, protection will reach desired levels at reasonable cost. This time lag in technical enhancement will also give the organization time to adapt to these changes.

5.8   AN INCREMENTAL PROTECTION PROCESS

Some people think that the piecemeal approach to protection has a major advantage in that it involves only incremental investment to meet current needs. Fortunately, you can have both a sound overall organizational approach and an incremental investment strategy. The result is lower cost and better protection. The incremental approach to organizational protection described here has been effective both from a standpoint of reducing loss and controlling protection costs for many organizations.

To give a frame of reference, when protection is implemented in this way, the overall cost is typically under one half of one percent of annual operating budget. Piecemeal protection commonly costs on the order of one percent or more of the overall operating budget and is far less effective. Unfortunately, piecemeal protection cost is often hidden in reduced productivity and expenses taken from operating budgets of small organizational units so it is rarely detected by top-level management.

Protection Posture Assessment

> An information protection posture assessment is normally the first step in addressing the protection issues in an organization. The purpose of this sort of assessment is to get an overall view of how the organization works, how information technology is applied, and what protective measures are in place.

This assessment should be comprehensive in its scope, cover all aspects of the information technology in use in the organization, and address the core issues of integrity, availability, and privacy. The reason a comprehensive approach is important is that there are interactions between components of the protection process. For solutions to work, they have to work well together.

Such an assessment is usually qualitative in nature, and the quality of the result is tied to the quality of the people used to perform the assessment. For that reason, it is important to apply the best available experts to this sort of assessment.

Such an assessment should be done over a fairly short time frame. I have done assessments like this for very large organizations, and time frames of only a few months are usually sufficient. For a small organization with only a few hundred employees, such an assessment can often be completed in only a week, and I have offered a one-day assessment service for small businesses with under 25 employees on a regular basis. The reason for the short time frame is that top-flight people know their field well enough to ask the right questions, determine the implications of the answers, and provide a well-supported result fairly quickly. It is also important to resolve the top-level issues quickly so that the rest of the process can proceed.

Assessments are normally provided in a form that can be easily read and understood by top management. This is vital in order for the issues to be meaningfully addressed from an organizational point of view. At the same time, the assessment has to withstand the scrutiny of the top expert available in the organization, and it may be passed through another outside expert if the implications are important enough. So it has to be technically solid and well-supported by facts.

If properly done, such an assessment yields a review of the information gathered in the process, a set of findings that describe the identified shortcomings in a systematic way, a plan of action that can be used immediately to carry out the rest of the protection process, and an estimate of the costs associated with the proposed plan of action. The result should be designed to provide metrics for evaluating vendors, considering time frames, and considering the financial rationality of the measures.

Emergency Measures and Long-term Planning

It is common for a protection posture assessment to call for two immediate steps: emergency measures and long-term planning.

Emergency measures are normally associated with exceptionally high exposures (i.e., areas with a high maximum potential for losses) that are not adequately covered by existing protective measures. In other words, situations where you could lose your shirt and the closet is left open with a *take me* sign posted in front. One example from a recent assessment included the following emergency measure:

"Secure the fungibles transfer capability. The current exposure is so great that a single incident could severely damage the corporation and there is currently no meaningful protection in place to prevent such an attack."

Long-term planning is usually required in the areas where inadequate plans are already in place, where previous planning didn't adequately consider alternatives, or where weaknesses were identified in the posture assessment. For example, in one study, a long-term plan included a quantitative assessment of the costs of alternative architectures and a list of protective measures for meeting the needs of a particular sort of installation. By implementing a plan over a multi-year period and properly selecting the mix of techniques, the overall cost of protection could be reduced by almost a factor of 2 from the previous plan and the effectiveness of protection increased along the way.

The time frame for completing emergency measures and long-term planning phases typically ranges from three to nine months, and a combination of people with different skills and experience levels are usually involved. In this activity, top experts are used to supervise the process and verify that things are done properly, while second tier experts are used for optimization studies, market surveys, implementing emergency measures, and making other plans.

Implementation and Testing

Once a detailed plan is in place and emergency situations are taken care of, the plan is implemented over an appropriate period of time.

It is quite common for a full-scale implementation to be put in place over a period of 1 to 3 years. In some exceptional cases, especially in large organizations where major investments in information technology are underway, the plan can call for action over a 3 to 7 year period. In infrastructure cases, the process may last as long as 10 years.

Implementation of an information protection plan typically involves many organizational components and, for large organizations, this may even involve substantial changes in organizational momentum. It typically involves a number of vendors, a substantial management component, cooperation throughout the organization, retraining of information workers, and a whole slew of other things that must be handled. If properly done, this is a relatively painless process.

In this phase of the process, second-tier experts typically supervise at a hands-on level, while top experts periodically spot check to verify that things are going well and review work underway with the second-tier experts to verify the propriety of any decisions made during the implementation.

Operation and Maintenance

Operation and maintenance of protection systems requires special attention, since protection, like any other process, doesn't just happen on its own.

The operational aspects of protection should be part and parcel of the overall protection plan, and will involve ongoing investments. Whenever possible, operation and maintenance should be handled internally. Some exceptions will likely include disaster recovery, which may use a leased site, and external audit, which by definition requires outside experts.

During normal operation, there will be incidents requiring special expertise that would be too expensive to maintain in-house, and the ongoing education process should include some outside experts or the use of widely available external short courses.

> Maintenance operations offer special challenges in the area of information protection because during maintenance, the normal safeguards may not be active or used in the same manner as during normal operating periods. Similarly, maintenance, by its very nature, involves testing under stress conditions. Under stress conditions, the likelihood of failure is greater, and thus special precautions must be taken to provide the necessary assurance even under these circumstances.

Decomissioning, Disposal, and Conversion

The decomissioning process typically begins by identifying any services provided by the system to be decommissioned, information residing in that system that has value other than in that system, and all resources related to that system.

Once these have been identified, replacement systems are normally put in place, information of value is converted to the new system, the new system is operated in parallel with the system about to be decommissioned, and finally, the system being decommissioned is shut down.

After shutdown, the system being decommissioned is normally cleaned of any residual information that might be left on disks, video terminals, or other obvious or subtle storage media. Any components with value are then stripped from the system and used or resold, and finally, the residual is recycled or disposed of.

After the system being decommissioned is shut down, elements of supporting infrastructure are normally made available for other purposes or decommissioned along with the rest of the system. For example, any wiring, cooling systems, power supplies, special lighting, fire suppression equipment, computer floors, security doors, video display terminals, printers, networking hardware, or other similar elements of the computing environment that are freed up may be used for other purposes.

CHAPTER 6

Protection Posture
Case Studies

The first step in providing protection is performing a protection posture assessment. Over the last several years, I have worked with a group of well-seasoned information protection specialists doing top-level qualitative analyses of the protection posture of many organizations. For this book, portions of several of these studies have been extracted and identities disguised to illuminate the topics discussed earlier.

6.1   HOW TO DO A PROTECTION POSTURE ASSESSMENT

Several people have asked how these studies can be done so that the same quality results can be attained with lower quality personnel. They ask for checklists and all sorts of other short cuts, but in the end, this is just not how you do a really good protection posture assessment. That is not to say that you cannot do a lower quality assessment with things like checklists and, in fact, many companies offer such a service.

In response to one request, I prepared a draft document describing what it takes to do such an assessment. What follows is a variation on that document in which company-specific information and references to previous studies are removed. This discussion concentrates on studies for large organizations, but many of the points apply to all organizations. This discussion is also oriented toward a 30-day study addressing a situation in which losses could have high value. This seems to be the norm for this sort of study in a large organization. It should be helpful both to those readers who are interested in performing these sorts of studies for others and for those readers who are considering hiring someone to do such a study.

Personnel

The information protection posture assessment requires a team of expert personnel with general knowledge and experience in a wide variety of areas, and special expertise in all of the aspects of information protection. Specifically:

- Consultants with 10 or more years of professional experience in the areas covered by the assessment are required in order to assure that their breadth and depth of knowledge is adequate. Since no single individual has this much experience in a broad range of areas, a team of well-seasoned professionals is required. The use of a team also implies the ability to work together and the use of a team leader who is in charge of writing the assessment document. Because of the highly technical nature of this sort of study and the requirement for the team leader to make technical and management decisions, this person must have substantial management and consulting experience and a great deal of expertise in all areas of information protection.
- Because this sort of assessment is done over a very short time frame and covers a wide range of topics, it is best done by a team of 3 or 4 people who have worked together before. Because this assessment involves the top-level people in the organization under study, the team members must be more knowledgeable about protection issues than the people working for the client in order to justify the use of outside expertise. This means that the people must be very good at what they do. They need the necessary experience in the proper set of interrelated areas, they have to be able to relate to the client, and they have to be able to get the necessary information quickly, efficiently, and without offense.
- Because the assessment must involve issues of protection, understanding of the computing environment, detailed understanding of the hardware, software, operating systems, networks, telecommunications equipment, standards within the industry, and other technical matters, it is important that each team member have a thorough background in computer hardware and software, a good working knowledge of how systems and networks work, understanding of the historical context of many current technologies, and deep understanding of information protection issues.
- At least one team member should be a specialist with more than 10 years of experience in the specific industry being studied. This background should include consulting work for a variety of companies in the industry, a good working knowledge of the standards and practices used by others in the industry, intimate knowledge of the hardware and software platforms used in the industry, their short-

comings, their features, their vulnerabilities, and methods used to protect them.

- By its very nature, the protection posture assessment is a qualitative analysis, not a quantitative one. For this reason, it depends heavily on the quality of the people doing the assessment. The people must not limit themselves to things like checklists or the result will almost certainly be poor. The people doing these assessments must understand many different viewpoints that may exist in the organization and reconcile the meaning of what different people say. They have to be able to judge the people in the organization by the way they act and make qualitative decisions about how to weigh their words. It is often necessary to ask a lot of questions in order to get a vital piece of information and, because each of the people interviewed has different biases, it helps to have experience interacting with similar people in similar situations.
- The people who do these assessments must be hard to push around or lead astray. This is hard to find in a large corporation because there is a tendency to promote those who don't make waves. By its very nature, such an assessment must make waves in the organization being assessed. If it does not make waves, either the organization was already very well protected, or the study didn't find the things it was supposed to find. That means that the people doing the assessment must expect and be able to deal with some hostility, lies, bizarre behavior, and other such things. It also means that they are there to make waves of a particular sort for a particular group within the client's organization. People who are afraid of losing their jobs by making a misstatement with a client are not going to do a good job of getting the necessary information.

Areas Covered

The areas covered (protection management, protection policy, standards and procedures, documentation, protection audit, technical safeguards, incident response, testing, physical protection, personnel issues, legal considerations, protection awareness, training and education, and organizational suitability) are detailed elsewhere in this book and I will not take the time to reiterate them here. It is important to use people who are well-versed in all of these areas because the language used by people in different corporate roles is quite different. In order to communicate effectively and be viewed as a professional, you must be able to switch languages while speaking to different people and understand the nuances of these different languages. For example, the term *wire room* means something very different to a facilities manager than to someone in charge of electronic funds transfers. Similarly, the abbreviations used are very different for different people with different backgrounds, so it is vital to have enough knowledge of these areas to be understood and to understand properly.

Process

The assessment process consists of the following steps:

- **Site visit:** This should take one or two days and should be scheduled so that client representatives that know how each part of the environment under consideration operates at the most detailed level are available for interview. Typically, the top-level manager and technical experts in each unique environment should be present. If there are tours to be taken, they should be taken on that day. Although experiencing everyone's job may be useful, it is far more important to have the details available in a concise form. The client should also provide copies of all relevant documentation at the site visit.

  The members of the assessment team should be well prepared to ask any question related to their areas and a very thorough record of what was said by whom should be kept. The goal of this effort is to reconnoiter the client operation. That means that, like a grand jury, it is appropriate to go anywhere and ask anything.

  For lack of a better analogy, this is very much like a tiger team where you get the best experts to tell you how they could attack. The difference is that you don't touch anything, you just ask questions and make observations that allow you to assess the current situation. If the client doesn't know the answers to the questions, this is an area they should do more work on. If they do know the answers, these answers will reveal the weaknesses and strengths.

- **Visit write-up:** In the write-up, each team member provides a copy of their notes to the team leader who combines them to provide as accurate a depiction of the site visit as is possible. This is then returned to the team members for verification of factual accuracy and to resolve any disputes between different viewpoints. The result is a detailed description of the visit that the client team members should agree is an accurate depiction of what they said. The visit write-up should be completed and agreed to by the end of the first week of the study. It is vital to do the write-up as soon as possible after the site visit because this will assure, to as high a degree as possible, that the write-up is accurate. Contemporaneous notes are the best resource.

- **Analysis and findings:** Each team member should concentrate on their areas of specialty as assigned by the team leader and perform a detailed analysis describing all of the weaknesses detected in the assessment process. In this phase, we rely on the experience and expertise of the team members to accurately and quickly detail the known weaknesses in the technologies in use. If the team members do not know this ahead of time, they cannot normally look it up at this point in the time frame of such a study, however, a good research team can help assure that these results are up-to-date. An important aspect of this activity is that the presentation not include all possible attacks, but rather systemic issues with examples of how systems can be exploited.

Another critical factor to the success of the findings is that they relate the results to comparable organizations so that the client gets a feel for what is normal and prudent, what is critical, etc. In the findings, it is the responsibility of the assessment team to make value judgments about the relative import of different issues. For example, in a glass factory, if a particular router is used to connect the Internet to a file server which is used for advertising, it is vital to understand that regardless of the potential for abuse, this component is inherently less critical to this particular company than the temperature control in the ovens. This combination of technical and business understanding is what makes the findings valuable to the organization being assessed.

In order to meet the typical 30-day time frame, the analysis and findings must be completed in draft form by the end of the second week of the study. Thus, the team members get only one week to generate, write up, and initially integrate their findings.

- **Plan of action and findings review:** Once a draft of the site visit and findings is available, the team members have to read the total document with an eye toward catching any errors, omissions, or poorly stated items. This should include each team member cross-checking other team member results, the team leader resolving disputes, and a copy edit to review the document for writing, spelling, sentence structure, and presentation. In the meanwhile, the team leader has the dual job of generating a proposed plan of action to mitigate the problems revealed in the findings. This is done at two levels. Since this is only a qualitative assessment, an overall plan separating the most time-critical changes from the long-term issues is appropriate. Then, a sample scenario for implementing this plan and estimates of costs are generated. This process should be completed by the end of the third week of the assessment.

- **Closure:** The draft document is now ready for review by members outside the assessment team. These reviewers should read the entire document with a critical eye. Final document preparation should be done. The executive summary should be written to summarize the report. Overhead viewgraphs should be made to summarize the document for a 15-minute presentation to top-level management. All of these should be completed and reviewed by the assessment team before the end of the fourth week so that the final presentation can be made on the last day of that week.

Alternatives

The protection posture assessment is designed to provide a very rapid, low-cost, top-level, qualitative assessment. For that reason, it depends on extremes in expertise. Some alternative approaches that are widely practiced in the industry include:

- A common alternative approach is to spend several months trying to get the same results by using less-qualified people for the assessment. The net effect is a lower assessment quality, a much longer delay in results, more inconvenience to the client, and a cost increase to the client of about one order of magnitude.
- Another common alternative is the use of a whole series of checklists that the client fills out and returns. This list is then analyzed and a report is generated (almost automatically). In some cases, even the data gathering for this checklist is automated. This type of assessment is less expensive in terms of assessment team time, but takes a lot more of the client's time, is often filled out by different people than would participate in the high-quality short-term assessment, misses many of the issues detected by a high-quality assessment, and is less satisfying to most clients I have encountered.
- Many of the major CPA firms have done assessments using a team of EDP auditors. These auditors are generally well-trained and interact primarily with the internal auditors of the client. They usually understand less about the business and more about the technical protection issues and spend several months in assessment. Another version simply reviews the internal auditor documents for completeness and accuracy.

Selling (and Buying) a Posture Assessment

"Nothing happens till someone sells something," is a famous quote from a well-known expert on marketing. Unfortunately, selling a protection posture assessment has not historically been a very easy task. Some have equated it to pulling teeth, but I must have a better dentist or a higher threshold of pain than they have, because selling a posture assessment has always been much more painful in my experience.

Political documents Despite their technical content and reasonable accuracy, all protection posture assessments are essentially political documents from the point of view of the customer. In particular, they are designed to address the specific desires of the client to make changes in their organization.

Why organizations don't get posture assessments Many people have legitimate concerns about information protection, but of those, very few do much about it. In some cases, the cost of an assessment prevents it from being done. In other cases, the person who wants the assessment done is not powerful enough to get it done without approvals that can never be obtained.

Probably the dominant reason that such a study is a rarity is that the person in charge of information protection doesn't want to have a report hanging around that describes inadequacies. Here are just some of the reasons such a report may be seen as undesirable:

- If the report demonstrates a weakness that is exploited at some later time, it will be impossible to claim that nobody knew such a weakness existed. Thus, it may force the people who requested the report to do something about protection, and nobody wants to have their hand forced in this way.
- In a substantial number of cases, computer crime in the form of embezzlement has been committed by high executives in companies. The last thing they want is some way to detect what they have been doing.
- If the report finds that a current way of doing things is inadequate, or worse yet, that a recent decision was not a very good one, then the person who made that decision may get into trouble. For that reason, the people in charge of protection are almost certain to claim that no such study is required and that they have things well in hand.

> There is a fundamental issue in here somewhere. And I think the issue is that people in most organizations are punished for being less than perfect. This means that it is better for the individual to cover up possible problems than it is to expose them and correct them. But a study of protection, by definition, is designed to expose problems. Even worse, it costs money to have such a study done, so you are spending money and identifying shortcomings, the two worst things you can do as an individual in an unenlightened organization.

Why organizations do get assessments Over the years, I have encountered five main exceptions to the rule of never buying trouble in the form of a protection posture assessment:

- The first exception is in cases when an attack has just taken place and it is impossible to cover it up. In this case, people are anxious to show that they are reacting strongly to the attack and are really clamping down. They already have trouble, so it's an ideal time to reveal all of the problems at once.
- The second exception is when an organizational change has just taken place. In this case, as part of the process of the organizational shakeup, a protection posture assessment can be used as a political tool to advance certain factions and consolidate control. It is politically acceptable to generate a report that documents the evils of the previous administration if the new one is interested in doing something about protection.
- The third exception is when someone who is high enough up in the organization has a legitimate concern about protection and a desire to address it. In a private corporation, this is the owner. In a public corporation, it is usually the CEO, or in rare cases when supported by the CEO, the chief information officer (or equivalent).
- The fourth exception is when someone is a lame duck and wants to do one last thing before departing. In the case of the lame duck, this sort of report is usually motivated by either revenge or an honest desire to do some good that couldn't be done while their career was still viable in the company.
- The fifth exception is during the early phases of a new system development project. This is fairly rare, but, in some cases, designers will have the foresight to consider protection in a serious way from the start of a project. When this is done, it dramatically improves protection and lowers protection costs, but few designers have enough knowledge or foresight today to take this approach. Even fewer work on large enough projects to have the budget for doing more than the minimum design required to get functional operation.

6.2   CASE STUDY 1: A MA AND PA BUSINESS

This information was extracted from a study done for a small restaurant corporation as a side effect of looking at other issues in their information technology area.

This situation is typical in that this business is not interested in keeping secrets, but they have a vital need for availability of information services and integrity in those services. They have a small network used in one location and they are considering using elements of the NII as a conduit for connecting a second location to their first location, but this is not emphasized in the particular report.

This study is also typical in that it is presented in the language used in the organization. For example, "servers" are the people that go out to the tables and "the system" consists of several PCs, a network, a file server, several printers in various locations, the point of sale terminals used by cashiers, and some office systems interconnected to the network. Many of the product names are known to those at this restaurant and several technologies are familiar to them, but in other areas, they know very little.

Executive Summary

- **Critical repairs:** Before the system will be fully suitable for the environment at Rest-O-Rant Corp., several issues must be addressed. These items are listed under "Critical Repairs."
- **Important changes:** Even though the system can be operated suitably in the Rest-O-Rant Corp. environment, once the critical repairs are completed, there are several important changes that should be made for the system to operate in a manner normally associated with such an environment. These items are listed under "Important Changes."
- **Aggravating factors:** Assuming the system is changed as described above, there are still substantial aggravating factors which make its use unduly difficult. These items should be changed, but the restaurant can continue to operate indefinitely even if they are not changed, without any obvious consequences other than the day-to-day inconvenience associated with them. These items are listed under "Aggravating Factors."
- **Long-term limitations:** There are long-term limitations to the suitability of this system due to design and implementation decisions. These limitations cannot reasonably be expected to change in the foreseeable future unless the vendor chooses to completely reimplement the product using more appropriate means. These limitations are particularly applicable to the long-term growth of Rest-O-Rant and the ongoing costs of operating the computer system in that environment. These items are detailed under "Long-term Limitations."

Critical Repairs

Software

1. There must be a way to quickly and safely "reset" the system to allow it to start processing a new day's activities regardless of other circumstances. When an error in closing the last day's activity prevents the business from opening the next morning, there must be an easy way to restart operations. As an example, on the Sunday morning after Christmas (one of the busiest shopping days of the year), the system could not be used because the "close" from the previous day had failed.

2. There appears to be a problem related to holidays that causes the system to fail when a day passes without the system being operated. This condition occurred on Thanksgiving and again on Christmas. This indicates that there may be many other date-related problems such as leap-year errors, leap-century problems (the year 2000 is a leap-century), and other similar problems. This is almost certainly related to design errors.

3. There are cases where the user is told to not change anything and contact the vendor representative in the morning. A restaurant cannot be out of business until the next morning because of a software failure of this sort. The system should be able to log errors and attempt to restart by saving critical files in a backup area and restoring the system to a usable state.

4. When components fail and those failures directly affect the moment-to-moment operation of the business, the system **must** adequately notify the affected users so as to cause them to act to repair these failures in a timely fashion. An example is the incident where the kitchen printer had an out-of-paper condition when it was not fully out of paper, and gave no other indication of the problem. For more than 10 minutes, the kitchen staff was unaware of many orders placed by the servers because the system did not notify either of the failure. Any and all known conditions of this sort must be addressed before the system will be suitable.

5. Software errors in noncritical functions must not prevent other critical functions from operating. An example is the software-induced error that prevents users from using the order entry system. In this case, the limited key pad used by servers is not capable of entering the necessary keystrokes to clear the error condition (i.e., 'y' in response to the DOS critical error handler to continue the batch file processing used for menu start-up). On a full keyboard, it is possible to clear the error condition and continue the order entry process, but the interaction of the limited key pad with the software's failure to properly handle the error condition causes the system to become unusable.

6. Security is cumbersome and inadequate. Specifically, it is trivial for anyone with access to a standard keyboard to bypass all protection by interrupting the system start-up process. Thereafter, all information on the file server is open to arbitrary examination and/or modification. For example, a cashier with minimal DOS user experience could easily delete all business records without a trace and without recourse. This is particularly disturbing considering the extensive requirements for using passwords throughout the system and the ease of implementing stronger access controls through the network software. In light of the substantial protection capa-

bilities provided by the LANtastic software used for networking in this environment, it would be an easy matter to implement controls limiting nonback-office users and computers from accessing those functions and files.

7. Backup and recovery facilities are nonexistent. In an environment such as this, a single disk failure (typical mean time to failure is only 2 operating years) will cause the entire business to stop operating and may result in total loss of all historical data other than that printed out in daily reports. The software vendor apparently didn't specify or provide for this requirement. This is clearly an accident waiting to happen.

8. All data collected and stored by the system should be made available for use by outside analysis programs in dBase-compatible form to allow further analysis via programmed means. This is critical to using the business information now being gathered by the system in ways not anticipated by the existing product.

Hardware and operations

1. Operation critical floppy disk drives and keypads must not be left unprotected in areas where they are exposed to food, drinks, spillage, smoke, and other similar environmental factors. These disk drives will almost certainly fail in 3 to 6 months in the present environment unless steps are taken to protect them from environmental exposures. Since these are critical to operations, the problem should be addressed posthaste. The best solution may be the use of mechanical barriers for the disks and plastic covers for the keypads.

2. The file server is currently in a very hazardous location and is in a high-traffic area. It is not adequately protected from environmental factors and is particularly critical to operations. This machine should be moved to the office area immediately.

3. The floppy disks used to bootstrap the computers are not write-protected. They should be.

Important Changes

Software

1. The software fails when a multitude of different menus are used in the course of a single user session. This causes the user to have to reboot the computer and test previous operations to assure that they were properly performed before continuing on. This sort of severe inconvenience should not be necessary at all, but in the worst case, should happen only in limited and well-documented

situations. Software interlocks should be provided to detect this condition before it happens and prevent it, even if in the process it requires the user to take remedial steps.

2. The software-induced warning message that states that only one user may perform a particular function at a time, requires that the user determine that no other terminal is currently using these functions. The result of a problem in this area can apparently be severe and there is no reason not to provide proper software interlocks or capabilities for simultaneous access by authorized users. This is clearly a case of poor design that could be easily resolved in a well-designed system. It also adds stress to the users and eventually causes them to ignore the warning because of the high rate (nearly 100 percent) of false positives.

3. Data is often lost when the system is used in a seemingly reasonably manner. For example, when two checks are combined, both are apparently lost. Many other examples are cited by those who have spent time using the system.

4. The system seems unable to undo erroneous steps easily. The general lack of editing capability is a minor inconvenience in some cases. For example, a server has to finish a bill and remember any incorrect entries instead of continuously being in an edit mode. In other circumstances, it results in substantial inconvenience and eventually will result in substantial limits on system use. For example, when the number of employees reaches the maximum, you can never add another employee because old employees cannot be removed.

5. Numerous bugs and unnotified dependencies prevent users from completing an operation which should not have been started without the appropriate preconditions existing. For example, you might enter a whole series of items before finding out that the entire process failed because some file that these operations depend on does not yet exist. The system should identify and, where possible, correct these conditions before permitting data entry to proceed.

6. Inadequate notice on error conditions causes users to "quest" for the cause of a problem rather than being directed to it or, better yet, being allowed to resolve it and continue the interrupted process. For example, doing end-of-day summaries often yields an error if a customer check is not closed. The user then has to search through all servers to find the unclosed check, and even then, the reason it is not closed may not be obvious and may require further effort. Similarly, people cannot check out until they have satisfied the computer. The computer doesn't provide them with the ability to resolve problems as they prepare to leave,

rather it requires them to figure out the source of a problem that the computer has already identified. If the computer can identify that there is a problem, it should be able to provide that information to the user so that, at a minimum, the user can resolve the problem. Ideally, the specific problem should be identified and its cure made directly available to the user attempting the operation.

7. Error messages are often presented in cryptic form and, in some cases, leave users in a position where they can type commands into the Basic command interpreter while files are opened. This presents substantial risks to data integrity. Furthermore, users with limited data entry key pads cannot recover without rebooting the computer.

8. Schedules don't provide information such as dates. Other reports are not easily reformatted by the user to suit specific reporting requirements of management. All functions that produce reports should be able to provide the same information in dBase-compatible format so that external programs can be used to manipulate it.

9. The networking package is unable to contend with momentary server failures and reboots. This, in turn, forces the users to reboot all of the workstations whenever the server has to be restarted. The workstations should be able to determine that this condition has taken place and automatically recover via periodic retries until successful.

10. There should be a way to enter orders via item numbers rather than via menu selections so that servers can enter a series of numbers and produce a whole check without having to look at the screen to find items.

Hardware

1. A short-term power failure, power spike, or lightning strike could cause the entire network to become unusable for a substantial period of time, and the resulting data loss could be catastrophic. The use of an uninterruptable power supply is advised.

Aggravating Factors

1. When examining information, the user is often *returned* to an unrelated on-line menu rather than a related one. For example, to look at current server activities requires repeated movement between three menus, when it could easily be made to return one menu level to allow the next person's information to be examined without the intervening steps. This seems to be common, in that you

cannot reliably predict where you will end up when you finish an operation. This seems to stem from a lack of a well-designed system structure.

2. Different menus and data entry types work differently. For example, passwords do not require an <enter> after entry but most other data does. Different menus appear differently, causing momentary confusion. This inconsistency again reflects a poor overall design strategy.

3. There is no universal escape from an on-screen menu, so that in each menu, a different strategy must be used to leave. This makes it hard to undo an error and, in many cases, makes it hard to figure out what to do. The delays caused by this are expensive.

Long-term Limitations

1. The underlying environment is not really suitable for a commercial product of this sort. Most critically, the use of Basic for implementing the system has resulted in very high error rates, poor design, inadequate structuring, terrible inconsistencies, and poor expansion of function. It is clear that the original design was augmented again and again to add new functions and features, and that in the process, a badly needed redesign was never done. It is unlikely that this problem can ever be resolved without a complete product redesign. For the foreseeable future, the problems encountered now will continue unabated. When combined with the selection of the networked DOS environment, this design decision caused the product to be more expensive, harder to maintain, and far less reliable than would be expected from a well-designed and well-thought-out implementation.

2. Inconsistencies in design likely stemmed from the choice of Basic as the implementation language and the design process previously described. These inconsistencies lead inevitably to the ongoing stream of errors, the inconsistency in user interface, the many user inconveniences, the inability to unify protection decisions, the difficulty in handling error conditions, the inability to resolve problems when they are found, and many of the other problems identified in this report.

3. The system is at or near its operational limits. For example, the vendor had problems adding drivers for a new printer. If they cannot add a new printer without problems, major problems are likely in adding other new interfaces and features. Anticipate problems with automated process control, new user interfaces, Lotus and dBase integration, new analysis and presentation methods, operation between multiple stores, and so on. It is unlikely that the system will be able to integrate well or adapt easily to these future

events. Expect to have to replace the system in a few years unless a major redesign is done.

6.3   CASE STUDY 2: A (NOT-SO) SMALL BUSINESS

This study was done for the information systems manager of a small manufacturing automation firm over a very short period of time. It represents a realistic view of the position of many small- to medium-sized companies today with respect to protection. The engineering orientation of this company places more emphasis on confidentiality than many other businesses.

Again, the language of the study is oriented toward the words and phrases used in this company. The study was done for the head of the Information Systems department and the entire firm is engineering-oriented. Little is provided in the way of explanation and many terms are used without explanation. The President of the company at the time this study was done had an engineering background and was familiar with these terms and phrases as well.

> One of the important issues detected in this study was the changing nature of their dependency on different portions of their information technology. This sort of change often creeps up on companies, and before they know what happened, their environment has completely changed and their protection plans are no longer meaningful.

Introduction

This report summarizes and comments on a brief review of information protection at ABCorp. The review was performed in the form of an interview with Mr. John Smith, the manager of information systems at ABCorp, and his chief system administrator. The review consisted of discussions of protection issues and a brief tour of facilities.

In addition to the normal business systems used by most modern corporations of substantial size, ABCorp survives as a company because it has unique information technologies and engineering expertise. To a large and increasing extent, it is information technology that differentiates ABCorp from its competitors. This is especially true in three areas:

- ABCorp has a standardized high-speed product that is based, to a large extent, on unique algorithms and implementation features that differentiate it on a cost and efficiency basis from competitors.

- ABCorp has a database of designs and design capabilities that make it more efficient than competitors at performing the engineering functions required for customized applications.
- ABCorp is now moving into the automated and integrated materials handling market. This market is driven very heavily by the efficiency of information technology. In order to remain competitive, it will be increasingly important to have efficient, properly operating, and proprietary information technology capabilities.

At present, the information requirements of these engineering areas balance with or slightly exceed the more common information technology requirements of business and operations. It is highly likely that within the next 3 to 5 years, information technology requirements in the engineering areas will come to far outweigh other business requirements. Correspondingly, the financial values associated with the engineering applications of information systems at ABCorp will come to far exceed the values associated with other areas.

This shift from business applications of information technology to engineering applications is not uncommon and is not proceeding without pain. The increasing use of PCs in the engineering functions is only one example of this shift. Another example is the movement toward far more complex and integrated information systems performing control and analysis functions in products. While the problem of providing backups for PC-based engineering workstations is becoming somewhat of an inconvenience, there is currently little or no centralized control over systems used for complex applications and no central storage of software provided to customers. These problems will only get worse as this shift continues, and without a well thought out plan, it is likely that the situation will get out of control within 2 years.

This study is primarily concerned with assuring that the right information gets to the right place at the right time, taking into account accidental and intentional events that may tend to prevent this from happening. This concern is usually considered in terms of three components: confidentiality of information, integrity of information, and availability of services.

In the case of ABCorp, there are substantial lapses that affect all of these areas, and yet from an overall perspective, the information systems specialists seem to have things reasonably in control. To the extent that the specific findings outline inadequacies, it appears that the people in the information systems department are ready, willing, and able to make reasonable improvements within reasonable time and cost constraints. Unfortunately, the trend seems to be toward a loss of control in the areas where responsibility is poorly defined, and even more unfortunately, this is the engineering area that will soon come to dominate the information component of ABCorp as a business.

The most important finding of this short review is that top-level management must work with engineering and information systems management to arrive at a well-defined policy and plan for this shift in information technology emphasis and that these people must come to work together as a team to regain and maintain control over this vital and growing area of concern.

Findings

It is important to note that the vulnerabilities detected in this review are not particularly unusual, that the presence of vulnerabilities does not necessarily indicate the presence of attacks, that exposures resulting from vulnerabilities are not always exploited, and that not all vulnerabilities have to be addressed by technical defenses or at high cost. In many cases, awareness of a potential problem may be an adequate defense.

- **Policy:** ABCorp has no written security policy that documents and describes responsibilities of personnel. This is a critical problem that must be corrected in order to address overall protection issues. Among other problems, there is no clear line of responsibility for the proliferating personal computers, and the lack of adequate long-range planning, if left uncorrected, may result in increased cost and ineffective protection as the client-server model of computing becomes more dominant in the ABCorp environment.
- **People:** ABCorp has no formal mechanism for mapping people to job function and relating job function and changes to authorization. Without such a formal mechanism, it is very difficult to properly manage protection in automated information systems. Notably, personnel and information systems do not have adequate communication and procedural safeguards. For example, when people leave ABCorp or go on vacation, the information systems department should be notified in a timely enough fashion to disable computer accounts over the period of inactivity.
- **Procedures:** ABCorp has no documented procedures and checklists for performing protection-related functions. Without documented procedures, implementation depends on people remembering what to do. Without checklists or some other form of tracking, there is no mechanism for documenting what was done by whom and when and assuring that responsibilities are properly carried out.
- **Physical:** Physical access to the main computer is relatively open. Minor improvements are apparently under consideration and the risk currently seems to be in the acceptable range. An uninterruptable power supply would have a positive effect on reliability, however, backup procedures and recovery contingency planning appear to provide an adequate, but poorly documented, recovery process.

- **Operating system:** Operating system protection is inadequately maintained, primarily because of inadequate manpower and/or automation, a lack of well-documented procedures, and too much reliance on applications for protection that is more appropriately implemented by the operating system. Password protection as implemented is inadequate, and the protection features provided for VAX VMS are not being used as effectively as they could be.
- **Protection enhancements:** Specific enhancements in the form of an outside vendor product called Watcher have been put in place to provide added protection for dial-in lines and the payroll application, but the internal VMS mechanisms that can also greatly enhance this protection are not being fully or properly exploited. Since internal VMS mechanisms are normally far more effective than third-party enhancement products, VMS protection should be set properly first, and then vendor enhancements should be used to provide added coverage which VMS is not capable of providing or to provide additional layers of coverage in vital areas. The enhancements specified for the Watcher product appear to be reasonable and appropriate, and are likely to be generally beneficial, but they should not be treated as a panacea and should not be used in place of proper VMS protection.
- **Networks:** Current networks are not well protected, but it is unclear that substantial protection enhancements would be cost effective in the short run. Some inexpensive enhancements would seem appropriate, but because ABCorp is not connected to outside networks, this is not a high priority. Some concern exists for the lack of adequate backup for PCs on the LAN, lack of controls over information leakage and/or corruption in the LAN, inadequate computer virus protection on the PCs in the LAN, inadequate protection against illegal copies of software, and a general lack of control and assigned responsibility for LAN-based PCs.
- **Applications:** Access to and within applications is the first line of defense against unauthorized activity at ABCorp, but this is inadequate for several reasons, including fundamental limitations on that technology, a lack of adequate protection in most vendor software, and well known methods for breaking out of the application into the command interpreter. Application-based protection should not be the first line of defense and should be treated as an auxiliary limitation more for convenience than for protection.
- **Users:** Users are not always given unique identities on ABCorp systems, their passwords are far too easily guessed, and inadequate controls and checks are in place to assure that only authorized activities are performed by authentic users. Inadequate tools are provided to assist users in behaving properly and to assure that errors or omissions don't result in problems.

- **Legalities:** Inadequate notice is provided for users entering and using the system. All users should be properly informed of their rights and responsibilities and should sign documents asserting their knowledge, understanding, and agreement to the rules of the road. Login screens should accurately describe the presence of monitoring and other restrictions on use. Users should be made aware of legal implications to the corporation and to themselves of their use of ABCorp systems.

- **Training:** ABCorp employees have inadequate education, training, and awareness of information protection. A properly designed regular awareness program, consuming only 15 to 30 minutes per quarter for most users, is required in order to keep protection in an appropriate perspective.

- **Personal computers:** Personal computers are predominantly used by engineering staff at this time, but as the process of moving toward a client-server environment proceeds, it will place increasing burdens on the information systems staff, and if not well thought out, may result in inadequate protection, poor performance, expensive retrofits, and many other long-term problems. In addition, management control over personal computing facilities is inadequate and is not properly defined. A top-level policy decision must be made and implemented regarding how these computers are managed, controlled, used, disseminated, connected, backed up, restored, repaired, replaced, stocked, purchased, paid for, and every other aspect of their use. Responsible parties must then be made aware of their responsibilities and provided with adequate tools, training, and budget to manage those facilities.

- **Major concerns:** The major concerns expressed were over the movement of all remaining financial functions from an outside corporate information-processing environment into the local environment. Further concern was expressed over the increasing value associated with information distributed on PCs, over the LAN, and over centralized databases stored on the VAX. In several cases, the conflict between usability and protection came up. These cases must be addressed on a case-by-case basis using innovative techniques. In many cases, people solutions appear to be overlooked in favor of technical solutions. It is important to find a more appropriate mix of automated and human solutions in order to afford the best protection at the lowest cost.

- **Budget:** There appears to be adequate budget in information systems to implement a reasonable program of protection if management can display appropriate resolve and if protection is made a key component of overall information systems and corporate planning. Affordable and well-conceived protection can only be implemented by making protection an integral part of overall information systems planning.

Perspective

A substantial amount of effort will be required in order to address the protection problems outlined in the findings of this report. A reasonable estimate is that 3 person-months worth of effort over the next six months will be required by the current information systems manager and staff in order to make appropriate improvements to existing information protection, and that an ongoing effort of 1 to 2 person-weeks per quarter will be required in order to maintain the enhanced protection levels once they are attained. In addition, a budget of $5,000 to $10,000 may be required in order to purchase software enhancements to address specific concerns that affect current networked systems.

The long-term planning requirement is somewhat more difficult to define in terms of costs because proper long-term planning which incorporates protection may not cost more, but it will probably lead to different planning decisions that affect corporate operations over a long period of time. A key component will be the increased awareness of the value of information and the requirement for information protection as a part of the corporate culture at ABCorp.

The change in corporate culture is key for two reasons. The first reason is that it brings the subject into the foreground, which increases the exchange of information, affects how people react when they see things that they used to ignore, changes what people talk about at lunch, and so on. The second, and perhaps more important, reason is that, if properly done, the cultural change creates an environment where people are brought into the protection process rather than disenfranchised.

Conclusion

This cursory review of protection revealed some simple problems with simple and inexpensive solutions, some more complex problems that require ongoing attention by the information systems staff, and some corporate challenges that are important to the long-term well-being of ABCorp.

Although a more thorough review may be appropriate at some future date, it is unlikely that such a review would be appropriate until information systems has time to address the issues pointed out in this study and management takes the time to consider and plan for the long-term implications of the changing information environment.

6.4   CASE STUDY 3: A BIG BUSINESS

It is nearly impossible to get permission to publish even disguised versions of studies done for a big business. Since this is infeasible, a pseudo-case study is used. This is done by taking several reports and combining them together, altering numbers to reflect similar deviations from average statistics, and then generating a report suitable for the case study. In other words, this report could come from any firm of a similar sort, but actually comes from no such firm. Any similarity between the people, places, or incidents in this case study and any actual people, places, or events, is purely coincidental.

In this study, language differences are even more stark. There is a very different language used in the executive summary than in the detailing of what their personnel told us, and a still different language is used in our findings. This is intentional.

- The executive summary was designed for the director of information technology, the chief executive officer, and the board of directors of this firm. They all have extensive background in the securities business and a lot of knowledge and experience in auditing and finance.
- The description of the site visit is designed to allow those who participated to read and agree or disagree on the accuracy of our depiction of their statements and to allow their managers to review what they said in detail.
- The findings section is in a protection-oriented language. It is designed so that technical managers can understand the issues and protection experts can act on the results. It is better organized than the site visit section because it reflects analysis rather than raw data.

Because this case study is quite extensive, only the executive summary is included here. The remainder of the study is included in Appendix B. It is well worth reviewing.

Executive Summary

We were asked to perform an initial protection assessment of XYZ Corporation. This assessment was accomplished by direct observation, interviews with key personnel, and comparison with comparable organizations.

Summary of findings   XYZ Corporation is highly dependent on information, highly vulnerable to attack, and at great risk of substantial information protection-related losses. Furthermore, substantial losses have been sustained in the past year and ongoing losses are being sustained as of this writing.

XYZ Corporation's assets are at great risk and immediate action is required to address this situation. XYZ Corporation's current overall protection posture is inadequate as the following summary assessment details:

Major Area	Assessment
Protection Management	Inadequate
Protection Policy	Inadequate
Standards and Procedures	Inadequate
Documentation	Inadequate
Protection Audit	Marginal
Technical Safeguards	Inadequate
Incident Response	Inadequate
Testing	Inadequate
Physical Protection	Inadequate
Personnel	Inadequate
Legal	Inadequate
Protection Awareness	Inadequate
Training and Education	Inadequate
Organizational Suitability	Adequate

In order for the protection situation to be properly resolved, significant enhancements must be made to XYZ Corporation's information protection posture. We recommend that the following program be undertaken:

1. Immediate controls are required to cover exposures currently being exploited and exposures with extreme potential for loss.

   - Secure the fungibles transfer capability
   - Make a comprehensive set of backups and store them off-site
   - Install audit reduction and real-time audit analysis
   - Perform a detailed protection audit of select information systems
   - Place sensors and alarms in key areas
   - Perform a comprehensive audit for illegal copies of software

2. Planning is required in order to institute a corporate information protection environment suitable to long-term protection of assets.

   - Form and implement a corporate information protection policy
   - Form an information protection advisory council

- Generate a cost-effective suitable information protection plan
- Incorporate information protection planning into overall planning
- Train select staff members in relevant information protection areas

3. After the first two phases are completed, a substantial set of technical, procedural, and personnel measures should be implemented to provide proper protection.
4. After appropriate protective measures have been instituted, the third and ongoing phase of activity will begin. In this phase, protection will be maintained and updated to reflect changes in environment, technology, and organizational priorities.

6.5 CASE STUDY 4: A MILITARY SYSTEM

This study analyzes protection for a military system that is currently being fielded. In order to understand the issues at play, it is important to understand that in military endeavors, the stakes are peoples' lives, and in extreme cases, the lives of nations. In a war, the enemy may send bullets, bombs, missiles, mortars, and/or martyrs in the normal course of events. When pressed, any biological, chemical, nuclear, or other sort of weapon might be used. In providing defenses, the military must also consider cost. For example, a system that will have a useful life cycle of only 10 to 20 years (a long time by modern information system standards) may never see a substantial combat role. If it never encounters a nuclear threat, it is unlikely that the protection from electromagnetic pulses (EMP) will be significant. On the other hand, if everything is designed to ignore the nuclear threat just because it hasn't been used in 50 years, the entire force may be wiped out by a single nuclear device blown up 25 Km above the battlefield.

When it comes to language, the military is in a world of its own. A multilevel secure (MLS) operating system may be used to implement a trusted Guard application which extracts Unclassified (U) information from a Top Secret (TS) database using government off-the-shelf (GOTS) hardware and commercial off-the-shelf (COTS) software. The military also has a myriad of standard operating procedures (SOPs) that specify everything from when Tempest (emanations) protection is required to how to do risk analysis. This particular system (called Alma in this book) is also required to connect to other military systems. In keeping with this long tradition, this report also makes up a series of words of its own to identify threats and countermeasures for the purposes of making charts and performing analysis.

This particular report was one small part of a larger report provided to the designers of Alma so that they could evaluate how to modify

Alma for use in the field. It may be that in the fielded version, none of the identified protective measures are taken. For example, many of the threats considered in this write-up are threats not generally addressed by military protection systems, and Alma is competitive with other projects throughout the DoD. Since price is a critical issue in the military (after all, we can buy a lot of bullets for this much money), the designers of Alma may decide that providing this protection will price Alma in a range where other less able systems will be chosen instead. It may be a better strategy to simply provide Alma as is, wait until a hundred of them are fielded, and then tell all the users that additional precautions are appropriate.

Only the executive summary of this report is included here. Much of the rest of this report is included in Appendix B.

Introduction and Executive Summary

We did an informal review of policies, procedures, and technical safeguards for Alma. During that visit and since that time, protection techniques to cover those threats cost effectively have been considered. This introduction and executive summary outlines the methods applied, the overall concerns that remain, and the conclusions of this analysis. The second part of this study details the identified vulnerabilities, available techniques that could be used to protect Alma, and the approximate costs associated with those protection techniques. The third part of this report details the method used to analyze Alma and results of the analysis.

Findings

Alma is a prototype system being deployed. As a prototype, the system demonstrates proper functional capabilities and a reasonable degree of protection, but in a deployed situation, far more care and consideration is warranted in the information protection area. Specifically, the following problem areas were identified and should be addressed:

Area	Rating
Tempest	Poor
Reliability	Poor
Protocols	Poor
Data exchange	Poor
Integrity protection	Poor
Security administration	Inadequate
Auditing	Inadequate
Availability protection	Inadequate
Rapid adaption	Inadequate
Future networking	Inadequate
Secure distribution	Inadequate

How Findings Were Analyzed

The findings were analyzed by creating and analyzing a covering chart which lists vulnerabilities along one dimension and defenses that cover those vulnerabilities along another dimension. Costs of defenses are approximated, and an efficient search of all single covers is performed to find the most cost-effective defense that would cover all of the threats at least once. The result is provided in the figure below.

Because of the interdependence of protection techniques and their synergistic effects, this analysis was performed for each of two distinct architectures. One architecture considers the existing Alma environment with enhancements performed on a step-wise basis. The other architecture considers the effect of moving to a multilevel secure implementation wherein Alma internals are redesigned to provide for protection enhancements. These two alternatives were chosen because they represent two key alternatives for future Alma systems.

Inherent in this analysis is the assumption that several Alma systems are to be implemented. In the cost analysis, it is assumed that 50 Alma systems are to be deployed over time, and that factor is used to amortize initial costs as opposed to unit costs. If fewer systems are to be implemented, the tradeoffs favor less redesign effort, while for larger numbers of systems, redesign has less effect on overall costs. Effects of inflation and the time value of money were not computed in this analysis, but the results are sufficiently clear that this will not substantially alter the end result.

The Two Architectures

The two architectures under consideration are pictured here:

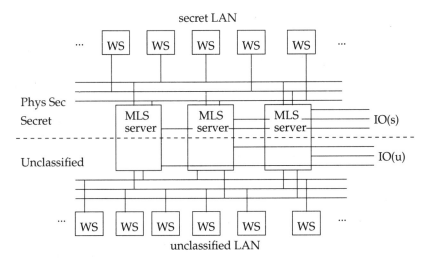

An MLS secure Alma architecture.

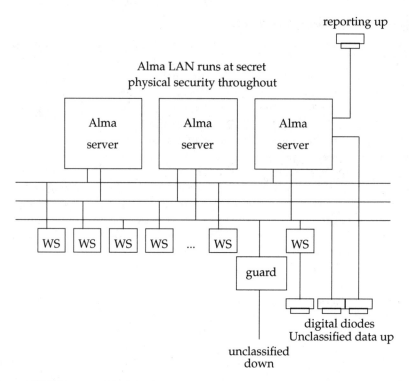

reporting up

Alma LAN runs at secret
physical security throughout

A non-MLS Alma architecture.

In the multilevel secure (MLS) version of Alma, a redesign central-
izes all database access to the 3 redundant Alma database servers, thus
eliminating a multiplicity of Oracle licenses, and saving several thousand
dollars per license eliminated. These servers run under multilevel security, and have two partitioned databases for secret and unclassified data,
respectively. The secret and unclassified sides of each MLS are linked to
2 of the 3 redundant LANs at each of the two security levels, providing a secure and reliable bridge between the security levels without any
additional hardware. An automated guard on the MLS systems automatically declassifies the appropriate portions of secret database transactions
so that unclassified databases are automatically and rapidly updated,
while unclassified entries are automatically available for secret access
by the normal operation of the MLS system. Thus, all redundant data
entry is eliminated and security becomes completely transparent to the
Alma users. Physical security need only be applied to the secret side
of this system and the MLS secure systems containing the database,
thus dramatically reducing the need for tempest coverage and other ex-

pensive protection requirements for nodes processing only unclassified data.

In the non-MLS version of Alma—shown in the second figure—the basic Alma system is left running system high and external devices and software are added to allow for declassification, incorporation of unclassified data, and so on. This has the advantage of requiring less effort in the redesign of Alma because only performance and stylistic changes are required, and the security enhancement of the database is easier. Database access is centralized so as to reduce Oracle license costs, but more systems are secured with physical protection. There is a single MLS system of smaller size and lower performance for the automated guard application, and unclassified Alma components are kept at system high. Similar reliability and redundancy are attained, and a lot of automated guard downgrading of information is used to reduce redundant data entry.

The basic difference in these architectures is the tradeoff between (1) the cost of physical security and custom protection implementations for the non-MLS version, and (2) the cost of designing to operate in an MLS environment and the added costs of MLS systems in the MLS design. Many components of this architecture can be changed without altering this basic difference, and these are not intended as final designs, but rather as the two most obvious alternatives from a cursory examination of the Alma design and function.

What the Analysis Showed

The following table summarizes the recommended protection and approximate costs associated with implementing this protection. It should be noted that several of these recommendations are badly needed for the wide-scale deployment of Alma for reasons not solely related to security (i.e., reliability, reduced life cycle costs, and so on).

Design Choice	Initial cost	Unit cost	ea.(1)	ea.(10)	ea.(50)
MLS w/shield	3,140,000	74,000	3,214,000	388,000	136,800
MLS w/o shield	4,390,000	54,000	4,444,000	493,000	141,800
NonMLS w/shield	2,690,000	184,200	2,874,200	453,205	238,000
NonMLS w/o shield	3,940,000	54,200	3,994,200	448,200	133,000

At quantity 50, the cost difference between an unshielded non-MLS version of Alma and a shielded MLS version of Alma is only $3,000, which is far less than the added life-cycle cost of maintaining a system-high classified information processing environment without shielding. Since an MLS environment with shielding costs less at this quantity level than an equivalent environment without shielding and a shielded environment is more effective, the MLS shielded version of Alma is the clear choice.

Further savings can be afforded by only protecting half of the Alma implementations (those deployed outside of the continental United States) with shielding. In this case, we don't have to design a special nonshielded version for the continental United States, but rather use the standard version without shielding.

In other words, (and per regulations) we can protect the Alma installations outside the continental United States with shielding, not provide an alternative to shielding for Alma systems in the continental United States, and get the best of both worlds. This, then, is our recommendation:

Implement the MLS Alma design shown earlier, placing Tempest protection (shielding) only in systems deployed outside the continental United States, and design for the following protection techniques (detailed descriptions are provided later in this report):

Protection technique	Initial cost	Unit cost
Cryptographic Checksums	200,000	0
Computer Misuse Detection System	250,000	20,000
Decentralized administration	20,000	0
Field installation requirements	0	5,000
Custom Alma Guard on MLS	500,000	0
MLS licensing fees	0	2,000
Multiple LAN configuration	20,000	2,000
New protection tools	100,000	0
New training programs	40,000	5,000
Alma redesign	1,500,000	0
MLS redesign overhead	500,000	0
Shielding	10,000	40,000(/2)
Overall Program Estimate	3,140,000	54,000

The total cost for a program of 50 Alma systems comes to $116,800 per Alma.

Conclusion

All of the items listed above should be implemented before Alma is deployed into widespread use.

6.6 CASE STUDY 5: THE DOD AND THE NATION AS A WHOLE

System designers can only do so much on their own. Obtaining information protection for the entire nation will require resources and hard work on a national scale. It will not come about as a serendipitous feature of the development of an information infrastructure based on open systems. The longer this matter sits on the back burner or is treated as a matter of academic interest, the greater the eventual costs will be to add resiliency to the infrastructure. Ultimately, neglect of this matter could result in major economic loss, the loss of military capability, and military defeat.

The study from which these results were extracted was done for the Defense Information Systems Agency (DISA) to address the question of information assurance in the Defense Information Infrastructure (DII). [63] The full study is not included in the appendices because of its substantial length and because everything covered in that study is reflected elsewhere in this book. Rather, the executive summary is provided here, and a more extensive summary is included in the appendices.

The DII is more than 90 percent comprised of the NII, so DII requirements are key to the NII design and operation. Information assurance in this context refers to the availability and integrity issues discussed earlier.

> The DoD has put a lot of effort into secrecy systems, but with the exception of a few very expensive special purpose systems, almost no effort has been put into availability and integrity of information systems under malicious attack.

Executive Summary

The United States depends on information as a key part of its competitive advantage. Operation Desert Storm was an object lesson in the critical importance of information in warfare, in that it demonstrated the DoD's ability to obtain and use information effectively while preventing Iraq from obtaining and using comparable information. This object lesson was observed and understood by other nations and organizations, but they also observed that the United States did not protect the massive information infrastructure it mobilized for the Gulf War against disruption. If the United States is to maintain a competitive advantage in future conflicts, then the National Information Infrastructure (NII) upon which the United States depends must be protected commensurate with its criticality. This analysis shows that:

- The nation is highly dependent on the accuracy and availability of information.
- The nation is dependent on the NII for information services.
- The NII is highly vulnerable to accidental and intentional disruption.
- These vulnerabilities are commonly known and widely publicized.
- Many individuals, groups, and nations have demonstrated disruption capabilities.
- The current ability to respond to disruption of NII functions is inadequate.

If the Department of Defense is to maintain operational readiness and fulfill its national security responsibilities, the information infrastructure upon which it depends for information services must be strengthened against accidental and intentional events that lead to disruption (corruption of information or denial of services). If the United States as a nation is to compete economically, the NII must be protected.

In order to sustain U.S. capabilities, the following information assurance (availability of services and integrity of information) considerations must be given priority attention.

- Information assurance should be recognized and treated as a critical readiness and economic survival issue.
- Defensive information warfare policy, doctrine, strategy, tactics, techniques, and procedures should be developed.
- Infrastructure design is different than systems design and should be treated as such.
- Existing technical and human vulnerabilities should be addressed.
- Information assurance standards, technologies, tools, and guidelines should be developed.
- Top-level technical management of information assurance should be improved.
- Real-time control mechanisms to enhance information assurance should be developed.
- Testing programs should be created and used to enhance assurance.
- Flexible, automated, prioritized responses to disruption should be implemented.
- Information assurance knowledge should be reduced to a usable and teachable form.
- Information workers should begin to train as defensive information warriors.
- Readiness exercises and war games for defensive information warfare should begin.

Information assurance for the NII must also be cost effective. This analysis shows that the costs associated with these tasks will increase dramatically over time if we do not act now. Furthermore, the efforts made to protect the NII will provide widespread benefits to U.S. commercial industries.

By the timely reinvestment of a small portion of the savings that will be gained from the current consolidation and migration to standard information and communication systems, the U.S. will avoid enormous future expenses, mitigate possibly catastrophic military consequences, and enhance its national competitive edge for years to come.

Is Information Assurance an Unsolvable Problem?

NO! We cannot make people immortal, but that does not mean we should abandon medicine. Nobody can provide perfect information assurance, but that does not mean that we should ignore a problem that may result in catastrophic consequences.

The issues that must be considered for proper information assurance in the NII span a wide range and a wide range of solutions exist to address these issues. There are some challenges in information assurance that are now and will likely remain imperfectly addressed for some time to come, but the vast majority of the challenges today can be adequately addressed with a reasonable amount of well-directed effort.

Perhaps a more enlightening view of this issue is the question of how much it will cost to address information assurance, and how much the United States will save as a result of wisely spending that money. In this limited report, we cannot even begin to address the specific issues for specific solutions in specific systems, but we advocate financial and military analysis before undertaking costly action. We also believe that early investment will pay enormous dividends in both the short-term and the long-term:

- By assuring the United States is able to win on the information battlefield.
- By dramatically reducing the long-term cost of information assurance.
- By reducing the costs of disruptions in the NII.

The information assurance challenge is not only one that can be met, but one that must be met, if the United States is to attain and retain a competitive edge in both the DoD and national information arenas.

What Are the Top Priorities?

Based on our study, we believe that the following three items are the most vital things the nation can do in order to provide a NII with adequate information assurance.

1. Design the NII for automated detection, differentiation, warning, response, and recovery from disruptions. It is absolutely vital that these capabilities be designed in from the start and that they be sufficiently automatic that they are effective without human intervention. Without these capabilities, the NII will not be able to sustain operation during substantial disruption attack.

2. Design the data centers, network components, and network control centers for repairability. Without the ability to recover from disruption of these facilities, under attack, the NII and the nation will grind to a halt and will not be able to reconstitute capabilities in any meaningful time frame.

3. Train today's information workers to become defensive information warriors capable of defending the NII against information attack. Without trained information warriors, the nation will not be able to sustain the NII no matter how automatically the NII reacts or how well it is designed.

CHAPTER 7

Summary and Conclusions

In one of my recent presentations before an executive committee at a multibillion dollar corporation, I discussed the issues of protection in the national information infrastructure and suggested ways in which they might get involved from a business standpoint. At the end of the discussion there was a break, and the president of the company came over and told me that he liked the presentation, but that it would have been better if I would have included more examples of actual break-ins to give a better idea of the magnitude of the problem. He will get a copy of this book, and if nothing else, I hope that the examples of actual attacks will satisfy his desire for some hard data.

I haven't done a detailed analysis, but I am certain that this book documents at least $10 billion per year of firmly supported, publicly disclosed losses in the United States alone. It also supports the notion that there are many billions of dollars per year in less firmly tied down losses in the United States.

We should all agree that we already depend heavily on our information infrastructure, and that this dependency is increasing rapidly. With increasing dependency comes increasing potential for harm, so we should expect these figures to rise substantially over the coming years. The current loss from disruption is on the order of $100 per year per capita, and it would be reasonable to conclude that over the coming 10 to 20 years, this will increase by a factor of 10 or more. The increase will be due to our increased dependency and the increased use of the information infrastructure for perpetrating crimes. Protecting the NII properly would likely cost far less than $100 per capita.

There are clearly many ways to attack modern information systems, and interconnecting them to the information infrastructure substantially increases the potential for attack. This book documents quite a few vulnerabilities, but it also makes it quite clear that approaching protection from a laundry-list perspective is unlikely to be effective. This should be cause for great concern because the vast majority of people working in information protection today are taking the laundry-list approach, costing their organizations a lot of extra money, and not getting very effective long-term protection.

Current protection in most organizations is inadequate to the task. One reason we have inadequate information protection is neglect, and I hope that this book helps to reduce the degree of neglect. Another reason we have inadequate protection is the lack of adequate knowledge by most people involved in information technology. This is due, at least in part, to failures of our educational system, but government must also take responsibility and the computer industry is certainly not blameless in this area either. The responsibility for correcting this situation now lies firmly in the hands of the organizations that depend on information systems.

It would be nice if we could simply buy our way out of this situation, but unfortunately, that doesn't work for this particular problem. We have to think and work our way out of it. Like most challenges in modern society, it is not enough to just attain knowledge and skills. We have to go through an ongoing and unending process of adaption in order to keep up with the rapidly changing environment. And unlike most areas of information technology, we cannot simply push this one off on some technologist and say: "Take care of it." Information protection requires an organizational approach and participation by everyone involved with information technology.

Fortunately, by reading this book, you have taken one of the most important steps toward attaining information protection. You have started to educate yourself. The next step is to take the protection process by the horns and begin to actively pursue it.

Details of the NII

The basic idea of the NII is to provide information channels over which information services can be provided. Just as the highway system provides for traffic flow from place-to-place and the American Automobile Association (AAA) provides routing from point-to-point for interested drivers, the NII has a traffic flow and routing function. Like the highway system, the NII will have limits on how much traffic can go how far how fast. Like the highway system, when too many things go to the same place at the same time, there will be delays. Like the highway system, parts of the NII will break down from time to time, and the result will be inconvenience and reduced service capacity over certain routes.

A.1 INFORMATION CHANNELS

The roads on the highway system have an analog on the NII called information channels, or simply channels. Just as roads have maximum flow limits, channels have channel capacities. Just as roads have intersections where cars can go one way or another, the NII has switching systems which route information from one channel to another. Just as roads have stoplights where cars line up, the NII has buffers where information queues up.

A.2 THE EVOLUTION OF THE INFORMATION INFRASTRUCTURE

The history that led to the NII of today started with the telegraphic systems of the mid-nineteenth century. By the end of the nineteenth century, there were under 100 electrical paths for getting information across the United States and the signaling rate was limited by human capabilities to about five signals per second, per line. The total U.S. signal capacity was only a few hundred signals per second.

Early telephone systems created in the first half of the twentieth century allowed people to call the operator and request a connection to another telephone. Since the number of wires was small, party lines, where many people shared a single telephone line, were common. You would pick up the telephone, and if the line wasn't busy, you could turn a crank that would put enough voltage on the line to sound a buzzer and light a light at the operator's station. The operator would plug a headset into your wire, ask if they could help, and you would tell the operator that you wanted to talk to Bill over at Tyson's Corners. The operator would try to hook a wire into Tyson's Corners, and ask the operator there to hook you up to Bill's line. If that line was available, that operator would hook the line up and signal that a call was coming in for Bill by ringing an appropriate number of rings in the right pattern. If Bill were in, he might pick up the phone, and the operators would tell each party to hold on while they plugged the wires in to connect you to Bill. You would talk till you were done, and then hang up. This would turn off the lights on the operator's console, and they would pull out the wires. This early telephone system allowed thousands of connections across the United States, each running at 4,000 signals per second of channel bandwidth. The total channel bandwidth across the United States was now up to several million signals per second. This is almost as much bandwidth as the computer network in my office provides.

The next great innovation was the introduction of broadcast radio stations throughout the United States. With the introduction of radio, a full voice channel was simultaneously broadcast to hundreds of thousands of potential listeners. With this capability, a small number of people could send audio information to a large number of people. The channel bandwidth of only a few thousand signals per second had an effective information rate far exceeding newspapers and, even more importantly, the listener could get the information quickly without having to read it. This brought large amounts of information to many illiterate people.

Soon after broadcast radio came on the scene, dial telephones appeared. In this case, automation was used to replace the human operator in local calls. This early circuit-switching technology reduced the labor required for the telephone system, made calls more efficient for everyone concerned, and brought down the price of local telephone calls. Long distance still needed an operator. The increased switching speed increased the number of simultaneous calls, which increased bandwidth again. By this time the total number of signals per second available in the United States was on the order of one billion.

Television came next. Many thought that this new technology would make radio obsolete and revolutionize education for the masses. Neither has come true yet, but the effective bandwidth for television and the presence of pictures dramatically increased the requirement for high quality signaling, reception, and programming. Problems arose with measuring listener response and getting advertisers to pay for time, and these problems remain to a certain extent even today. Three nationwide affiliations were formed to compete for the market and these television networks dominated broadcast television until the 1980s when cable television took hold. Their larger market gave them more watchers which meant more advertising money and allowed them to create more expensive and better-looking programs. This, in turn, made competition more difficult and created a sort of a *triopoly* (i.e., a three-party monopoly—also the name of a board game).

Direct-dial long distance soon became available and this advancement in switching systems again changed the economics of telephones. International calls still needed operators, but the number of international calls compared to cross-country calls is relatively small. Automated switching systems were now getting to the limit of the complexity feasible for mechanical systems and repair costs were increasing substantially while reliability became an increasing concern.

Soon, electronic switching systems became a vital advancement to the telephone company and the effort to link electronic switching systems began in earnest. To send the digital switching information needed over analog wires, the modulator/demodulator (i.e., *modem*) was invented. As a general purpose tool for linking digital systems over analog wires, the modem became a core technology for linking computers, which were starting to come into widespread use. By this time, the total communications bandwidth in the United States was about 10^{11} signals per second.

With the introduction of the integrated circuit, and the subsequent introduction of microprocessors and single board computers, the number of computers increased dramatically. Soon, there were millions of personal computers, and modems became increasingly important in linking distant computing sites together over telephone circuits.

Satellites began to be used for communication in the early 1960s. At first, relatively low bandwidth retransmitters were put into orbit and only a select few military installations had the knowledge and ability to use them, but soon, high bandwidth commercial satellites became available. By the 1980s, suitcase-sized satellite transmitters and receivers were available for use in the field, and by the Gulf War, CNN was broadcasting live video direct from Bagdad during the initial bombings.

Cable television became available in major metropolitan areas and the effect on broadcast television was dramatic. Large local stations that had some of their own programming were now able to transmit over cable systems to other cities. In a very short time, a single station could become a nationwide mini-network and, if the programming was popular enough, it could make inroads against even the three major networks. As more of these niche channels became available over cable, the three major television networks began to decline in popularity and influence. Their death grip on television was broken.

Soon, there was enough money going into cable television to afford such wonderful capabilities as the Cable News Network , which was the first 24-hour-a-day cable news station, and Court TV, which broadcast courtroom proceedings directly into the common person's home. There is C-SPAN which broadcasts congressional hearings and other political events direct from the source. Astute viewers were now able to see the news first hand over live television feeds, watch the subsequent news stories, and make value judgments about how the media was interpreting the facts.

Today, the total communication bandwidth in the United States is on the order of 10^{15} signals per second, and the vast majority of it is digital (1 or 0) signals.

A.3   THE NII TODAY

As it exists today, the NII is a jumble of different networks. I will try to give a general idea of the different technologies currently in the mix.

As an overview, the NII consists of a set of communications technologies (e.g., satellite links) combined with commercial communications systems (e.g., telephone systems) to support protocols (e.g., NTSC video channels) which are used by information service providers (e.g., your local cable provider) to provide information services (e.g., the O.J. Simpson case live from Los Angeles).

In the United States, free enterprise rules. Anyone who has the money to spend can launch a satellite, create a telephone system, implement a new protocol, provide access to services, provide programming, or in most cases, combine these together in any way they wish. There are some restrictions brought about by the federal licensing procedures relating to radio frequencies and satellite launches, but historically, anyone with enough money can buy these rights as long as that person doesn't monopolize the market.

The cost of implementing communications technologies on a large scale normally limits this part of the market to big players, but on a local level, Ma and Pa operations have started cable television systems for investments of a few thousand dollars, servicing as few as 10 or 20 customers.

When AT&T was broken up by the now famous Consent Decree, local phone companies covering only a few hundred people in a small town were fairly common. Today, many businesses have Private Branch eXchange (PBX) systems that turn their phone system into a local telephone company.

Novell, Banyon, 3-COM, LanTastic, and Little Big LAN are all commercial network protocol providers with their own communications protocols. Although standards such as TCP/IP are freely available and widely used, many companies opt for other protocols for the advantage of restricting access to their markets except by providers that pay them for the protocol development tools or because their protocol is a bit more efficient for some special application they want to implement.

Information service providers are springing up very rapidly today because the market for information services has not yet matured. For example, the number of computers on Internet has increased by a factor of 10 every two and a half years for quite some time. But in this case, it has to stop soon because at this rate, before the year 2000, every person in the United States will have their own computer on the Internet.

Communication Technologies

Communication technologies are roughly broken down into radiated energy waves (e.g., radio, television, microwave, and satellite transmission) and physically connected energy waves (e.g., shielded twisted pair wires, coaxial cables, fiber optics). The dominant infrastructure components today are copper wires, coaxial cables, fiber optic cables, microwave links, broadcast radio and television, and satellite links.

Commercial Communications Systems

Commercial communication systems currently include cable television systems (e.g., Warner Cable, TCI), long-haul telephone systems (e.g., AT&T, MCI, Sprint), regional and local telephone systems (e.g., New York Telephone, SouthEast Bell) and computer communications systems (i.e., Tymnet, NSFnet).

Packets and Protocols

Regardless of the physical means by which information is transmitted and received, the flow of information is organized and controlled by switching systems. Whereas historically, line switching or leased lines were used to make end-to-end connections, today, almost all computer communications and an increasing portion of the telephonic and video information is put into finite-sized *packets* which are switched in a *store and forward* network.

Store and forward networks transmit packets of information which are stored in switching computers along the route and forwarded to the next computer along the line until they reach their final destination. It is sort of like taking apart a 100-page report, numbering each page, and handing pages out to people in the front row of a classroom. The people then pass the pages around with the object of getting them to someone at the back of the room who reassembles them.

In order for these networks to operate, the intermediate computers must make routing decisions about which outgoing communications path to use to forward a packet to a particular destination when it came from a particular source. These decisions are based on the design of the network and information stored in the packets used to contain the information. The control of the network is carried out through a communication protocol, a formalized way in which the switching systems communicate with each other.

The same protocol can be used over almost any communication technology, so that the protocol creates a virtual communication environment that abstracts the physical nature of the media. The protocol is typically divided into a set of layers, each forming a packet which contains information at other protocol layers. By using the packet and protocol system as a virtual infrastructure, applications are implemented to provide user services. This is the so-called application layer of a protocol.

A.4   INFORMATION SERVICE PROVIDERS

This was discussed in some detail in the introduction to the book.

A.5   POSSIBLE FUTURES

Information is rapidly becoming a commodity. Information is already sold by the bit without regard to content or value. For example, for $29 or so, you can buy several thousand software packages on a CD-ROM, including spread sheets, databases, and all manner of other packages that high-priced vendors sell for hundreds of dollars per program. It's hard to tell where the real value lies without spending a lot of time and effort in analyzing the differences between products. Consumer reports may be good for looking at which car to buy, but there are only a few hundred choices of cars on the market today, while there are tens of thousands of software packages and information services, and Consumer Reports doesn't have a clue about where the value lies.

Good information is still expensive, and it is likely to remain expensive for some time to come, but the public as a whole is poor at differentiating good information from poor information, and very often chooses based on price and marketing rather than content and quality.

It is increasingly the *meta*-information (information about information) that has more value, and soon, the meta-meta-information (information about the meta-information) may become the real value. Round and round it goes, and where it stops, nobody knows.

The race is on to wire every home and office in the United States with fiber optic cables, to connect them to packet switching systems capable of handling the traffic, and to connect services of all sorts to this network. But the race is also on to regulate the NII and to find ways of attacking and defending it.

Current Plans

Current plans for the cable system are for regional wide-area networks (RWANs) that go between cities in a region of the continent with a capacity of 3 billion bits per second and are capable of supporting up to 50 cities, and national wide-area networks (NWANs) that serve an entire continent and have a capacity of 10 billion bits per second or more. Current plans for telephone companies include wiring far more fiber optic connections between central offices (COs) and implementing digital compression to allow moderate quality video phones, integrated computer and communications services, and many other functions.

Futuristic Visions

The next advancement may be implementing fiber optic switching systems that have similar switching capabilities to current telephone switches, but which switch optical fiber channels that have channel capacities of a trillion (10^{12}) bits per second, and are multiplexed into a million simultaneous channels. One of these sorts of connections could serve a thousand households with a thousand channels each, and would last well into the future without substantial enhancements. To give you an idea of how much information could be moved with such a system, just one hundred of these fibers channels could carry as many bits per second as all of the personal computers in the world combined can now generate.

In fact, it is hard to comprehend how an individual household could use a thousand television channels worth of information. If 10 family members were each engaged in a 10-person conference call, this would only use 200 channels.

SouthEast Bell seems to believe in the fiber optic concept and they are now in the process of rewiring all homes receiving their service with fiber. Some of their competitors, on the other hand, take the position that fiber optic cables will never go to every home. [180]

Case Studies

The rather extensive case studies are summarized in the body of the text. The main bodies of the larger reports are included here for completeness, to more thoroughly support the conclusions, and to give deeper insight to readers interested in the details.

B.1 CASE STUDY 3: XYZ CORPORATION

The Site Visit

The site visit was used to interview key members of XYZ staff and to personally view the operations. The remainder of this assessment is based on this single visit, and its accuracy and completeness are limited by that constraint.

The site visit involved interviews with several different groups of staff members, walkthroughs of several key areas and typical workspaces, and minimal off-hours investigation.

> *Comments on the facts gathered during the site visit are indicated in specially formatted areas such as this. These comments would not normally be included in a report to a client, but they should give the reader a sense of what goes through the analyst's mind while listening to this information.*

Operations overview XYZ Corporation has about 100,000 full-time employees.

Information systems at XYZ Corporation consist of approximately:

Quantity	Type
50,000	Unix workstations
100,000	PCs running DOS
50,000	Terminal emulators
1000	External client dial-in systems
10,000	Authorized at-home dial-in systems

This is probably far too many home dial-in systems for an operation of this sort. It may make protection very expensive to effectively control.

Physical security is staffed by a poorly paid and transient outside guard force directed by an internal staff member.

Low-cost guards are susceptible to bribes, tend to be transitory, and usually aren't willing to risk much for information protection. They tend to miss work, miss scheduled walkarounds, do not remain very alert when performing their duties, rarely notice and report minor inconsistencies, and are not highly motivated. It is also easy to get hired into such a position with minimal background checks, and once in place, it is easy to get assignments guarding high-valued information assets.

Information Technology (IT) staff accounts for about 12,000 full-time members (about 12 percent of the total work force).

There is no comprehensive and well-defined corporate information protection policy. It is the feeling of staff members that the general corporate policies regarding honesty and integrity are adequate to cover this issue.

This is a typical situation that is generally perceived as unimportant when, in fact, it is a key element in detecting a more serious protection problem. Not only is there no comprehensive policy, but people think they are covered by some other policy. The effect is that protection falls between the cracks, and this misperception indicates just how inadequate the training and education process in the organization is.

There are no training or awareness programs in information protection, and protection is currently handled by line managers who independently make piecemeal improvements as they determine a need, using their own budgets.

Not surprisingly, there is no training or awareness program and respon-sibility is pushed to the lowest levels of management. This is a strong reflection on the lack of policy.

Internal audit covers some top-level elements of the IT department, but only performs an in-depth protection audit when specifically re-quested and paid for by a line manager. This is rare indeed. For example, no audit trails are generated or analyzed in most systems, of the systems generating audit information almost none are periodically examined, and except for the electronic funds transfer system, none are currently exam-ined or analyzed in real-time.

Typically, internal auditors are understaffed for this sort of work and should not be tasked with it, but we see that nonauditors don't appreciate this and expect auditors to do tasks normally associated with systems ad-ministrators. The auditors are likely to expect the systems administrators to do this, and so this vital protection issue slips through the cracks.

About one quarter of XYZ Corporation staff members are replaced each year. Many of the employees with major responsibility for informa-tion protection have been on staff for less than two years.

This is not good. Financial industries have high turnaround rates, but it is important that people tasked with protection be longstanding employees because it makes it more difficult for outsiders to penetrate the layers of protection by getting and holding positions of increasing responsibility. If you are willing to risk 10 years in prison to take a few million dollars, why not spend a few years as an employee, get paid along the way, and then take tens of millions of dollars?

XYZ corporation currently uses consultants for much of its infor-mation technology work, and is rapidly increasing its use of outside resources for this purpose.

There is a major movement toward outsourcing information technology today, but there is also a great risk in that it places people over whom you have no direct control in a position to cause great harm.

Group 1 The physical security force consists of a contract guard force and is directed by a single responsible staff member. This staff member sets and implements policy, which he states as protecting facilities. Equipment is only peripherally involved. The value of information is ignored by the guard force.

Individual staff members should not be setting policy on their own. Policy must come from top-level management. Protecting buildings is not an adequate policy for protecting valuable information assets, and this is reflected in the lack of attention to the value of information.

There are no written physical security standards or procedures. Informal and undocumented standards are said to exist, but differing actions of different guards in response to the same events indicates that the standards are inadequate to the task.

The guards each take their responsibilities differently, so that with minimal probes, it is simple to find guards that will allow or even facilitate entry and exit.

In most locations, the guards are only concerned with perimeter security. Although there are walkthroughs at night, there is no specific notion of what to look for in these walkthroughs, and since employees often work at all hours, the guards don't react inquisitively to people sitting at desks in the middle of the night typing into computers.

The guards ignore protection of wire rooms, computer disks and tapes, temperature and environmental controls, and other special facilities or components that are important from an information protection perspective.

Some outside doors have card-key or coded entry pad access, but almost every employee knows the entry codes and during the day, these doors are almost always left propped open to facilitate traffic.

Anyone in a decent looking suit who acts like they belong can come and go unnoticed.

No theft prevention devices are used.

Since entry is not prevented, no physical security is used for computing facilities, and no theft prevention devices are used, it would be simple to enter a facility, place several backup tapes in your pocket, and leave unnoticed. Similarly, it would be easy to enter a facility with a floppy disk (perhaps containing a program to initiate communications with the Internet or a custom-made virus intended to disrupt the global network), place the disk in a networked computer, run the program, and walk away with the disk. The damage could be severe and protracted, and the attacker could go completely unnoticed.

The staff member tasked with physical security responsibility is apparently unaware of any incidents of physical intrusion or theft involving information systems.

Other staff members reported several minor incidents to us. This indicates that the physical security team is out of touch with the rest of the organization and that there is inadequate collection and reporting of data in this area. This is probably a reflection on inadequate policies and procedures.

There are no testing programs for guards or physical security systems, and no alarms to detect illicit entry.

This reflects a lack of protection policy which should require regular testing of all components of the protection system.

Sweeps for physical intrusion and bugging devices are not performed and there is no consideration of emanations security.

Since these sorts of attacks are common against high-value targets, it would be advisable to have regular sweeps of select areas where key meetings are held.

Pay scales for guards range from $6 to $12 per hour, and guards have a turnover rate of about 50 percent per year.

Bribery is almost certain to work against some of these employees, and resentment is likely. Consider that they are guarding the offices of people who, in some cases, make more money each day than they do in a year.

During the site visit, we were able to enter facilities without badges or passes by simply walking in next to employees. We were never questioned when we entered an employee's desk area during lunch and typed commands on their computer, which was logged in. Once inside the outer perimeter, no guards were seen, and access to areas such as the mail room and rooms containing file servers went unchallenged.

This seems to be a reflection of a general lack of concern for protection that is deeply embedded in the corporate culture.

Physical security is funded on a per square-foot basis, and no priority is assessed to the value of the assets being protected in the assignment of protection to those assets.

This is a very common situation and is incongruous with rational allocation of resources in an information-intensive environment.

Line managers dictate physical security requirements in their own areas. The cost for physical security is also budgeted out of a line manager's operating budget.

The natural result is that physical security is inconsistent and there is a reward for inadequate physical security in the sense of increased budget for other operational requirements. Since the security of each area depends on the security of surrounding areas, those who spend less lower the level of protection for neighboring areas and get some benefit from neighboring areas with increased protection.

Physical security is generally viewed as a service organization that is supposed to react to incidents and not try to prevent them.

The reactive approach in physical security presumes that incidents are detected, but in practice, such attacks as the placement of listening devices and tapping of cables is rarely detected without an explicit search. For example, almost none of the listening devices commonly used by law enforcement are ever detected.

The personnel department and physical security department don't communicate effectively, so an ex-employee's physical access is typically unrestricted for a substantial period of time.

This is a symptom of inadequate protection management.

Physical security receives reports of about 25 stolen laptop computers and 50 other stolen hardware components per year. No follow-up investigation is done and no suspect has ever been arrested.

Apparently, there is not even a deterrent effort. One wonders what the physical security force does.

Group 2 Data is transferred to clients via direct-line dial-out from PCs using standard modems. This is implemented by users with almost no knowledge of information protection who must respond to the promises of salespersons. There is a general lack of control over this sort of process.

This is not likely to be very important because the employees sending information out have legitimate access to the information. As a mechanism to leak information, this is probably less effective than hand-carrying a backup tape out of the facility.

Poor passwords are common, passwords are commonly placed on computer screens, and the Crack password guessing program commonly used by attackers guesses 75 percent of passwords in a few hours.

This indicates a lack of training and education, a lack of effective protection management, and a general disregard for corporate information assets.

Viruses infect local area networks about once per week. So far, they have all been cleaned up by commercial products and they are more of a nuisance than anything else.

This indicates very poor controls and inadequate user awareness. Even a moderate effort should reduce this rate dramatically. The idea that they are only a nuisance indicates that the people charged with protection are unaware of the serious nature of this threat.

Group 3 The corporate computing environment consists of:

- A mainframe computer that clears all financial transactions worldwide. The mainframe uses the RACF operating system protection package to enhance access controls.

   Centralized systems tend to lead to severe damage during downtime, but are easier to maintain than a distributed version of the same thing. For a large financial institution highly dependent on computers, it would seem appropriate to have a backup site in a physically secure location. The RACF operating system is highly vulnerable to attack, has minimal integrity and availability controls, and has many widely published weaknesses.

- A global network provides voice, data, and video communications over leased lines between offices in key cities throughout the world.

   This has the potential for abuse because it tends to distribute trust very widely. With billions of dollars at stake, there had better be some additional coverage for this network.

- 50,000 UNIX workstations run a variety of applications. About 1 percent of these systems are file servers, and many of the file servers also act as gateways between network segments.

There's nothing fundamentally wrong with this configuration, but the use of file servers for gateways introduces a lot of potential for harm unless they are properly secured.

- 100,000 DOS-based PCs are in place. About 90 percent are networked into Novell file servers and about 10 percent are used as terminal emulators to access mainframes.

All of these systems are almost certainly vulnerable to viruses, all manner of insider attacks and, if any of them are connected to the outside world, they may all be vulnerable to external attack.

- 60,000 terminal emulators are connected via the network or telephone lines to the mainframe.

These are of special concern because the mainframe is responsible for the entire financial assets and has an insecure operating system. The sheer number of access points leads to concerns that auditing and detecting abuse are likely to be inadequate.

- An unknown number of modems are connected through central sites and auxiliary ports on computers throughout the corporation.

The unknown numbers of external connections spread throughout the corporation indicate a severe lack of control. It is likely that many of these access points are being probed for weakness and that if weaknesses are found, they are being exploited on a regular basis. It is very hard to audit and detect abuse on connections when you do not even know they exist.

- Several ISDN and T1 connections link networks at client and user sites onto XYZ Corporation's global TCP/IP network.

This extends the protection requirement to all of the interconnected systems at all of these sites. There should almost certainly be a secure gateway used to connect all of these sites in order to prevent the extension of global privilege to these locations. A comprehensive real-time auditing and audit analysis capability should also be used for these connections.

About 60,000 people at XYZ Corporation have user identities, but the total number of user identities reported by systems administration is several times this many. Apparently, the same user gets different identities on different systems throughout the corporation.

This indicates poor control and inadequate central administration. Multiple user identities also introduce numerous entry points for attackers, many of which are probably not used very often by their legitimate owners.

XYZ Corporation currently allows dial-in by vendor maintenance personnel and has no special mechanism to control this activity.

This is a very common entry point for attackers. For example, most PBX systems and timesharing systems can be easily taken over by well-publicized methods over maintenance channels. Furthermore, the privileges available from maintenance channels are generally sufficient to do a great deal of harm in a very short time.

Electronic mail is used throughout the organization for internal memos, altering policies, making hiring and firing decisions, and most other aspects of business operations. This includes changing access to information systems.

E-mail is very handy, but it is also very easily forged and examined in most current environments. Without a secure mail system, it is easy to forge memos, examine mail traffic between specific parties to track corporate strategy and tactics, look for specific sorts of memos to learn about potential scandals, and disrupt operations by misdirecting or relabeling mail.

When connecting to the mainframe computer and UNIX machines, a minimal notice that unauthorized users are not permitted is placed on the login screen, but no other information or technique is currently used to notify or discourage potential attackers or legitimate users of restrictions or responsibilities. Remote logins proceed as plaintext transactions containing a user ID and password, which are normally used for all access by an individual throughout the organization.

In New York State (where most financial institutions have major offices) notice is required if civil cases against attackers are to proceed. The lack of adequate notice makes many forms of entry impossible to successfully litigate. Also, the use of plaintext passwords from remote sites opens them up to attack. Additional precautions may be called for.

XYZ Corporation is connected to the Internet by way of UNIX-based computer systems designed to act as gateways between the Internet and XYZ's internal computing facilities. These systems allow bidirectional computer mail, Telnet terminal access, and File Transfer Protocol (FTP) from XYZ Corporation to other Internet sites. They are not supposed to allow incoming access other than via electronic mail.

Unfortunately, this sort of protection is rarely done correctly, and requires at least one full-time expert in order to operate the gateway with reasonable protection. For example, the FTP protocol can often be exploited to allow other activities, electronic mail can be used to send in an attack which then opens a channel for external Telnet access, and the sorts of activities performed over this channel for such an organization rarely justify its unlimited access to internal networks.

PCs are operated in Novell Netware networks and as standalone computers. There is no added protection on most PCs, but there are site licenses to Norton Antivirus, McAfee Antivirus, and Norton Encryption, none of which are used very uniformly or updated often. No evaluation process was undertaken to determine the effectiveness of these products when purchased.

Many big companies purchase from major providers of anti-virus software without realizing that this is very risky. The first problem is that many of the attackers writing viruses explicitly design them to bypass the most popular products. Another problem is that in large organizations, there is a higher probability of entry by viruses, and thus it is more likely that viruses undetected by these packages will enter and spread unnoticed. A third problem is that in large financial organizations, there is enough potential for financial gain to warrant writing a custom virus for a specific attack, and these products are useless against such an attack. In some cases, these defenses actually spread viruses faster than they would spread without these mechanisms in place.

There is an effort to provide remote control over networks to LAN servers and PCs. Some of these systems are already operated on a remote-controlled basis without any special protection to prevent active tapping. LANs are uniformly used throughout the corporation with no special protection.

Remote control is a very interesting feature, but the potential for abuse is staggering. In essence, this permits any other user to act as if they were sitting at your computer.

XYZ Corporation implements databases on UNIX-based machines and PCs using an off-the-shelf database product. In the case of UNIX-based machines, file servers operate as database servers.

File servers are now seen to perform network gateway services, file services, and database services. This introduces further dependence on these few computers. A way to exploit this might be to overload the file server with unimportant requests, thus tying up the gateway and disrupting database access. If this database is like most, data integrity will suffer as distributed locking mechanisms time out and computers attached to these databases may not even report these errors or perform retries.

Servers are rebooted monthly to force users to reauthenticate. Users are unwilling to enter a password to use a system and request staff members to disable screen lockout programs requiring password entry.

Clearly, this environment permits any insider to access another user's account. This is probably viewed as unimportant because, despite the longstanding security statistic that insiders are more of a threat than outsiders, most people don't believe their fellow employees launch attacks. On the other hand, this also permits maintenance people and guards that are hired by outside firms unlimited access during off hours. Perhaps even more importantly, this environment displays a lack of concern about information protection.

The mainframe is used to store financial transactions and to allow employees and clients to execute transactions. Mainframe data is controlled by a commercial database product which has an inadequate protection that staff does not depend on. The mainframe operates under the RACF operating system security package which is used to protect libraries used to generate and manipulate application data. Prepackaged software is used to perform database structural modifications. This software includes an automatic test and installation facility that detects errors in field use and other similar problems.

Upon detailed examination, this test system is likely to be inadequate for protection purposes. It probably only verifies that tables are properly accessed and not that the proper operations are performed on them or that only authorized programs manipulate them.

Applications are written in a special language. Several thousand applications programs exist and all requests to add or modify libraries are subject to approval. Backout mechanisms exist for program changes. Ad hoc testing is performed by IT staff responsible for program alterations, and a general attitude of quality assurance is a part of the data center environment. No other change control is in place.

Accurately controlling several thousand programs requires a substantial effort and adequate controls had better be in place to assure that the proposed changes match the actual changes. Because of the high value of the data and the ease of attack from an authorized program, it is vital to have a program of strong change control, but they apparently have none. Ad hoc testing is not adequate for this type of application. At a minimum, there should be a very well structured testing program including regression analysis.

There have been several thefts of laptop computers and other computer hardware, including the theft of several backup tapes. Other thefts may be taking place, but it is impossible to tell because most small equipment is purchased under line manager budgets and there is no comprehensive inventory control that crosses organizational boundaries.

The lack of a good inventory control system means that there could be systematic attacks underway that go undetected because there is no method to correlate them.

This group is aware of many protection problems and has requested funding from management to correct the known deficiencies, but to date, no funding has been forthcoming. Furthermore, they are generally too busy keeping systems operational to spend the time required to implement information protection.

One of the things this organization doesn't seem to realize is that by spending more time on protection, they will save time spent in keeping systems operational. For example, a reasonable change control system would make emergency change backouts rare instead of common, and good protection management would eliminate a lot of extra work required to administer thousands of systems independently.

The staff is aware of many of the current protection problems but has no resources to pursue solutions. Poor password selection is a common problem and no enhancement has been made here either. In a simple test using a public domain password guessing program, over three-fourths of the passwords were guessed within only a few hours. About one-fourth of the passwords were the user ID, the user's first or last name, or their employee number.

There is a pattern here indicative of sloppy overall controls, lax policy and procedure, and poor management of the protection function. The password examples are typical.

More than 500 people from all around the world perform systems administration and all of them have unlimited access to systems throughout the organization. This is done to allow remote management and because no simple technological solution is currently in place to allow better control.

Any of these people could modify the passwords on all of these systems and thus deny services worldwide for at least several hours. With a more concerted effort (e.g., typing a simple command on each of those systems), information could be wiped out worldwide in a matter of an hour or less, and it would take at least a day to get even a few of these systems operational. Massive loss of financial data could result, the organization may not be able to meet the clearing requirements for completing transactions for several days, and the long-term implications could be devastating in such an institution.

Many automated administrative functions are implemented as command scripts. These scripts are stored on file servers and used to automate mundane management tasks on many systems. These scripts are launched remotely and in many cases contain user identities and passwords required to perform restricted functions. They are commonly left readable on file servers in order to allow them to be centrally maintained and run from remote computers without the need to allow those computers special access.

These scripts can thus be read by anyone on the network and the user identities and passwords can be exploited to break into highly sensitive areas in vital databases.

There is no special network protection such as encryption or physical security in place.

This leaves the entire global network open to (1) observation with public domain software, (2) corruption with somewhat more effort, and (3) disruption with widely publicized techniques. Unless special precautions are taken, outsiders as well as insiders will be able to exploit this in any number of ways, ranging from theft of long haul communications services, to transfer of fungibles, to theft of confidential information.

Group 4 Group 4 provides redundant communications lines in case of failures on primary circuits, and locally manages telecommunications through a variety of PBXs.

The use of redundant communications increases resiliency against disruption, but care must be taken that the apparent redundancy is real. For example, in this case, the supposedly redundant lines are provided by the same carrier through the same cables. Any common mode failure such as a cable cut would sever the redundant pair, leaving no communication channels.

PBX break-ins occurred during the last three holiday weekends, despite the best efforts of the staff to prevent them. Nevertheless, the staff members charged with this effort are now convinced that their system will not be broken into again.

It seems almost certain that further break-ins will occur. If the last two attempts at repair were inadequate, why should we believe that they did it right this time? Upon more detailed study, it is likely that more entry points will be found.

There is no cryptographic or physical protection for voice or data lines, but staff believe that the protocols used to transmit data are so complex that nobody could ever decode the information. The main concern of the staff is the increasing use of wireless communications.

If this were true, then how would they be able to decode the information at the other end of the lines? The staff members appear to believe that because they don't know how the protocols work, nobody else can figure them out, but of course this is foolish. This demonstrates their lack of knowledge in this field and indicates a need for a strong program of education.

The major concern of this group is the broad access to data. Physical (i.e., paper-based) information is seen as most critical.

This is not a very healthy attitude in the information age. Clearly, the value of the information in electronic form is far higher than the paper information in this business.

Dial-in lines are seen as a more serious threat than other telecommunications lines, but no risk assessment has been done to associate numbers with these risks.

Without a detailed analysis, this is guesswork, and there are good reasons to believe it could be wrong. For example, if the Internet gateway were bypassed, it would provide a very high bandwidth connection to the global network.

There is concern over electronic transfers of fungibles which are easy to initiate and alter from anywhere on the internal network. There is no protection against an active tapper in the network.

Combined with the serious concerns about unlimited access to the internal network, this appears to be a very serious threat indeed.

Leased lines and microwave radio links are used for high speed communications circuits between offices. There is no encryption or authentication on any communications line other than an authentication used for UNIX systems.

Without encryption and authentication, it may be impossible to determine if any systematic attacks are underway.

Several toll frauds that exploit loopholes in PBX systems have been successful. They were detected after the fact by the presence of large telephone bills on holiday weekends. The loss from each incident was in excess of $100,000.

The detection of these incidents by excessive telephone bills indicates that other toll frauds may be ongoing at levels below the threshold of detection. For example, it would be an easy matter to take $1,000 per day during regular business hours in telephone tolls without detection.

Group 5 Background checks are performed on all new employees to comply with corporate policy and government regulations.

This is good, but upon deeper questioning it was determined that this does not apply to short-term consultants or outsourced work. Since these comprise a substantial portion of the staff working on information technology, additional effort is required.

Employees complete a form and an outside service provider does background checks of education, credit history, and military service records over the last seven years.

It is pretty easy to create a false history for many of these checks, especially if it is planned as a means for infiltrating an organization that has enormous potential for insider financial abuse.

Employees start to work while background checks are done, and the checks are usually completed in two or three weeks. No background check has ever resulted in an employee being terminated.

It is hard to believe that a thorough background check of an average of over 20,000 people per year (two-year average turnaround and 100,000 employees) has never come up with any case where an employee had to be terminated. Something is not right here.

All new employees are subjected to a drug screening by urinalysis. If a new employee does not pass the drug test, it is retaken. Four failed tests result in termination.

It is hard to believe that none of the 100,000 employees uses illicit drugs. Since nobody has ever been terminated, but several employees have failed the first several tests, we suspect that after a few failures, employees resign rather than face the potential of being fired.

During new employee orientation, employees are asked to sign a certificate of compliance with the corporate policy statement which mentions the value of information but has no explicit protection information. No training on information protection is performed during orientation.

Signing a compliance certification related to a general document is not a very strong assurance measure. Most people who are presented with these documents don't thoroughly read them before signing, and few ask questions about the contents. I have been repeatedly astonished to find that people are surprised when I read documents before I sign them. When asked questions, they invariably say that I'm the first person who has asked them a question, and they have to refer the document to someone else for interpretation.

Equipment signed out to an ex-employee is supposed to be returned before the final paycheck is sent and a procedure is in place to implement this policy.

The problem is that equipment is not usually signed out to an employee, so there is no tracking to assure that this procedure reflects reality.

Procedures are also used to remove access and authorization from information systems.

This is a direct contradiction to other statements that no procedure is in place to do this and is at odds with the reports of internal auditors. It seems that the beliefs of this group do not meet the reality seen by other groups. This implies a serious management problem.

No attempt has been made to link particular jobs with information sensitivity or access or to include protection responsibilities in job descriptions or personnel evaluations.

How can employee access possibly be removed when there is no linkage between employees and their information-related job functions?

Exit interviews are conducted, with particular attention paid to employees terminated for cause. According to staff members responsible for this function, there is no reason to believe that ex-employees are motivated to do harm.

History shows that employees terminated for cause are indeed likely to do harm. This indicates a lack of adequate training and education.

Group 6 The most desirable situation would be an environment in which authorized users could perform legitimate operations unhindered and unauthorized users could not. The less effort required by the user for protection, the better.

We all wish this were possible, but in today's environment, it is not.

Substantial access problems exist for staff members who travel. Entry requirements are different in different sites, and being identified as a legitimate employee sometimes presents a problem. A single universal identifier would be highly desirable.

This is another common problem. Although technically it is feasible to solve this problem, legally, there are restrictions on export and import of these technologies that prevent universal identification without a great deal of effort.

In current database systems, access to the entire database is either permitted or denied with no middle ground for limited access.

This means that when several people use the same database, there is no way to audit or control individual behavior. For example, the database used to store sales commission data is accessible by all of the sales people, so a clever sales person could take credit for other peoples' work or assign themselves select accounts.

Viruses consistently disrupted one area.

It is hard to understand why the people in this area haven't resolved this situation. It clearly indicates inattention to the problem.

A bomb destroyed offices in one city. A second bomb was found by chance at a new site.

This obviously indicates a serious concern that has to be addressed.

Personnel doesn't provide data in a timely enough fashion to allow accounts to be managed properly when people change jobs or leave the organization.

The result is potential access to or modification of sensitive information by unauthorized people.

Consultants are responsible for many of the trusted systems, and there are no standards or bonding requirements placed on them.

Outsourcing is becoming popular, but the implications of this to informa- tion protection may be severe. This issue should be seriously examined.

Illegal copies of software are used throughout the organization.

This potentially introduces civil and criminal liability, and a concerted effort should be made immediately to resolve this problem. The clear implication is that the legal department is not adequately involved in protection, and that policy, standards, procedures, and training are in- adequate.

Confidential information is thrown out without concern for proper destruction.

This indicates inadequate policy and procedures.

Group 7 In light of the recent World Trade Center bombing in New York, business continuity planning is now being completed for all corporate facilities worldwide.

Late is better than never.

There is substantial concern about implementing such a plan prop- erly, since it depends heavily on the inputs from business units about what is critical to them. There is currently no way to test the accuracy of the assessments made by the people in business units.

Experience shows that this sort of activity works best in the context of an overall information protection program. In this context, more cooperation and better testing can be achieved.

Several systems have on-line audit trails implemented, but the vast majority of systems do not use the audit capabilities available to them. Audit reduction tools are used periodically to analyze the available audit data. These tools generate reports of potential violations. All current information systems have been examined at least once. No audit trail or attempt at analysis is in place in any system other than those explicitly listed in the audit reports.

This helps address select attacks on select systems, but does not reflect an overall audit policy, probably has inadequate testing, almost certainly detects only the most obvious attacks, and will almost certainly be bypassed by most serious attackers.

User identities are audited periodically, and in every audit to date, unauthorized user identities have been detected.

It appears that systems administrators wait for auditors to detect problems and then react to them rather than proactively maintaining an adequate protection posture.

Many critical bookkeeping computers have no detection capabilities.

Modified books would not be detected unless they triggered financial changes detected by financial audit. For example, shifting profits and losses between clients or commissions between employees would not be detected unless they were so large as to attract obvious attention.

Information system related purchases are not tracked and for that reason, accurate inventory control is impossible.

This confirms the previous concern about inadequate inventory control.

Numerous incidents have been detected or reported:

- An audit for illegal copies of software in a small percentage of the organization's computer systems indicated that $10 million worth of illicit PC software is probably in use throughout the corporation. The illegal copies were removed as they were detected.

The fact that this much illegal software is detected indicates inadequate policy, awareness, training, education, and procedures. It also introduces the potential for very large civil and criminal penalties.

- Virus incidents are detected about once per week.

This confirms previous reports and indicates a lack of adequate attention to long-term prevention.

- An attempt to tap the CEO's PC was detected by chance.

  This indicates that a more serious problem may exist.

- A laser printer disappeared one day and observation cameras intended to detect such behavior showed nothing.

  This suggests an insider theft.

- Password guessing is fairly common, and in at least one case, an attempt was definitively determined to be an illicit attempt at access.

  This should result in serious action, but according to previous interviews, nobody has been fired for any such incident. This seems to imply inadequate personnel policy.

- There was one case of E-mail being used to get a computer operator to illicitly transfer more than $1 million. The money was eventually recovered and the person was caught.

  This clearly indicates inadequate standards and procedures.

- Fungibles are commonly sent to the wrong account. Detected errors are repaired and reported monthly to the managers in charge of those areas, but no further action has ever been taken.

  This indicates inadequate integrity controls.

- Forged accounts payables have been used to move fungibles.

  Clearly, there is an insider threat.

- One copy of PC-based usage logging detected unauthorized access on the average once per month. No follow-on investigation was carried out.

  This could easily indicate a systematic attempt to examine data in information systems throughout the organization, but without more auditing, there may never be a definitive determination.

- There have been instances of terminated employees and consultants entering facilities without authorization and for unexplained reasons.

Unexplained reasons means that they were never questioned and inadequate follow-up was done. Entry by terminated employees indicates a lack of adequate physical controls.

- Intruder incidents have occurred at several facilities. At least one entry was made through a maintenance elevator.

This indicates inadequate physical perimeter control.

Tapes used for server backups are stored in the same physical location as the servers they back up, and are not physically protected from theft or alteration.

This indicates a lack of adequate education, policy, procedures, and standards.

More than one quarter of policy and procedure documents are out of date at any given time.

This shows that the personnel department's attempts to get everyone to sign policy statements is not effective. Improved policies, procedures, and management supervision is required.

Group 9 On the mainframe, passwords are set to a minimum length of four characters and a maximum length of eight. Vendor-supplied passwords are left in place, and passwords are commonly programmed into hot keys.

Any other mainframe security depends on this authentication process, and yet four-character passwords are used. This is the system that stores all financial data. This indicates a poor policy decision and inadequate standards and procedures.

Transfers of stocks and bonds are essentially unprotected, even though the financial values of these transactions can be as high as several billion dollars.

An outsider can guess a four-character password within only a few minutes, and is then able to transfer billions of dollars worth of stocks and bonds. This is clearly not a very good situation. It certainly indicates inadequate policy, standards, procedures, technical safeguards, training, education, and an overly lax attitude.

Users have expressed a desire for automatic terminal inactivity lock-out, but *security* deliberately took this capability out.

Perhaps insecurity is a better name for this group.

No formal risk assessment has ever been done.

Why am I not surprised?

Additional information   The information provided during the site visit contained several inconsistencies and seemingly unsubstantiated reports of incidents. In order to clarify these issues, we asked the point of contact to follow up. Every incident was denied, including those that had already been publicized in the press and reported to the police. Internal management sources assert that the denials of attacks are false.

The staff members are becoming defensive and are probably nervous about their jobs. They figure that denial of everything is the safest position.

Findings

When taken on their own, the many shortcomings identified in this report are cause for concern, and some of them justify immediate action. But when taken in combination, they reflect an overall lack of attention to an area that will likely have a great impact on the future of XYZ Corporation.

Protection Management   Protection management is inadequate. This inadequacy appears to stem from the management of information technology by line managers and a general ignorance of the issues of information protection. Even when members of technical staff reported incidents and potential problems, management did little or nothing to address these problems.

The inadequacy of protection management is reflected in many ways, but perhaps the most obvious one is the lack of an incident reporting system. The result is that even when incidents occur, the knowledge of the incident is so localized that nobody can see an overall trend. There could have been over a thousand locally detected incidents in the last year, and management would never be aware of it. Without knowledge of the nature and extent of a protection problem, it is not possible to coordinate an effective protection program.

The many lapses we found reflect most clearly on inadequate protection management. Until the protection management problem is properly addressed, great risk will remain for the organization as a whole.

The list of protection management problems is essentially endless. The only way these problems are likely to be resolved in a meaningful way is by a concerted effort by top-level management to put an appropriate management structure in place, place an appropriate person at the top of that management structure, and provide adequate independent assurance that the structure operates properly.

Protection Policy A formal information protection policy should be established. At a minimum, this policy should include:

- Protection management personnel and responsibilities
- Individual, organizational, and corporate responsibilities
- Incident reporting and investigation requirements
- Protection requirements in all areas listed in this report
- Sanctions for policy violations
- Exceptions to the policy

Standards and procedures Current procedures are the product of individual initiative. They are not consistent across organizational lines, and thus are not standards. Overall standards and procedures should be developed by consolidating existing procedures where possible and developing new ones where appropriate.

In order to be effective, standards and procedures must be:

- Documented in writing
- Detailed enough to allow measurement of compliance
- Practical and understood by those who implement them
- Of real value to the business units they apply to
- Tied to protection awareness, training, and education
- Facilitated by knowledgeable and properly trained people
- Periodically reviewed and revised to meet changing situations

Emphasis on the need for standards and procedures is a management responsibility and should be implemented through the protection management structure created with the implementation of a protection policy.

Documentation There is a notable lack of necessary documentation. The lack of documentation is evident both corporate-wide and within the business units we observed. The existence of select pieces of documentation does not reflect an overall approach to creating, maintaining, distributing, and using documentation.

At a minimum, documentation should include:

- System hardware and software configurations
- Formal risk assessments

- Software acceptance testing
- Protection countermeasures
- Protection test and evaluation
- Contingency plans
- Disaster recovery plans
- Business continuity plans
- Incident response guidelines
- Software change control
- Proper use of licensed software

Documentation should be located where it will be used, clearly identified, and backed up by accessible copies in disaster recovery and regional sites.

Protection audit The internal audit department has made a substantial effort to regularly audit information systems despite a serious lack of adequate funding and personnel. Internal auditors have done a good job of identifying obvious deficiencies, but in order for audit to become an effective protection tool, a great deal more must be done. Internal audit had the most comprehensive list of incidents and was more aware of the overall protection posture than any other group interviewed. Auditors also had a good sense of where inadequacies existed and how they might be dealt with.

This suggests that internal auditors should play a key role in improving information protection and that they should be intimately involved in the creation of all aspects of the protection program.

External protection audit should be performed at least once per year to assure that internal audit teams are properly performing their function.

Technical safeguards Almost all of the appropriate technical safeguards required for effective protection in this environment are lacking. Furthermore, the environment actively promotes practices which cripple the effectiveness of existing technical safeguards. Current safeguards don't detect or prevent even a small percentage of known incidents. It is possible, perhaps even likely, that there are numerous ongoing attacks at this time and that technical safeguards are not acting to alert anyone of their presence.

Appropriate technical safeguards must be determined and implemented as soon as possible. The highest exposures, such as the ability to transfer large amounts of fungibles, should be defended against immediately, while other technical safeguards should be implemented in concurrence with newly developed protection policy over time.

Incident response Incident response is reactive and ad hoc, and this is inadequate to the task at hand. An incident response team should be put in place and centralized reporting and response should be implemented with all haste. This team should maintain a database of incidents and assure that all incidents are resolved in a timely fashion.

Testing Testing needs to be enhanced. Although minimal testing is done according to vendor specifications, this only verifies that software is properly configured and compiled, and does not verify that it operates properly. A rigorous test program for all aspects of information protection should be instituted as part of the process of developing new protection.

Physical protection Time did not permit full investigation of a number of physical security and facilities issues reported by staff members; however, it is clear that physical protection is inadequate.

If physical protection is to be effective, there must be an atmosphere that challenges outsiders and an organizational will to have physical security. XYZ Corporation must evaluate the atmosphere it wishes to maintain in conjunction with the protection to be afforded to determine an appropriate mix of physical security measures.

Personnel issues There is a sense in the personnel department that there are adequate policies and procedures in place with respect to information protection issues, but this is not supported by the facts.

Personnel department enhancements that support information protection should be implemented, including but not limited to enhanced new employee training, employee awareness programs, new standards and procedures for employee termination, and improved communication with other departments.

Legal considerations The legal department is supposed to keep track of both domestic and international requirements. They apparently do not. Notice and consent is required in many jurisdictions in order to enforce restrictions on use. The legal department has apparently not made any effort to have this requirement enforced. Due diligence requirements are not met by current corporate policies and procedures. Widespread use of illegal copies of software indicates a lack of attention to legal requirements. The list goes on. The legal department should be trained in areas related to information protection and should be tasked with providing appropriate advice regarding all aspects of the protection program.

Protection awareness No protection awareness program is currently in place. A concerted effort should be made to implement a comprehensive program of protection awareness. This program should include at a minimum:

- One hour of training per quarter for all staff members
- Coverage of all of the protection issues discussed in this report
- Detailed instructions and documents on how to detect and respond to incidents
- Explanation and discussion of corporate protection policies
- Discussion of personal and corporate responsibilities
- Discussion of recent protection-relevant events in the media

Training and education There is no substantial training and education in information protection at XYZ Corporation today. A concerted effort should be made to provide adequate training and education to all personnel with information protection responsibilities. This effort should, at a minimum, include training and education in relevant specialty areas for:

- Managers
- Auditors
- Systems Administrators
- Programmers
- Guards

Organizational suitability XYZ Corporation seems well suited to the introduction of information protection at this time. Current restructuring efforts make the environment amenable to change. At this time, staff members strongly resist even minimal effort in support of information protection. If adequate protection is to be attained, either these staff members have to change, or the corporation has to pay for protection that requires no effort by these people. The latter will almost certainly be too expensive to attain.

Staff levels may require some adjustment. Typical figures for properly protected environments are 20 users to each systems administrator. There may be special features of the corporate environment that affect these figures, but none were observed.

A Plan of Action

We recommend a comprehensive realignment of information protection posture. In order to accomplish this realignment, the following four-phase plan is proposed.

Phase 1 Extreme exposures should be immediately addressed:

- Secure the fungibles transfer capability. The current exposure is so great that a single incident could severely damage the corporation and there is currently no meaningful protection in place to prevent such a loss.
- Make a comprehensive set of backups and store them off-site. This is necessary in order to assure that existing information assets are not lost due to accident or abuse.
- Install a corporate-wide real-time audit analysis and reduction system. This system should automatically analyze audit trails currently being generated, generate and analyze audit trails not currently being generated, and detect a wide variety of known attack patterns as they occur.
- Perform a sampled protection audit of critical systems. This is necessary in order to determine at a detailed level how systems currently in place are being used, whether there are widespread ongoing attacks, what weaknesses are poorly addressed by administrative controls, and what vulnerabilities must be covered in each class of system to provide adequate protection. A complete audit would be far too time-consuming, so random samples are used to provide statistical data.
- Place minimal sensors and alarms in key areas. This is required in order to provide some level of assurance that equipment and information critical to ongoing operation is not tampered with or stolen.
- Perform a comprehensive audit for illegal copies of software and either remove the software or purchase legitimate licenses. This is necessary in order to address possible criminal liability, lawsuits, and negative publicity.

Phase 2 Planning should be initiated as soon as possible to provide long-term protection suitable to the need.

- Form a comprehensive corporate information protection policy and implement it throughout the corporation.
- Form an information protection advisory council. The purpose of this council is to act as a focal point for making policy decisions about information protection, investigating reports on protection incidents, hiring an appropriate corporate staff member to manage long-term information protection requirements, and assisting that staff member in carrying out their duties.
- Find a cost-effective set of long-term protective measures suitable to the environment.

- Make information protection part of the overall planning process of the corporation. By involving protection as early in the planning process as possible, large cost savings and improved protection result.
- Train staff members in the technologies implemented during the first phase of this effort.

Phase 3 After the first two phases are completed, a substantial set of technical, procedural, and personnel measures should be implemented to provide proper protection.

Phase 4 After appropriate protective measures have been instituted, the fourth and ongoing phase of activity will begin. In this phase, protection will be maintained and updated to reflect changes in environment, technology, and organizational priorities.

B.2   CASE STUDY 4: THE ALMA SYSTEM

Vulnerabilities and Protection Techniques

Three categories of vulnerability will be considered:

Vulnerability	Protection issue
Leakage of classified data	Secrecy
Corruption of information	Integrity
Denial of services	Availability

Other aspects of protection will not be considered in this study, except in as far as they relate to these issues of concern.

Alma secrecy requirements are fairly well understood in a general sense and are addressed by existing regulations. The other issues are less well understood and are not adequately covered by regulations. This assessment will primarily address the threats that are realistic over the operational lifetime of Alma, and regulations will be largely ignored in our analysis.

There are several disturbing vulnerabilities in Alma as it currently exists and in light of its potential deployment. These are briefly outlined here and detailed more fully below:

- Alma was originally designed to operate in a Tempest environment. It was not designed to withstand any sort of threat in a non-Tempest environment. The move from a Tempest environment to an open environment creates numerous and various vulnerabilities ranging from problems of securing the hardware and software during distribution to maintaining operational safeguards against field threats.

- Alma was designed as a prototype and, as in many such cases, is now being deployed operationally. The prototype requires some rework in order to improve performance, audit high level events, improve systems administration, augment database labeling and integrity, improve reliability, and for other reasons not related to protection.
- The use of standard protocols for sharing information presents a number of vulnerabilities that may weaken Alma protection and enable attackers to succeed with a very low workload. The use of these protocols has to be examined in some depth to determine if the vulnerabilities presented by them are worth the expense of covering them with additional safeguards and, if so, to determine whether they can continue to be used in some cases or must be completely redone.
- The data exchange between Alma and other systems has not been adequately addressed either from a performance standpoint or from an integrity standpoint. The low bandwidth digital diodes currently in use should probably be replaced by high bandwidth devices capable of handling Ethernet speeds while providing protection against covert channels. There are also cases where redundant data entry is being performed and in which the time differences between Alma entry and other entry is inadequately addressed. Several other interface issues are also likely to cause problems in the future.
- Protection administration is inadequately addressed for a widely distributed set of Alma systems. Although the current administrator appears to be quite well versed and probably performs his duties quite well, there is no proper mechanism for training, testing, and assisting in the systems administration process. History has shown this to be a key area of vulnerability.
- Integrity is not adequately addressed in Alma. There are almost no safeguards against corruptions in the LAN, in individual systems, of personnel, of software, of data, of protection functions, of peripheral devices, or of external communications.
- Auditing is inadequately handled. The current mechanism does not provide a realistic way for the systems administrator to read and understand audit data, but only a simplistic way to view it.
- Availability is not adequately addressed. There are several single points of failure that could seriously cripple or completely disable Alma, including a single corrupt systems administrator, a single corrupt program propagating through the network, and various jamming techniques.
- Rapid adaption over time to new situations and inputs should be considered. It is likely that Alma will be interfaced to many new input sources over its life cycle, and each of these connections introduces a potential protection problem for Alma.

- Future networking enhancements are likely, and there is no protection plan in place for dealing with such changes. If Alma is networked with other systems using imperfectly matched protection techniques, this networking is likely to introduce vulnerabilities to both environments.
- Field deployment introduces new problems of secure distribution. If rapid field deployment is permitted, security provisions must cover distribution, installation, and maintenance of all hardware and software components.

In the remainder of this report, threats will be designated with **boldface** abbreviations and protection techniques with *[bracketed italics]* abbreviations. These abbreviations will then be used in the tables for ease of presentation. For vulnerabilities, abbreviations begin with capital letters as follows to designate our major areas of concern:

Letter	Area of concern
T	Tempest
R	Retrofit/Redesign
P	Protocol
D	Data exchange
PA	Protection Administration
I	Integrity
A	Audit
AV	Availability
F	Field deployment

Tempest problems The move from a Tempest environment to a non-Tempest environment changes everything about the hardware and software vulnerabilities.

- **T-SWdist** Software and hardware distribution have to be secured in the Alma deployment process because anybody in the environment could place a device or a disk in a shipping container and have a reasonably high degree of assurance that it would be inserted into the system and used. [167]
- **T-HWleak** A transmitter/receiver in a computer or LAN hardware device could be exploited to cause arbitrary denial, corruption, leakage, or accounting failure. [228]
- **T-defect** The use of off-the shelf hardware is a vulnerability in itself because of the ease of modifying standard components, interrupting the commercial distribution environment, the possibility of a known

defect being exploited, the possibility of jamming to cause selective denial, etc. [8] [187]

- **T-Ebeam** An incoming energy beam could be used to cause heating of select components causing false input signals, reduced reliability, or even complete denial of services.
- **T-HWjam** Energy signals of sufficient strength can jam LAN cables, serial cables, keyboard connectors, mouse cables, and other electromagnetic devices. [27]
- **T-bugs** Short wave-length radar can be exploited to listen to larynx movements and observe subliminal speech commonly used by operators while entering data such as passwords, cryptographic keys, and other vital information. [107]
- **T-emanate** It would be a simple matter to plant or drop Van Eck devices proximate to an Alma system and through them to retransmit emanations to extract timely mission specific information. [220]
- **T-IOjam** Jamming can be effective against the cryptographically covered radio links used in current Alma sites, which can disable portions of the network.
- **T-target** The emanations from Alma systems could be exploited to guide weapons against Alma installations, thus easing the targeting problem for enemies. [219]
- **T-visual** Video display outputs, keystrokes entered at keyboards, and lip movements could be observed with cameras at visible or invisible frequencies and that data could be retransmitted or magnified by observers at substantial distances (including airborne, satellite, ground-based, and underground observation sites). [173]
- **T-conduct** Conducted emanations over power lines can be exploited to extract data from computer systems. [220]
- **T-physical** Clothes, gifts, or other items shipped into the environment or distant observation posts could be used to include audio or data receivers/transmitters to leak information from the environment. This includes keyboard sounds which yield input sequences, voices, etc. [229]
- **T-audio** Audio output devices can be exploited to transmit audio versions of electronic data at nonhuman-audible frequencies. These could be observed and retransmitted or directly observed at considerable distance. Audio input devices could be exploited to introduce commands in a similar fashion, producing a bi-directional high speed covert data channel. [194] One technique used to find certain types of hidden microphones is to use two ultrasonic generators at different frequencies, with a difference frequency in the audible range, to combine in the microphone and produce enough tone to hear. This might be used to produce audio "voice" commands in microphones

used for voice control of systems. Likewise, the ability to produce an audio varying small voltage on microphone leads could accomplish this. These would bypass normal authentication procedures for a workstation in use. Microwave pulses with the correct timing pattern could probably generate enough voltage to simulate keyboard output to the workstation. It may be possible to detect and interpret the ultrasonic horizontal sweep signal from monitors to reproduce the display, through a tent, using a directional microphone. Directional microphones are useful for 300 feet, or perhaps farther using speech signal processing for conversation in tents.

- **T-keys** Cryptographic device emanations may be exploited to detect the cryptographic keys or secret data during operation. Keys could be further exploited to introduce false information into the network. [202]
- **T-EMP** EMP attacks operate far more easily against non-Tempest equipment. [92] [91]
- **T-Radar** Normal air traffic control radar can cause interference and intermittent failures in computer equipment within a radius of several hundred yards. [13]
- **T-future** In the future, the governments currently engaged in these sorts of activities will likely expand considerably on these attacks. [63]

Two basic techniques are involved in reducing the threat from Tempest attacks. One is to reduce the emanations that can enter or leave an area, and the other is to introduce sufficient noise so as to make the detection or modification of signals too difficult to attain at a reasonable price.

[noise] Noise can easily be introduced into the Alma environment to reduce the emanations threat, but the amount of noise required to reduce existing threats to acceptable levels is not yet known. This analysis would require the use of special-purpose hardware devices to test for radiated and corruptive emissions effects in a real Alma environment under simulated or actual load conditions. This would require several weeks of time and the use of specialized equipment. Once proper levels are determined, hardware noise generation devices can be designed and implemented to generate appropriate noise characteristics so as to reduce signal to noise ratios appropriately. An appropriate plan would also be required to guide and train Alma installers on how and where to place these devices to achieve proper effect. The estimated affect would be about one-third as effective as emanations controls and no reasonable amount of improvement is feasible beyond that.

There are also devices available which sample both emanated and conducted signals from workstations, and adjust to output proper levels of confusing signals. They require a wire loop around the workstation and cost several hundred dollars each.

[perimeter] Emanations can also be reduced by increasing the distance between sources and sensors. Protective measures could be put in place so as to reduce the emanations threat by searching and securing large perimeters on an ongoing basis. This is the least reliable of the techniques considered here. Although it has low initial costs, it involves substantial amounts of people time and training in order to be effective, substantially increases perimeter sizes and search requirements, and is far less likely to be effective than the technical alternatives.

[shield] Emanations and introduced signals can also be greatly reduced by providing a tempest protection environment specially designed for field use. Training would be required for installers and a limited production run would be required in order to produce sufficient supplies to create enough suitable hardware to supply numerous Alma systems. For a multilevel secure version of Alma, we estimate the cost of shielding at $20,000 per 100 sq. ft. of floor space in a deployed setting. Assuming that only classified components of Alma require coverage, this cost could be limited to under $40,000 per installation. There is an added cost of about $10,000 for the first implementation associated with finding and assessing vendors, testing the implementation to assure that it meets the specifications, training installers, and so on. For a single level Alma implementation, the area to be secured would likely be at least three to four times this large, for a cost of at least $150,000 per installation.

There is available material designed for portable shelters to shield emissions from observation and targeting by RF missiles. If this were used several feet outside a tent, it might cut Tempest problems enough to be worthwhile, if the main threat is from less than 20 or 30 degrees elevation.

Prototype conversion Although effective protection may be feasible without modifying the Alma software, there are some substantial opportunities to save time and effort, reduce vulnerabilities, and enhance performance through this effort.

- **R-dbase** A major problem in the Alma design is that there is no single interface to the underlying (Oracle) database. Since each Alma call to the database comes from a different module, there is no central way to introduce auditing at the Alma call level, authenticate database contents, label data by security level, or encrypt data stored in the database.
- **R-flex** There is a potential vulnerability in only allowing one underlying database (Oracle). A flaw or unknown limitation in that system, a vendor-placed intelligence threat, a protection problem, a problem

in Oracle distribution, a business failure, or other similar problems are a serious threat to Alma's future, and the DoD should move toward database independence as much as possible. Moving the database calls into an independent module allows vendors to compete for price and function in future Alma installations and allows Alma to adapt to more environments more quickly.

- **R-X11** The X11 interface to Alma has not been thoroughly examined and approved by the NSA, and the protection mechanisms added to X11 are not adequate from an audit or integrity perspective. [83, 79]
- **R-stress** From a reliability standpoint, it is likely that under high-load conditions and other stresses, the current Alma system will have substantial failures. Even if current needs are met under stringent test conditions, it is highly likely that as time passes, the nature and scope of things Alma will be asked to do will greatly increase. By doing this work now, the DoD will clear the path for future enhancements to Alma functionality and scope of operations, while increasing current system reliability and reducing dependence on single-vendor database solutions. [204]
- **R-MLS** Redesign will be critical if a multilevel secure version of Alma is to be implemented, as this is required in order to effectively separate data of different levels, cover them with cryptography, and track their movement through the network.

[redesign] A redesign of Alma for improved auditing, performance, reliability, authentication, and classification would cost on the order of $1,500,000, and would dramatically reduce the overall cost of securing the Alma environment.

[redoMLS] If a redesign were made toward a multilevel secure Alma implementation, the redesign cost would likely be about $500,000 higher.

Both of these are one-time costs.

Protocol issues Alma currently uses four types of protocols, each of which has little or no protection capability as currently implemented.

- **P-TCP** The TCP-IP protocol suite has known vulnerabilities, including but not limited to the ease of corruption and spoofing, ease of service denial, ease of leakage, and traffic analysis. [18] These vulnerabilities result respectively from a lack of cryptographic integrity checking, hardware limitations of media, the inability of TCP-IP to exploit redundancy for reliability, a lack of cryptography for secrecy, and the exploitation of low channel usage as a technique for scheduling. [93]
- **P-NFS** NFS is also used in Alma and this introduces additional problems including but not limited to disk-caching-induced protec-

tion failures, different protection algorithms used for remote versus local file access, and limited local denial of services when remote file systems become unavailable. [40] NFS also has no coverage against the sorts of vulnerabilities specified for TCP-IP.

- **P-YP** The network protocols currently used for remote authentication are inadequate to provide proper protection, again due to the same sorts of deficiencies as TCP-IP, but also including inadequate auditing capabilities, inadequate protection against password guessing attacks, no protection against downloading password files and attacking them off-line, and inadequate protection of automated update spoofing of local file system copies. [119]
- **P-dbase** The database-specific protocols used for performing remote database access also have the same problems just described for TCP-IP.
- **P-IO** A different protocol suite is used for communications with peer systems and this suite may also have similar problems.

The protocol vulnerabilities are particularly important in light of the lack of strong physical security in the deployment of Alma. Any physical breech of the network or any of the computing components introduces the possibility of corruption, denial, and leakage.

[*newprotocols*] The cost of rewriting protocols would be far too high to be of great value. An estimated cost of $1,250,000 would be required to augment the existing protocols to include a modicum of protection, but this would negatively affect long-term reliability, performance, and compatibility.

[*mls*] + [*shield*] By moving to a multilevel secure version of Alma with cryptographic LAN protection and Tempest protection for classified areas, the secret level components of the Alma system could be secured. Shielding costs were discussed earlier, MLS software adds about $1,000 to the cost of affected workstations, and cryptography is already used between Alma areas.

[*cmds*] Another partial solution to the protocol problem would be the use of network-based computer misuse detection systems to detect protocol attacks in real-time. The cost of this protection would be on the order of $250,000 plus $20,000 per Alma site.

Data exchange Alma data exchange with other systems generally falls into five categories: peer exchanges with other systems now existing and to be implemented in the future; read-only inputs from unclassified systems and future systems; write-only outputs to other systems; downgrading of information from other systems; and downgrading of information from Alma to unclassified systems. At present, each of these exchanges is a problem.

- **D-peer** Peer-to-peer exchanges are not covered by any protection at present. There are no audit records of these exchanges except as stored through editable Alma database entries, which means that problems cannot be traced to their source and audit trails cannot now be automatically and reliably analyzed for signs of abuse. There is no integrity checking to allow the contents of messages to be properly assured, which means that protection relies entirely on people noticing and correcting errors. This may be effective in some areas where targeting information only makes sense with proper routing information, but in other areas, such as the peer-to-peer connection with other systems and the future links to soon-to-be peer systems, it is and will likely remain ineffective unless we do something about it. Furthermore, merely detecting a problem without being able to correct it produces either reduced integrity or denial of services.

- **D-up** Read-only inputs from unclassified systems are currently limited to 2,400 baud incoming serial lines implemented as digital diodes. The current implementation suffers from low performance and poor reliability because it is over a serial line and because the digital diode is implemented in a non-optimal fashion. Bandwidths up to 19.2K baud could probably be reliably attained by improvements to the digital diodes currently in use, but higher (i.e., 1–10M baud) connections require hardware that does not yet exist. There is also no assurance that this information cannot contain interpreted code which could result in Alma corruption. Any information that is automatically interpreted or can be caused to be automatically interpreted by misuse of Alma should have additional constraints placed upon it including, but not limited to, syntax and semantics checking, and restraint to a limited function environment.

- **D-up** Write-only exchanges are currently assured by the recipient and the line used to perform output. If these connections are not currently protected, Alma should implement protection to assure that no protocol attacks can have an effect on Alma and to assure that Alma does not receive any information via covert channels that it should not receive. There should also be some sort of internal Alma cryptographic coverage to assure that if signals go out over the wrong wire or if the cryptographic hardware covering the transmission should fail, signals cannot be easily read by an enemy in a time frame that could harm a mission.

- **D-down** Information downgraded for use by Alma from TS systems is currently sent without assurance that it cannot contain information that could be interpreted by Alma so as to cause corruption. This risk should be handled in the same manner as the risk of read-only inputs from unclassified systems is handled.

- **D-down** Information downgrades from Alma to base-management systems are not currently provided. In order to provide these downgrades, it will be necessary to implement a guard application and enhance internal Alma controls to assure that only unclassified data in unaltered form is downgraded.
- **D-reenter** Redundant data entry is currently used because of the inability to downgrade Alma data to other systems. In addition, the one-way links from current unclassified systems cause integrity problems with database entries because there is no accurate date and time information about when events took place, only about when the data was entered. Thus, a more current status in Alma can be overwritten when a less timely entry is subsequently made in an unclassified system and that information is transmitted to Alma. By allowing automated downgrades in Alma, we can eliminate much of the incoming data from other systems and some of the redundant data entry into those systems. This both lowers costs and enhances integrity.

The most important items for providing enhanced performance and reliability while providing strong protection for data exchanges are the implementation of high-speed digital diodes and a secure automated downgrade facility.

[*p-diode*] For medium speed (i.e., 19.2K baud) digital diode applications, we can easily enhance the existing digital diode design at fairly low cost and over a very short time frame. Something like one person-month will be required in order to implement and test a digital diode of this sort ($10,000), and the cost per unit will be on the order of $100 each (assume 5 per site) in quantities of several hundred. This would seem a reasonable solution for most of the Alma interfaces with external systems. A medium speed digital diode would also be fairly easy to get approved by security certification groups because it would be very similar to the existing approved design.

[*e-diode*] For high speed (i.e., Ethernet) digital diode applications, the cost will likely be far greater in design time, in price per unit in quantity, and in time to get approval. Design time would likely be on the order of six person-months ($60,000), and would result in an operational prototype. Depending on the design, unit cost (not including design costs) will likely be in the range of $500 to $1500 per unit in quantity 100. The approval process will likely take longer because it is not a simple enhancement to an existing approved technology, but the principles are the same, and approval should not be excessively difficult to attain.

[ccs] [guard] [guard-HW] [cmds] [mls] Portions of this problem could alternatively be covered with enhanced change detection and control via cryptographic checksums *[ccs]*, automated guards *[guard]*, and the use of CMDS or a similar misuse detection system *[cmds]* in conjunction with a multilevel secure implementation of Alma *[mls]*. A custom Alma guard for automated real-time downgrading would cost about $500,000. If the guard hardware *[guard-HW]* were also required (i.e., in a non-MLS version of Alma), it would raise the price by $10,000 per installation.

Protection administration Protection administration is a universal problem that has never been adequately addressed in off-the-shelf systems. In Alma, at least the following problems exist today:

- **PA-doc PA-man PA-train** Current practices are not well documented, **PA-doc** + **PA-man**, and no training program **PA-train** is in place for training and maintaining the several hundred systems administrators that may be managing Alma systems when they become widely used. A protection manual should be developed to address this issue and a training program should be designed to provide training and education.
- **PA-Tprot PA-Tauthen PA-Taudit PA-Tpwd PA-Tadmin** Current tools are inadequate to assure to a reasonable degree that workstations in Alma are properly configured and used. This problem includes, but is not limited to, the inability to verify and correct protection settings **PA-Tprot**; inadequate assurance in the distribution of authentication databases, **PA-Tauthen**; inadequate audit analysis **PA-Taudit**; inadequate password complexity assurance **PA-Tpwd**; and high complexity of administration. **PA-Tadmin** [119]
- **PA-Aaccess PA-Ainteg PA-Apasswd PA-Aspoof PA-Aproc PA-Aactive PA-Aexec PA-Afiles PA-Aattack** Inadequate alarms are currently available for real-time or even delayed detection of attack or abuse. This includes such areas as illicit access attempts **PA-Aaccess**; integrity problems **PA-Ainteg**; password guessing attempts **PA-Apasswd**; spoofing attempts **PA-Aspoof**; process and file system problems **PA-Aproc**; activity and inactivity **PA-Aactive**; execution of unusual programs **PA-Aexec**; access to unusual files **PA-Afiles**; and known attack patterns **PA-Aattack**.

[newdoc] [newman] [newtrain] [training] Alma documentation *[newdoc]* and *[newman]*, and training *[newtrain]* can be addressed by about five person-months of effort ($50,000) in conjunction with several person-weeks of effort by current administrators. This is a one-time cost. As further enhancements to Alma are made, documentation and training can be upgraded with an additional 10 percent level of effort. Once man-

uals and training techniques are developed, training can also be provided for time and materials, or select Alma personnel can be used for training purposes as desired *[training]*. This is estimated to cost about $5,000 per Alma system per year.

[cmds] *[simptools]* *[newtools]* Systems administration tools should be augmented to include the capabilities just listed. This might best be done by a combination of CMDS or a similar system *[cmds]* which is very strong in the area of alarm generation and audit consolidation, and a set of simple tools *[simptools]* and new tools *[newtools]* for augmenting administration. Simple tools are commonly available, and with only about $10,000 of effort, they can be integrated. More effective tools would require about $100,000 of effort.

[mls]-[simptools]-[newdoc] In a multilevel secure version of Alma *[mls]*, both simple tools *[simptools]* and protection documents *[newdoc]* are provided, which should reduce these costs significantly, leaving only the Alma-specific protection techniques to be implemented.

[redesign] *[cmds]* *[mls]* *[redoMLS]* *[custaudit]* Most of the auditing and control problems are addressed by the redesign of Alma *[redesign]*, the implementation of CMDS *[cmds]*, and an MLS operating environment *[mls]* + *[redoMLS]*. Without this option, the cost of covering audit *[custaudit]* will be fairly extreme (on the order of $2,500,000 initial cost plus ongoing time required of systems administrators that could otherwise be spent on useful work). Such an implementation would be inadequate without at least the minimal redesign of Alma *[redesign]*.

Integrity protection Integrity is widely ignored in the computing community and Alma is no exception. The following broad categories of integrity problems exist in Alma today:

- **I-lan** LAN corruption, forgery, active tapping, and aliasing are all possible in Alma. Without additional coverage of the LAN, any physical attack on hardware devices can potentially result in widespread denial of services, corruption, leakage, and audit destruction. This includes hardware manufacture, test, distribution, assembly, shipping to forward installations, installation, and use. This problem can only be addressed by very good hardware and personnel security throughout the process, or by the use of cryptographic authentication of LAN traffic. [7, 53]
- **I-SW** Software and/or data corruption, **I-data**, inside computer systems in Alma are not covered. Database data corrupted intentionally or by hardware error is undetectable. Corruption of system-critical files including audit trails, password files, and configuration files is not covered and any of these can result in widespread corruption. Corruption in the operating system, support systems, or applications

software is not covered and any of these can result in widespread corruption. Any corruption in one system can easily propagate throughout Alma, thus extending the effect to widespread denial, leakage, corruption, and repudiation. This requires, at a minimum, built-in integrity checking in an integrity shell mode in order to provide effective protection. [52]

- **I-prot** Protection facility corruption is also possible in the Alma systems including, but not limited to, modification of protection settings on files and the resulting effect of these modifications on devices and local and remote file systems. To properly address this problem would require substantial enhancement of the UNIX systems to include mandatory access controls or the movement to MLS or other similar Unix environments at greatly increased cost. A fall-back position would be to create a set of controls including internal monitoring software on each file server, and the enhancement of the Alma and X11 software to provide additional protection setting checks and real-time warnings.

- **I-phys** Peripheral devices are often treated as limited function devices, but most modern peripherals contain general-purpose computers and, in some cases, they can be exploited to attack systems. Network printers are particularly common as sources of denial, corruption, and leakage. Other peripherals can sometimes be exploited so as to modify the operating system in memory. This does not currently appear to be a serious threat to Alma, but as technology appears and is integrated into the environment, this may become a serious problem. Protection techniques include tracking and securing peripheral hardware from the womb to the tomb and digital diodes to restrict activity to output or input as appropriate to the device. Medium bandwidth digital diodes seem most appropriate to this application. [125, 205, 86]

- **I-HW** Hardware integrity has been addressed elsewhere.

- **I-IO** External communications and data integrity have been addressed elsewhere.

- **I-inputs** Inputs from other systems should have limitations on input syntax and semantics, and labeling, authentication, and encryption should be applied to all input from all sources both before its arrival and as it is integrated into the environment. This would integrate well into the effort to secure external communications and move Alma from a prototype to a production environment.

- **I-other** Other input sources including software distribution, backup tapes, and other maintenance media represent avenues for the introduction of corruption and the leakage of data. Policies and procedures should be in place for the use of these peripherals, and technical controls should be considered including backup encryption and authentication, secure software distribution via encryption and authentication, and adequate change control over software. [172, 75]

- **I-transitive** Transitive effects should be considered in all integrity analysis since the current design of Alma is highly integrated and allows very rapid dissemination of information throughout the system, and thus a corruption will rapidly have widespread effect. [209]

[ccs] [embedccs] [mls] The majority of the software problems require cryptographic authentication [ccs] that can be attained for costs on the order of $150,000 in software and five person-months of effort for an additional $50,000. In untrusted systems, this capability should be embedded in other facilities [embedccs] which increases cost by an estimated $250,000. At present, there is no alternative to this solution for attaining enhanced integrity other than using an MLS [mls] to reduce the need to embed protection as heavily. With an MLS many of these requirements can be reduced because of the ability to use the MAC capabilities to prevent corruption (e.g., system software is at system low).

Auditing In the current environment, no systems administrator can effectively use the audit data provided by the system to detect or counter attacks either in real-time or on a post-mortem basis.

- **A-OS** Operating system data is too voluminous and difficult to understand to provide meaningful audit analysis by a systems administrator. A minimal effort of three person-months could eliminate this problem to a substantial extent. [138]
- **A-lan** Network-based attacks cannot be reliably detected without combining information across platforms and there is no facility to provide this capability. This can only be addressed by a network monitor. [203]
- **A-dbase** Database auditing is inadequate because it is meaningless at the level audits occur and does not associate actions with people and understandable Alma events. A more rational approach would be to provide audit trails in the interface between Alma and Oracle or whatever other database may eventually be used. This would be a natural side effect of the movement to a production environment described earlier.
- **A-Alma** Alma level auditing is nonexistent and will be vital to detecting correlations or the lack thereof between user actions and database and operating system events. Effective application would also require a correlation between Alma events and database events by a network monitor.
- **A-extern** No auditing of external information sources or sincs is provided, which makes tracking attacks to their source very difficult.

All incoming data should be audited, authenticated, marked with its source and security level, covered by a cryptographic checksum to detect corruptions, and encrypted if it is classified.

- **A-meaning**   No mechanism exists to combine the various levels of audit that are or eventually may be available into a form that permits meaningful review. The combination of audit information from multiple levels of auditing is one of the key ways we can assure proper operation, and this can only be effectively done with a network monitor.
- **A-monitor**   Network activity monitoring is nonexistent in Alma. This would be necessary in order to detect network-based attacks, statistical anomalies indicative of many physical attacks, and other similar scenarios, assuming they were not otherwise covered. A network monitoring and analysis system would be required to cover this vulnerability unless it is covered from other protection mechanisms such as LAN encryption, authentication, and so on.

It is clear that if auditing is to be effective in detecting attacks and acting to mitigate problems that occur, it will be necessary to expend a substantial effort toward audit automation if only to provide effective means for administrators to deal with the volume. Other aspects of auditing cover various vulnerabilities, but may not be the most cost-effective covering technique or may be best applied in conjunction with other techniques.

[cmds] [redesign] [custaudit] It appears that misuse detection *[cmds]* in conjunction with Alma redesign *[redesign]* is the best solution to this problem. Alternatives require custom auditing and analysis which likely cost on the order of $2,500,000 and end up less effective and less flexible over the Alma life cycle. *[custaudit]*

Availability   Availability is not adequately addressed. There are several single points of failure that could seriously cripple or completely disable Alma, including:

- **AV-admin**   A single corrupt systems administrator could bring down any given Alma installation with ease in a very short time frame and keep it down for an extended period. Similarly, administrative error could disrupt services for several hours. [167]
- **AV-prog**   A single corrupt program propagating through the network could easily disrupt services, corrupt data, leak secrets, or repudiate responsibility. This could be sustained over a long period of time and cause great damage.
- **AV-power**   A power failure of sustained duration or of the uninterruptable power supply could bring an entire Alma network

down. Alma currently uses both an uninterruptable power system and backup generators. These should be retained and properly managed. [92]

- **AV-HWfail** A single hardware failure in a processor or an IO port could cause substantial damage to the current Alma implementation. This should be addressed for deployed versions.
- **AV-lanfail** A LAN failure could bring down a substantial portion of Alma in the current design. This should be covered by proper redundancy.
- **AV-jam** Jamming techniques and other similar attacks could be used to cause Alma to fail for sustained periods. [12, 77]

[decenter] [ups] [multilan] [multiserver] [redesign] The availability issue requires that systems administration of a Alma network be decentralized *[decenter]*, that emergency power be provided in a distributed fashion *[ups]*, that multiple networks be implemented to cover single failures *[multilan]*, and that the database be replicated on multiple servers *[multiserver]*. Redundant servers are already planned. Decentralizing network administration requires a slight redesign of the Alma networking administration scheme. This would cost about $20,000. Redundant emergency power would double the cost of current uninterruptable power supplies. A generator should also be included with every Alma system as a backup, and should be tested regularly for proper operation and adequate fuel supply. Multiple networks in Alma must be addressed if Alma is to be implemented as an MLS system, and the addition of redundant networks would cost only about $2,000 per Alma system. Efficient redundant file servers would require the Alma redesign effort described earlier *[redesign]* and would be included in that effort.

Rapid ongoing adaption In the current computing environment, rapid adaption of operational systems to differing sources of input is vital to operational continuity in deployed situations and as technologies and capabilities change. This presents an ongoing design problem for Alma which will likely require retrofits throughout its life cycle because of its high degree of interoperation with other systems. The current design permits this sort of adaption in a fairly straightforward manner, but in order to facilitate protection in such an environment, it is advisable that these considerations be included in any redesign effort. This requirement also contributes to the increased cost of using nonstandard protocols and the savings afforded by an Alma redesign at this time. Otherwise, no specific coverage is indicated.

Future networking enhancements Future networking enhancements are likely and there is no protection plan in place for dealing with this issue.

If we allow Alma to be networked with other systems using imperfectly matched protection, we may introduce vulnerabilities to both environments that neither had without the other. It is advisable that every time a system is networked to Alma, a similar analysis be performed for that system, and that an analysis of the interactions of the mechanisms on these different systems be performed for each such connection. Otherwise, no specific enhancement is required for this problem.

Field deployment issues Field deployment introduces new problems of secure distribution:

- **F-distrib** Secure distribution of hardware and software must be used to prevent the hardware and software from being corrupted at the point of manufacture, during shipment, or at any other step in the process. Without secure distribution, arbitrary leakage, corruption, denial, and repudiation can be easily attained by an attacker at very low cost.
- **F-install** Secure installation requires that corruption during installation be prevented and that at installation, the integrity of the secure distribution and installation be verifiable.
- **F-maint** Secure maintenance requires that protection be maintained during maintenance as well as normal system activities. This includes secure backups, secure reconfiguration and restoration, secure channels for updates, suitably cleared maintenance personnel, secure supplies and supply channels, and secure change control over hardware and software modifications.

[noTro] Hardware and software must be securely distributed from the manufacturer to prevent the introduction of Trojan horses into the system. This cost is nominally covered by secure distribution costs and a slight fee for increased assurance from vendors.

[preconfig] Field-deployed systems should be preconfigured at a central site to avoid the protection problems associated with performing full installations in the field.

[sectransit] The fully configured system should then be broken down into components, labeled for reassembly, and packaged for physically secure transit to the field location. Only fully sealed packaging should be used for distribution because of the ease of introducing Trojan horses in relatively small and innocuous looking packages.

[field-proc] Field installation should consist of physically securing the site and introducing all required Tempest, power conditioning, and other components before computers are introduced. Computers and related components should be assembled last and only removed from their packaging in the secured areas. We estimate that this will require about

$5,000 of additional packaging and other personnel costs for each distribution.

[replacements] Replacement parts should be included in the distribution and an additional secure distribution capability should be provided for further replacement parts.

None of these requirements has substantial direct costs not already born in Alma deployment. They require only good procedural controls and training.

Summary The following tables summarize by listing each vulnerability, the sets of protection techniques that cover it, and the costs of each protection technique, broken up into initial, per unit, and total amortized over 50 units. A "*" is used to indicate that this solution only applies to the MLS architecture, a "+" is used to indicate that this solution applies only to a non-MLS architecture, and a "!" is used to indicate items that only apply to systems without shielding.

Vulnerabilities and Protection Techniques

Vulnerability	Protection	Vulnerability	Protection
T-SWdist	*[field-proc]*	**R-MLS**	*[redoMLS]*
T-HWleak	*[noTro]* + *[sectransit]*	**P-TCP**	*[mls]* +*[shield]*
T-defect	*[noTro]* + *[sectransit]*	**P-TCP**	*[newprotocols]*
T-Ebeam	*[shield]*	**P-NFS**	*[mls]* +*[shield]*
T-HWjam	*[shield]*	**P-NFS**	*[newprotocols]*
T-bugs	*[shield]*	**P-YP**	*[mls]* +*[shield]*
T-bugs	*[noise]*	**P-YP**	*[newprotocols]*
T-emanate	*[shield]*	**P-dbase**	*[mls]* +*[shield]*
T-emanate	*[noise]*	**P-dbase**	*[newprotocols]*
T-IOjam	*[shield]*	**P-IO[B**	*[mls]* +*[shield]*
T-target	*[noise]*	**P-IO**	*[newprotocols]*
T-target	*[shield]*	**P-IO**	*[cmds]*
T-visual	*[noise]*	**D-peer**	*[cmds]*
T-visual	*[shield]*	**D-peer**	*[mls]*
T-conduct	*[shield]*	**D-up**	*[e-diode]* +*[guard]*
T-physical	*[shield]*	**D-up**	*[p-diode]* +*[guard]*
T-audio	*[shield]*	**D-up**	*[mls]* +*[guard]*
T-keys	*[noise]*	**D-down**	*[e-diode]* +*[guard]*
T-keys	*[shield]*	**D-down**	*[p-diode]* +*[guard]*
T-EMP	*[shield]*	**D-down**	*[mls]* +*[guard]*
T-Radar	*[shield]*	**D-reenter**	*[mls]* +*[guard]*
T-future	*[shield]*	**PA-doc**	*[mls]*
R-dbase	*[redesign]*	**PA-doc**	*[newdoc]*
R-flex	*[redesign]*	**PA-man**	*[newman]*
R-X11	*[redesign]*	**PA-train**	*[newtrain]*
R-stress	*[redesign]*	**PA-Tprot**	*[newtools]*

Vulnerabilities and Protection Techniques (continued)

Vulnerability	Protection	Vulnerability	Protection
PA-Tprot	[mls]	I-data	[cmds]
PA-Tprot	[cmds]	I-prot	[cmds]
PA-Tauthen	[ccs]	I-prot	[custaudit]
PA-Taudit	[cmds] + [mls]	I-phys	[cmds]
PA-Taudit	[custaudit]	I-phys	[custaudit]
PA-Tpwd	[simptools]	I-HW	[cmds]
PA-Tpwd	[mls]	I-HW	[noTro] + [sectransit]
PA-Tadmin	[newtools]	I-IO	[custaudit]
PA-Aaccess	[mls] + [cmds]	I-IO	[cmds]
PA-Aaccess	[newtools]	I-inputs	[guard]
PA-Ainteg	[ccs]	I-other	[cmds] (weak)
PA-Apasswd	[mls]	I-other	[custaudit]
PA-Apasswd	[cmds]	I-transitive	[ccs]
PA-Aspoof	[mls]	A-OS	[cmds]
PA-Aspoof	[cmds]	A-OS	[custaudit]
PA-Aspoof	[custaudit]	A-lan	[cmds]
PA-Aproc	[newtools]	A-dbase	[redesign] + [ccs]
PA-Aproc	[cmds]	A-dbase	[redesign] + [cmds]
PA-Aproc	[custaudit]	A-dbase	[redesign] + [custaudit]
PA-Aactive	[newtools]	A-Alma	[redesign] + [ccs]
PA-Aactive	[cmds]	A-Alma	[redesign] + [cmds]
PA-Aactive	[custaudit]	A-Alma	[redesign] + [custaudit]
PA-Aexec	[newtools]	A-extern	[guard]
PA-Aexec	[cmds]	A-meaning	[cmds]
PA-Aexec	[custaudit]	A-monitor	[cmds]
PA-Afiles	[newtools]	AV-admin	[decenter]
PA-Afiles	[cmds]	AV-prog	[ccs]
PA-Afiles	[custaudit]	AV-prog	[cmds]
PA-Aattack	[newtools]	AV-power	[ups]
PA-Aattack	[cmds]	AV-HWfail	[multilan] + [multiserver]
PA-Aattack	[custaudit]	AV-lanfail	[multilan] + [multiserver]
I-lan	[cmds]	AV-jam	[multilan] + [multiserver]
I-SW	[ccs]	F-distrib	[noTro] + [sectransit]
I-SW	[cmds] (weak)	F-install	[noTro] + [preconfig]
I-data	[ccs] (weak)	F-maint	[noTro] + [sectransit]

Protection Techniques and Their Costs

Protection	Initial cost	Unit cost	at 50 units
[ccs]	200,000	0	4,000
[cmds]	250,000	20,000	25,000
[custaudit] +	2,500,000	0	50,000
[decenter]	20,000	0	400
[e-diode] +	60,000	1,000	2,200
[embedccs] +	250,000	0	5,000
[field-proc]	0	5,000	5,000
[guard]	500,000	0	1,000
[guardHW] +	0	10,000	10,000
[mls]	0	2,000	2,000
[multilan]	20,000	2,000	2,400
[multiserver]	n/a	n/a	n/a
[newdoc]	50,000	200	1,200
[newman] +	50,000	200	1,200
[newprotocols] !	1,250,000	0	25,000
[newtools]	100,000	0	2,000
[newtrain]	40,000	5,000	5,800
[noTro]	n/a	n/a	n/a
[noise]	10,000	20,000	20,200
[p-diode] +	10,000	500	700
[perimeter] !	n/a	n/a	n/a
[preconfig]	n/a	n/a	n/a
[redesign]	1,500,000	0	30,000
[redoMLS] *	500,000	0	10,000
[replacements]	n/a	n/a	n/a
[sectransit]	n/a	n/a	n/a
[shield] *	10,000	40,000	40,200
[shield] +	10,000	150,000	150,200
[simptools] +	20,000	0	400
[training]	20,000	5,000	5,400
[ups]	n/a	n/a	n/a

Analysis Method

The chosen analysis technique is designed to find the minimum cost
covering for the vulnerabilities considered. This technique uses a covering table like the example depicted here (this sample depiction is not
accurate):

					Protection Technique	
Vulnerability	**Integrity**	**CMDS**	**Guard**	**Noise**	**Walls**	...
Downgrade Leakage	yes	no	yes	no	no	...
Upgrade Leakage	yes	no	no	no	no	...
Program Corruption	yes	yes	no	no	no	...
Network Corruption	no	yes	no	no	no	...
Tempest	no	no	no	yes	no	...
...	...	...	...	...	...	...

At least one "yes" is required in each row if we are to "cover" each
vulnerability with a protective technique. The following algorithm can
be used to derive a list of candidate covers:

1. If only one yes covers any given row, the technique in that column
   is required in order to cover the corresponding vulnerability. Select
   the column with that yes as "necessary." Since all rows covered
   by the necessary column are now covered, remove those rows
   from further consideration. In the preceding example, CMDS and
   Integrity checking are necessary because they are the only covers of
   Network Corruption and Upgrade Leakage, respectively. Tempest
   is also necessary to cover noise.
2. If there are columns left without a yes, remove them from the
   matrix. In this example, Guard is removed, since it provides no
   required coverage. We are now left with only trade-offs between
   competing techniques.
3. For each remaining technique, if any one technique both costs
   less than or the same as another technique, and covers everything
   the other technique covers, remove the more expensive technique.
   This selects in favor of techniques with equal or superior coverage
   and lower or equal costs.
4. For each remaining technique, select that technique, act as if it
   were necessary under the preceding criteria, and proceed through
   these steps until there is nothing left to cover. This process will
   generate a set of all possible minimum cost covers.

5. Add the costs of the list of items selected for each minimal cost cover, and select the cover with the lowest total cost. This will produce the lowest cost single cover.

The correctness of this technique will not be shown here, but it is very similar to covering problem solutions used in other fields and follows the same theoretical process.

MLS Implementation Protection Techniques and Their Costs

Protection	Initial Cost	Unit Cost	at 50 units
[ccs]	200,000	0	4,000
[cmds]	250,000	20,000	25,000
[decenter]	20,000	0	400
[field-proc]	0	5,000	5,000
[guard]	500,000	0	10,000
[mls]	0	2,000	2,000
[multilan]	20,000	2,000	2,400
[multiserver]	n/a	n/a	n/a
[newdoc]	50,000	200	1,200
[newtools]	100,000	0	2,000
[newtrain]	40,000	5,000	5,800
[noTro]	n/a	n/a	n/a
[noise]	10,000	20,000	20,200
[preconfig]	n/a	n/a	n/a
[redesign]	1,500,000	0	30,000
[redoMLS]	500,000	0	10,000
[replacements]	n/a	n/a	n/a
[sectransit]	n/a	n/a	n/a
[shield]	10,000	40,000	40,200
[training]	20,000	5,000	5,400
[ups]	n/a	n/a	n/a

Non-MLS Implementation Protection Techniques and Their Costs

Protection	Initial Cost	Unit Cost	at 50 units
[ccs]	200,000	0	4,000
[cmds]	250,000	20,000	25,000
[custaudit] *	2,500,000	0	50,000
[decenter]	20,000	0	400
[e-diode]	60,000	1,000	2,200
[embedccs]	250,000	0	5,000
[field-proc]	0	5,000	5,000
[guard]	500,000	0	10,000
[guardHW]	0	10,000	10,000
[mls]	0	2,000	2,000
[multilan]	20,000	2,000	2,400
[multiserver]	n/a	n/a	n/a
[newdoc]	50,000	200	1,200
[newman]	50,000	200	1,200
[newprotocols] !	1,250,000	0	25,000
[newtools]	100,000	0	2,000
[newtrain]	40,000	5,000	5,800
[noTro]	n/a	n/a	n/a
[noise]	10,000	20,000	20,200
[p-diode]	10,000	500	700
[perimeter] !	n/a	n/a	n/a
[preconfig]	n/a	n/a	n/a
[redesign]	1,500,000	0	30,000
[replacements]	n/a	n/a	n/a
[sectransit]	n/a	n/a	n/a
[shield]	10,000	150,000	150,200
[simptools]	20,000	0	400
[training]	20,000	5,000	5,400
[ups]	n/a	n/a	n/a

The covering table results The covering tables for MLS and non-MLS designs with and without shielding were generated from the Alma data previously described. These results are summarized by the following cost table:

Non-MLS Implementation Protection Techniques and Their Costs

Design Choice	Initial Cost	Unit Cost	ea.(1)	ea.(10)	ea.(50)
MLS w/shield	3,140,000	74,000	3,214,000	388,000	136,800
MLS w/o shield	4,390,000	54,000	4,444,000	493,000	141,800
Non-MLS w/shield	2,690,000	184,200	2,874,200	453,205	238,000
Non-MLS w/o shield	3,940,000	54,200	3,994,200	448,200	133,000

The key to understanding the tradeoffs for substantial numbers of Alma systems seems to lie in assessing two issues:

1. Is it worth forgoing the coverage of shielding for a savings of $3,000 per Alma? (This is the cost difference between the lowest cost nonshielded version of Alma with coverage and the lowest cost shielded version of Alma with coverage.)
2. Is the extra operating expense of running a system high (non-MLS) Alma more than the $3,000 saved on each Alma by using a nonshielded, non-MLS implementation?

It seems clear that the expense of running system high will greatly exceed $3,000 per system, and that the cost of shielding the classified portions of Alma is far less than the potential benefit in reducing attacks.

B.3   CASE STUDY 5: THE DOD AND THE NATION AS A WHOLE

Throughout the rest of this case study, the term *we* is used. In the original report, this referred to the information security organization within DISA for which this report analysis was performed, but in my opinion, the responsibility lies with all of us to assure that these things get done.

Information Assurance Is a Military Readiness Issue

We should strive to ensure that senior decision-makers come to understand that the assured availability and integrity of information are essential elements of U.S. military readiness and sustainability, so that they will provide adequate resources to meet this looming challenge.

Military capability is: "The ability to achieve a specified wartime objective (win a war or battle, destroy a target set). It includes four major components; force structure, modernization, readiness, and sustainability." [117]

a. force structure—Numbers, size, and composition of the units that comprise our Defense forces; e.g. divisions, ships, air wings.
b. modernization—Technical sophistication of forces, units, weapon systems, and equipment.
c. readiness—The ability of forces, units, weapons systems, or equipment to deliver the outputs for which they were designed (includes the ability to deploy and employ without unacceptable delays).
d. sustainability—The ability to maintain the necessary level and duration of operational activity to achieve military objectives.

Readiness assessment generally involves such factors as people authorized and on hand, their skills and training; operational status of equipment, the time to repair, degree of degradation; training status of units, recency of field exercises, command-post training; and other more detailed factors. In the age of information warfare, everyone in the military must recognize that the readiness status of forces, units, weapons systems, and equipment depends on the status of the information infrastructure. An assessment of readiness should include such questions as:

- Are there enough information workers and managers on hand?
- Are they properly trained in detecting and reacting to information attacks?
- How recently have they undergone defensive information warfare training?
- What is the readiness status of the information infrastructure?
- How much stress can the infrastructure take at this time?

Currently, the DoD appears unable to take comfort in the answers to these questions. Training programs to prepare information workers for the prevention of attack, detection of intentional attacks, differentiation of malicious from mischievous from accidental disruption, and the recovery steps to undertake do not exist. Worse, there is no analysis indicating how many people with what sorts of training and skills are required to operate successfully in an information warfare environment.

The DoD depends on the DII at least as much as it depends on its logistics structure for battle readiness, and yet the DoD does not treat them in the same light. The DoD must assess information assurance as a readiness issue. It must incorporate information infrastructure readiness into the overall military readiness assessment, and it must treat DII readiness as a component critical to overall battle readiness. A recent awareness campaign has had a substantial effect on the top levels of government; however, the awareness must be spread throughout the DoD in order to have lasting effect.

National Planning Should Reflect Information Age Warfare

> In any conflict against an information warfare opponent, the information infrastructure will take battle damage. Whether the war is military or economic, and whether the weapons are bombs or computer viruses, in order to continue as a nation under this sort of attack, the NII must automatically detect, differentiate, warn, respond, and recover from disruption.

There must be enough redundancy to meet bandwidth requirements during anticipated levels of disruption, sufficient firewalls to prevent disruption from spreading, sufficient mechanisms to make recovery and reconstitution of the NII feasible in an appropriate time frame, and sufficient training and support to allow that reconstitution to safely take place. In order to meet budget constraints, we must find ways to do this at a tolerable cost.

It is not reasonable to expect that technicians will be able to detect, differentiate, warn, respond, and devise work-arounds for each attack in real-time, and in the case of remote components, they may be unable to gain access to do these things at reasonable cost. For this reason, the designers of the NII must devise mechanisms that are as nearly automatic as feasible, and have built-in resiliency that, at a minimum, puts these mechanisms into known and controllable state sequences when they become ineffective over a period of time. This is very similar to the requirements on remote space exploration vehicles, except that the NII must be designed to behave in this fashion, even during hostile attack and at a far lower cost.

We must retain flexibility In order to spend money wisely and still be properly prepared, the NII must retain flexibility to adjust to changes in direction and applications over the next 20 years. Compare U.S. war fighting in 1975 to 1995. Predicting 2015 is not a simple matter. Compare business computing over the same time frame. Rather than trying to make a 20-year prediction and hinging enormous amounts of money on being right, we should use designs that ensure an NII capability that is flexible enough to adapt with the times. Fortunately, information systems are easily made flexible, but unfortunately, that flexibility leads to vulnerability to disruption. The designers of the NII must devise information assurance techniques that allow flexibility without increasing vulnerability.

Information assurance policies and standards are needed Most current information protection policies include requirements for availability and integrity, but these features are always mentioned along with secrecy. When this policy is translated into implementation, the information assurance elements are usually ignored. An example of this is the recent draft versions of the Defense Information Systems Network (DISN) specification. The top-level goals include almost equal emphasis of these three elements of information assurance, [66] but in the design process, there is often a deemphasis of information assurance and an emphasis on secrecy. [67] There seem to be two reasons for this, and top-level attention is required in order to resolve them:

- Information assurance is usually brought up in conjunction with protection of classified information. Even though these areas are distinctly different, they are specified, discussed, and addressed together.

  In order to assure that information assurance is adequately addressed, policy makers should separate the information assurance requirements from the secrecy requirements, and make it explicit in policy documents that they are separate and different.
- There are no information assurance standards explicitly referenced in top-level specifications. When specifications are translated into implementations, standards influence a large part of the design process. Standards are commonly viewed as checklists that have to be met. Where no standards are specified, there is no checklist, and thus no features are implemented.

  To assure that information assurance is properly and consistently practiced, we should develop a set of information assurance standards for the NII that address disruption.

We should engage on a program of education to ensure that the top-level technical managers responsible for designing and operating the NII understand the issues of infrastructure design as opposed to typical system design and can help make design decisions that will satisfy the changing requirements over the lifetime of the infrastructure.

We Should Address Current Weaknesses

In order to transition existing systems into the NII while providing appropriate information assurance, we must first understand the weaknesses of existing systems, and then find ways to provide these systems with the information assurance features required in order to operate in the NII environment.

A key step in this process is performing a threat assessment which can be used as a baseline for vulnerability analysis. If properly done, such a threat assessment will bring to light a variety of new threats and threat sources that have not historically been considered.

Once the threat assessment is completed, vulnerability analysis of the most common classes of systems can begin in order to create baseline vulnerability assessments of the major classes of systems without performing an expensive and unnecessary exhaustive analysis of each system on a piecemeal basis.

While vulnerability analysis is underway, mathematical life-cycle cost and coverage analyses of potential defensive measures against identified threats in different classes of environments can be performed. As vulnerability assessments become available, the results of these assessments can be used in conjunction with defensive measure analysis to identify minimum cost protective measures required to cover identified threats.

As threats, vulnerabilities, and defensive measures are made available to program managers, they can make risk management decisions and implement appropriate controls in keeping with budget and other constraints.

Technical vulnerability should be assessed NII planners should undertake a substantial study of existing and planned NII components in order to understand their vulnerabilities to offensive information warfare and determine appropriate actions to provide information assurance during the interim period before the NII and enhanced components are fully developed. Specifically:

- Perform disruption-oriented assessments to identify potential vulnerability.
- Perform safe and authorized experiments to more precisely assess the extent to which accidental and intentional disruption has been addressed in the NII components in place today.
- Analyze the overall NII in conjunction with these analytical and experimental results to assess overall NII vulnerability to disruption today.
- Determine methods by which existing and proposed NII components can or should be cost effectively upgraded or replaced over time to provide enhanced information assurance for the NII.

There are some limited but proven scientific theories about vulnerability to intentional disruption, [44, 43] and these theories can be used to form hypotheses about potential information assurance problems. From these hypotheses, the government and key industry members should sponsor the development of experiments to confirm or refute the existence of actual vulnerabilities, provide immediate awareness of their existence to information assurance personnel, and form approaches to removing or reducing their impact on the NII.

Something that should be clear from the start is that it will be infeasible to analyze software in most existing systems for potential vulnerabilities. The DoD alone has more than 500 million lines of customized software in operation today, and the vast majority of it has never been examined for information assurance properties. With that much unexamined software, it is prudent to assume that malicious logic weapons have been implanted.

One way to enhance assurance in networked systems at a very low cost is to provide an external misuse detection capability at the network level. These sorts of enhancements can provide substantial protection improvement at minimal cost, remain flexible enough to be adapted as the NII expands, and can provide a backbone for long-term automated detection and response. Such systems exist today and anyone with a substantial network should consider using them. [72, 137, 136, 105, 176]

In the course of assessment, improved procedures, standards, and documents should be generated to capture and disseminate the limited expertise currently available in this field. A mentor program might also be used to develop more expertise in this area.

Human vulnerability should be addressed According to one recent report, [80] the root cause of 30 to 40 percent of failures in digital cross connect systems is human procedural errors and this is the cause of more disruption than any other single source. Many industry studies show similar results for other classes of information systems and networks. One report claimed that more than 80 percent of reported intrusions could have been prevented by human procedures. [17] Another author posted to the *risks* forum that the lack of information from the current computer emergency response team (CERT) caused numerous disruptions to take place and kept them from being prevented, detected, and corrected. [181]

"High reliability organizations are defined as high-risk organizations designed and managed to avoid catastrophic accidents. The organization is high-risk due to the high complexity of the technology. Examples include air traffic control and nuclear reactors. ... increasing numbers of serious errors will occur in high-reliability organizations, ... data is lacking on ways to avoid exceeding human capacity limits, and ... design and management strategies to allow safe operation are not understood. ... These organizations have several distinguishing characteristics in common: hypercomplexity; tight coupling of processes; extreme hierarchical differentiation; large numbers of decision makers in complex communication networks (law of requisite variety is cited); higher degree of accountability; high frequency of immediate feedback about decisions; compressed time factors measured in seconds; more than one critical outcome that must happen simultaneously." Another study is cited to show that designers are often unaware of the human limits to operating such systems. "However, as Perrow points out ... Designers tend to believe that automatic controls reduce the need for operator intervention and errors, while operators frequently override or ignore such controls due to the constraints ... ". [183]

We have to assure the resolution of the role of human components of information assurance to properly protect the NII. There are generally three strategies for improving this situation:

- Automate more human functions
- Improve human performance
- Use redundancy for integrity

It is generally beneficial to automate functions for enhanced reliability whenever automation enhances performance, reduces cost, or provides other desired benefits. Unfortunately, while we spend a lot of money on enhancing automation for other tasks, one of the areas where automation is severely lacking is protection management. A simple example is the lack of administrative tools in most timesharing computer systems. Systems administrators are expected to keep systems operating properly, and yet:

- There are typically millions of protection bits that have to be set properly to prevent disruption and there are virtually no effective or supported tools to help set, validate, verify, or correct them. [43]
- The DoD requires systems administrators of many systems to examine audit trails daily for signs of abuse, but it is virtually impossible for people to detect intentional disruption by this process, and the time and effort consumed in this activity is quite substantial. [2] According to one report, audit records for a system with seven users executing an average of one command per minute over a period of six hours results in 75 Mbytes of audit data! [176]
- Current audit analysis requirements don't require real-time analysis or response. Even automated audit reduction tools are inadequate in today's environment if they cannot act in near real-time, because disruptions can spread through a network at a very high rate unless response times are very short. For example, one AT&T switching system will disrupt the local central office unless failures are detected and responded to within 1.5 seconds of their occurrence. [165]
- Local area network administration tools are just now emerging, and the few tools that are commercially available open unlimited opportunity for intentional disruption. Some of the most powerful tools for network analysis are available for free and allow even an unsophisticated user to observe network packets. In many current local area networks (LANs), this allows passwords to be observed as they are entered.

"Research has shown that performance of certain types of control room tasks increases if the operator has some knowledge of the functioning of the process." [116]

Improving human performance is most often tied to motivation, training, and education, and again, there is woefully little of this in the information assurance area. Educational institutions do not currently provide the necessary background to make training easy, [44] and existing training programs in information assurance are not widely incorporated in the military or industry. These areas must be addressed if we are to provide information assurance for the NII.

Real-time Prioritization Should Be Addressed

In order for the NII to react properly to malicious disruption, it must be able to prevent disruptions where possible, and detect and respond appropriately to disruptions when prevention is not possible. In plain terms, the operators of the NII must be able to manage the damage. During periods of substantial disruption, there are likely to be more tasks to perform than bandwidth available to perform them. In an economic model of a high demand, low supply situation, the value of services naturally increases and usage decisions change to reflect the relative values.

It would be prudent to create an analogy to this economic theory for NII priorities so that the network manager can design a priority assessment and assurance scheme so that the value of information passed through the degraded NII is higher per bit than that passing though the non-degraded NII. Someone needs to specify metrics for, assess value of, and assign priority to information as a function of value at that time and the NII must use these metrics to prioritize its behavior. A sound start in this area could be achieved by developing a national version of the commercially oriented *Guideline for Information Valuation*. [113]

If the priority assessment scheme is not a fully automatic process, the NII may have a profound problem in reacting in a timely fashion. The first problem is that if people have to react, they are inherently limited in their reaction time. If the attack is automated, and peoples' reaction times limit the defense, it may be possible to design attacks that vary at a rate exceeding the human ability to respond. A knowledgeable attacker who understands reflexive control may exploit this to create further disruption by misleading the people into reflexive response, and exploiting those responses to further the attack. [95] A fully automatic response may have similar reflexive control problems except that it is potentially more predictable and normally far faster. This is where design flexibility must also come into play.

Priorities should be properly addressed over time and circumstance In- formation assurance issues must be flexibly prioritized and adapted as needed in order for the NII to behave properly over the range of oper- ating and disrupted conditions. The metrics associated with information should be evaluated differently in different situations and should include such factors as time, value, criticality, locality, and redundancy. Each of these values should have an effect on the manner in which the NII prior- itizes activities, while each should be controlled by different mechanisms to assure that an attacker cannot circumvent a single mechanism and exploit this to dominate activities.

Even in the most dire of circumstances, unconditional pre-emption should not be the method of choice for prioritizing scarce services. The problem is that pre-emption results in service denial for the pre-empted and, if the assessment of priorities is not accurate, it may be highly desirable to apply some, albeit reduced, bandwidth toward all legitimate needs. It would be preferable to have a scheme whereby higher priorities have a higher probability of domination of resources at any given time, but over any significant period of time, even the lowest priority process has a reasonable expectation of some limited service. This concept is often called "graceful degradation."

Criticality of function should be properly addressed A more fundamental issue that must be resolved is how to prioritize between the basic information assurance measures. If it is better to have wrong information than no information, then availability is more important than integrity. If it better to have no information than wrong information, then integrity is more important than availability. The former appears to be the case from a standpoint of infrastructure recovery, where even low-integrity information may assist in service restoration. The latter appears to be more appropriate when making strategic or tactical decisions where a decision based on corrupt information can be fatal.

In most modern databases, it is a simple matter to make undetected modifications. Whereas an outage would be noticed and cause a response and modern database techniques detect inconsistencies in a database, there is no protection provided in most modern databases for erroneous data entered through the legitimate database mechanism or malicious modification by a knowledgeable attacker.

> Subtle corruptions typically produce a different sort of failure, such as a missile defense system detecting hostile missiles as friendly or an airplane flipping upside down as it enters the southern hemisphere. [181]

In DoD logistics, command and control, and medical databases, such an error can not only be fatal, but can cause the DoD's automated information systems to be used as a weapon against it. In the national power grid, such a failure could literally wipe out electrical service throughout the country.

Priorities should interact properly across components Prioritization in the NII will involve both communication and computation, and the prioritization schemes must meld together in a suitable fashion across these boundaries. Furthermore, many of the computation components of NII will not be under the operational control of the network managers. For example, embedded systems interacting with the NII will have to interact in specific ways in order to assure that no mismatch occurs. The NII will have to be able to deal effectively with intentional mismatches created to disrupt interaction between communication and computation resources.

Most current network protection strategies are based on the concept that all of the systems in the network behave properly and many local area network protocols are based on well-behaved hardware devices and software products in all of the nodes. When connecting these networks to global systems, imperfectly matched protocols or processes can snowball causing widespread disruption. The priority assessment scheme must not be based on trusting the network components and must be designed to detect and react properly to limit the spread of network-wide disruptions, regardless of their specific characteristics. There are some theories for addressing protocol inconsistencies, but new basic understandings are needed at the process and infrastructure levels. We must promulgate standards that provide assurance based on the assumption of malicious components, and not based solely on lists of known attacks.

We Should Train for Defensive Information Warfare

Information workers cannot be expected to react properly under stress unless they are properly prepared for defensive information warfare. This involves several key actions by those who manage components of the NII:

- NII components must act together to develop proper policies and procedures, to define specific defensive information warfare tasks to be carried out, and to specify the manner in which they are to be performed.
- NII components must train information workers in how to properly carry out their duties under stress, so that they are able to efficiently carry them out as required under *battle* conditions.
- NII components must hold readiness drills and regular exercises so that the skills developed and honed in training do not decay with time.
- NII components should hold *war games* in order to determine weaknesses in strategies and improve them over time.

In the long term, education and training for defensive information warfare must rest upon a well-conceived, articulated, implemented, and tested body of strategy, doctrine, tactics, techniques, and procedures. In turn, this body of knowledge must be based, in large measure, on a fairly detailed knowledge of the offensive capabilities available to potential adversaries and the nature of possible attacks on the information infrastructure. In the short term, however, there are several actions that should be undertaken to mitigate disruptions of the information infrastructure.

As a first priority, everyone associated with the operation, management, and maintenance of the NII should become familiar with the concept of information assurance and the nature of likely disruptions, and should undergo regular training and awareness drills to reenforce this training. Primary emphasis should be given to proper prevention, detection, differentiation, warning, response, recovery, analysis, and improvement.

The operators of the elements of the NII must be trained to consider, as a matter of course, the possibility that there are hostile disruptions being undertaken and that nobody, other than the attacker, is aware of them. Without awareness, advanced training, and education, the human elements of the NII are unlikely to be able to detect attacks unless and until advanced technology-based warning enhancements are implemented. Even then, awareness, advanced training, and education play a vital role in installing, maintaining, and using the automation.

As a second priority, training and awareness should be given to NII users. While this training may be more narrow in scope, it is essential that the users of the NII be aware of the information assurance issues, how their function can be impacted by NII disruption, what they should do to avoid causing disruption, and what they should do in the event of disruption.

Extensive use of simulation capabilities is called for in training individuals and groups. This training should be reinforced through the conduct of frequent readiness drills and exercises. These drills and exercises may initially be conducted as standalone events, but must eventually be integrated into the day-to-day operations of the NII components.

Information assurance should become part of the curricula of technical and professional courses of instruction offered throughout the nation. Information assurance should be embedded in all courses related to information systems, sciences, and management, and courses concentrating on information assurance should be offered as a part of the required curriculum for students concentrating on computer or information science or engineering.

Bibliography

[1] *2600. The Hacker Quarterly* 10, no. 2 (Summer 1992). Middle Island, N.Y. [This quarterly magazine has provided technical details on vulnerabilities of information systems for more than 10 years. It commonly publishes technical details extracted from technical support manuals and details how the features can be used to defeat protection.]

[2] DoD Directive 5200.28. "Security Requirements for Automatic Data Processing (ADP) Systems." [This specification details the DoD requirements for security in information systems.]

[3] Anonymous. Central Intelligence Agency, [Accused double agent Aldrich Ames may have sold information about the Clinton administration's Clipper initiative to the Russians, a development that could doom the controversial scheme to deliver low-cost encryption via a government-developed chip.]

[4] "Army Enterprise Strategy: The Vision," April 1993. [This strategic planning document describes the U.S. Army's approach to integrating information systems for reduced cost and increased efficiency.]

[5] AP Online "AP 07/21 01:17 EDT V0289" (July 21, 1994). [In this short article, some details of the results of attacks against DoD computers are described, including quotes from the head of computer security for the Defense Information Systems Agency.]

[6] Associated Press. "Strike Bares Just-in-time Fatal Flaw" (August 27, 1994). [This article briefly describes the impact of the three-day strike and its implication toward just-in-time delivery systems.]

[7] M.D. Abrams. "Observations on Local Area Network Security," *Computer and Network Security*. IEEE, 1985. ["For a commercial LAN Network Interface Unit, the trust is based on commercial practices. This should not make us exceptionally confident, for our experience probably indicates that many commercial products are released following the implicit decision that the customer will detect some latent errors."]

[8] M. Alexander. "Computing Infosecurity's Top 10 Events." *Infosecurity News* (September/October 1993). [This article describes 10 catastrophic events that the author believes demonstrate the degree to which the nation's information infrastructure is vulnerable.]

[9] M. Alexander. "Industrial Espionage with U.S. Runs Rampant." *Computerworld* (March 4, 1991):64. [The FBI head of foreign counterintelligence is quoted that French DGSE tried to hire employees to furnish research data from IBM, TI, and others.]

[10] Sir Peter Anson and Dennis Cummings. *The First Information War.* 125. "The First Space War: The Contribution of Satellites to the Gulf War." [This article details how satellites were used by the allied forces in the Gulf War.]

[11] John Arquilla and David Ronfeldt. "Cyberwar is Coming!" *Comparative Strategy* 12:141–165. [This paper describes some of the issues related to military operations in the increasingly information-intensive environment.]

[12] "Ground Wave Emergency Network Should Be Operational Next Spring." *Aviation Week & Space Technology* (July 16, 1990):78–79. [GWEN is the only strategic defense communications system hardened to survive a high-altitude electromagnetic pulse (HEMP).]

[13] "Business Flying." *Aviation Week & Space Technology* (October 2, 1989):85. [FAA measurements at one U.S. high-density airport peaked at 14,000 volts per meter from surveillance and satellite tracking radars. The FAA set a 200 v/meter no adverse effects limit for one aircraft, partly due to rapid movement of both aircraft and radar beam.]

[14] "BOC Notes on the LEC Networks—1990." SR-TSV-002275. March 1991 (Issue 1). Bellcore.

[15] N.V. Bakhmet'yeva, Yu.A. Ignat'yev, S.A. Dmitriyev, P.B. Shabin, "Observations of the back-scattering of radio waves from an artificially disturbed region at a frequency of 1.68 MHz." *Geomagnetism and Aeronomy* 32, no. 3:464–65. [Results of observations are cited of the back-scattered signals at 1.68 MHz from artificial ionosphere inhomogeneities produced in the F region of the ionosphere by the action of powerful radio radiation. The scattered signals were observed from a height of 100 to 130 km below the reflection level of the powerful radio waves. The appearance of inhomogeneities at these heights is associated with the heating of the ionosphere along the lines of force of the geomagnetic field.]

[16] Melinda-Carol Ballou. "Survey Pegs Computer Downtime Costs at $4 Billion." *Computerworld* (August 10, 1992):53. [This is one of many surveys done in an attempt to understand the financial impact of information system disruption. It does not 'peg' the value, but it gives some good information which can be used as a starting point.]

[17] Bellcore. "Unix Security Awareness Alert." Bellcore Technical Education JobAid. (May 1990). [This is one of an increasing number of security awareness alerts published by information providers.]

[18] S.M. Bellovin. "Security Problems in the TCP/IP Protocol Suite." ACM SIG-COMM. *Computer Communications Review* (April 1989):32–48. [According to R. Ramaswamy, this paper covers sequence number attacks, source address attacks, routing attacks, network management attacks, and authentication attacks.]

[19] S.M. Bellovin. "There Be Dragons." *Proceedings of the Third Usenix UNIX Security Symposium.* Baltimore (September 1992). [In this paper, numerous

foiled attacks from the Internet against AT&T are described and the author details how some of these are traced and what is done about them.]

[20] D. E. Bell and L. J. LaPadula. "Secure Computer Systems: Mathematical Foundations and Model." The Mitre Corporation, 1973 (cited in many papers). [This was the classic paper in which Bell and LaPadula described a model for maintaining secrecy in timesharing computer systems.]

[21] Joanna Smith Bers. "Telecom and Network Security: Sealing Up the Leaks." *Facilities and Design Management* 13, no. 4 (April 1994):42–45. [FBI and AT&T figures are cited as examples of the extent of the telecommunications security problem today.]

[22] K. J. Biba. "Integrity Considerations for Secure Computer Systems." USAF Electronic Systems Division, 1977. [In this paper, the dual of the Bell-LaPadula model is used to achieve integrity levels in a computer system for the first time.]

[23] Barry W. Boehm. "Software Engineering Economics." Prentice-Hall, 1981.

[24] Scott A. Boorman and Dr. Paul R. Levitt. "Software Warfare and Algorithm Sabotage." *Signal* (May 1988).

[25] N.D.Borisov, L.M. Gorbunov, A.V. Gurevich, and A.B. Romanov. "Generation of Low-frequency Emission by Powerful HF Radio Waves in the Earth's Ionosphere." Inst. of Terrestrial Magnetism, Ionosphere & Radio Wave Propagation. Troitsk, Russia, *Physics Letters A* 177, no. 3:241–47 [The authors discuss artificial low-frequency emission generated via a decay process during the heating of the ionosphere by HF electromagnetic waves. The spectral characteristics of the emission and its intensity are found.]

[26] *The Bottom Up Review of the U.S. DoD*, 1993. [This was a major internal review of the U.S. military which was used to determine appropriate downsizing requirements in the Gulf War environment.]

[27] R. Brewer. "Design Tips for EMI Shielding." *Machine Design* (March 23, 1989):85–88. [This paper explains the difficulty in deciding whether enough shielding has been used and mentions that ElectroMagnetic Interference (EMI) was suspected in Army Blackhawk helicopter crashes because the Navy version has more shielding and fewer crashes. A graph is used to show shielding effectiveness versus frequency for electrical and magnetic fields using two different materials.]

[28] Bob Brewin and Elizabeth Sikorovsky. "Hackers Storm DoD Nets." *Federal Computer Week* 8, no. 18, [Dept of Defense (DoD) networks are under daily attack by hackers who are gaining control of hundreds of unclassified, but sensitive, systems . . . including those of the Joint Chiefs of Staff, the Navy, the Defense Logistics Agency, and the Air Force's Rome Laboratory.]

[29] E. M. Brodie. "CIA Chief is Accused of Being a Spy." (February 23, 1994). *New York Times*. [This article broke the story of the Ames case.]

[30] Ralf Burger. "Computer Viruses—A High Tech Disease." *Abacus*. 1988. [This book details how computer viruses work and provides source code which can be used to implement simple viruses. Many security pundits have claimed that this book is partially responsible for many of the viruses in the world today.]

[31] CJCS MOP 30, "Command and Control Warfare." March 8, 1993. [This document describes the doctrine of Command and Control Warfare used by the U.S. DoD. This doctrine basically calls for the use of information as a replacement for force by emphasizing speed and agility in offensive operations and intelligence, disruption, and deception for defensive operations.]

[32] D.E. Campbell. "The Intelligent Threat." *Security Management*, Special Section 33 no. 3 (March 1989):19A–22A. [The author describes incidents and threats for computer exploitation for a variety of motives other than innocent hacker exploration. Among other incidents recounted are: the 1970 bomb at the Army Mathematics Research Center, University of Wisconsin, resulting in one death and several damaged computers, attributed to antiwar activists; four attempts to damage the computer center at Wright-Patterson Air Force Base; a 1969 attack on a chemical company computer center in Midland, MI by five members of Beaver 55, which damaged 1000 tapes with small magnets as an antiwar protest; the Earth First environmental group's publication called *Ecodefense: A Field Guide to Monkeywrenching*, 2nd ed., pages 213 to 218 discussing computer sabotage through hardware and media destruction, stored information disclosure, and use of logic bombs.]

[33] Alan D. Campen, ed. *The First Information War*. AFCEA International Press, 1992. [This book consists of a series of papers describing in some detail how the Gulf War was fought from an information infrastructure standpoint.]

[34] Bill Cheswick. "An Evening with Berferd in which a Cracker Is Lured, Endured, and Studied." AT&T Bell Laboratories. [In this paper, a secure gateway at AT&T is used to observe and forge responses to an attacker and to gather data on the techniques used to try to break into AT&T from the Internet.]

[35] Bill Cheswick and S.M. Bellovin. "Firewalls and Internet Security—Repelling the Wiley Hacker." Addison-Wesley, 1994. [This book is one of the most authoritative sources of information on network firewalls. It includes many details of attack and defense techniques as well as case studies of attacks against AT&T.]

[36] Seyhan Civanlar and Bharat T. Doshi. "Self-Healing in Wideband Packet Networks." *IEEE Network Magazine* (January 1990).

[37] D. Clark and D. Wilson. "A Comparison of Commercial and Military Computer Security Policies." *Proceedings IEEE Symposium on Security and Privacy*. Oakland, CA (April 1987):184–194. [This paper describes the substantial difference between historical requirements for military secrecy and commercial requirements for information system integrity and availability.]

[38] Teresa Cochran and Joseph M. Mellichamp, "AUTORED: An Automated Error Recovery System for Network Management." *IEEE Network Magazine* (March 1990). [This paper describes one mechanism for automating fault detection and recovery for network management.]

[39] F. Cohen. *It's Alive*. New York: John Wiley, 1994. [This book describes the impacts of reproducing programs on the current and future computing environment and introduces many potential positive and negative effects of this technology.]

[40] F. Cohen and S. Mishra, "Experiments on the Impact of Computer Viruses on Modern Computer Networks," IFIP-TC11 *Computers and Security*, 1993. [In

this paper, a series of experiments on the effectiveness of computer security capabilities in modern UNIX and Novell computer networks are described. The results showed that only very specific protection settings were effective and that protection settings are not what the normal systems administrator might think they are. It also pointed out several major protection flaws in current networking technology.]

[41] F. Cohen. "Information Warfare Considerations." SAIC's Strategic Assessment Center under a contract for OSD/Net Assessment's study on Information Warfare. [This paper outlines some expectations for information warfare over the next 20 years.]

[42] Many administrators have found and reported examples of this, and some unpublished experiments by F. Cohen and S. Mishra at Queensland University of Technology, Brisbane, Australia, in 1992, confirmed these results.

[43] F. Cohen. "A Short Course on Systems Administration and Security Under Unix." ASP Press, 1991. [This short course details many methods of attacking UNIX-based systems, and details the management functions required to deal with these attacks.]

[44] F. Cohen. *A Short Course on Computer Viruses*, 2nd ed. New York: John Wiley, 1994. [This is widely considered one of the most comprehensive books on computer virus attacks and defenses, and it details most of the current state-of-the-art in this field.]

[45] F. Cohen. "A Cost Analysis of Typical Computer Viruses and Defenses." IFIP-TC-11. *Computers and Security.* 1991. [This paper provides a detailed cost analysis of the financial impact of certain classes of defense against computer viruses. One of the major results is that in many cases, the defense costs more than the attacks it is designed to defend against.]

[46] F. Cohen. "Computer Viruses—Theory and Experiments." IFIP-TC11 Conference. Toronto, 1984. [This is the most famous paper on computer viruses and forms the basis for most of the current understanding of that field.]

[47] F. Cohen. "Computer Viruses." Ph.D. diss. University of Southern California, 1985. ASP Press. [This is the most comprehensive theoretical coverage of the topic of computer viruses.]

[48] F. Cohen. "Design and Administration of Distributed and Hierarchical Information Networks under Partial Orderings." IFIP-TC11 *Computers and Security* 6(1987). [This paper describes how integrity and confidentiality can both be maintained in modern information networks by extending results previously applied only to individual systems.]

[49] F. Cohen. "Protection and Administration of Information Networks under Partial Orderings." IFIP-TC11 *Computers and Security* 6(1987):118–128. [This paper describes how integrity and confidentiality can both be maintained in modern information systems.]

[50] B. Cohen and F. Cohen. "Error Prevention at a Radon Measurement Service Laboratory." *Radiation Protection Management* 6 no. 1 (January 1989):43–47. [In this study, redundancy in automated and human-entered data was exploited to verify the integrity of medical measurements.]

[51] Some unpublished results of a small study by F. Cohen, 1993. [Many experiments with the integrity, confidentiality, and availability properties of modern computer networks were performed without publication in early 1993 by Dr. Cohen and other researchers. These results were not previously published.]

[52] F. Cohen. "Models of Practical Defenses against Computer Viruses." *Computers and Security* 8:149–160. [This paper models and analyzes various computer virus defense techniques and shows a technique which is optimal from the standpoint of the protection that can be provided by a general purpose automated system and the amount of time required for such a mechanism to operate. This is the basis for modern integrity shell and virus monitor technologies.]

[53] F. Cohen. *A Short Course on Information Protection in Personal Computers and Local Area Networks.* ASP Press, 1991:28–30. [Discusses unauthorized packets, leakage, corruption, disruption, electromagnetic disturbances, forgery.]

[54] Rebecca Cox. "Wire Fraud on Rise Despite Efforts to Control It." *American Banker* 154, no. 236 (December 5, 1989):3. [FBI figures on reported banking losses due to fraudulent wire transfers over the 18 months ending in December of 1989 exceeded $300 million in the New York region alone. Most of the crimes were perpetrated by insiders.]

[55] Myron L. Cramer and Stephen R. Pratt. "Computer Virus Countermeasures— A New Type of Electronic Warfare." *Defense Electronics* (October, 1989). [This article describes how computer viruses are becoming military weapons in the age of information warfare.]

[56] Martin van Creveld. *The Transformation of War.* Free Press, 1991.

[57] Martin van Creveld. *Technology and War.* Macmillan, 1991. (revised and expanded from 1989)

[58] Barton Crockett. "Manhattan Blackout Cripples User Nets." *Network World* (August 20, 1990):1. [This article describes how a blackout in Manhattan affected information systems and networks.]

[59] DoD Directive TS3600.1. "Information Warfare (U)." (unclassified extract), December 21, 1992 [This is a DoD directive which directs the use of information warfare techniques and defines the responsibilities of various agencies and departments of the DoD for the various aspects of this activity.]

[60] DISA. "Instruction 630-230-19, Security Requirements for Automated Information Systems (AIS)" (August, 1991). [This document specifies the security requirements for automated information systems in the DoD. It is particularly important to know that the vast majority of the specification lacks any specific requirement.]

[61] DISA. *Draft Specification/Statement of Work for the Integrated Network Management Systems (INMS) Program.* August 31, 1992.

[62] DISA. *The Defense Information Infrastructure Architectural Guidance.* Draft. February 1, 1993. [This document describes the architecture for the objective Defense Information Infrastructure, about 85 percent of which is the National Information Infrastructure.]

[63] F. Cohen, et al. "Planning Considerations for Defensive Information Warfare—Information Assurance." Task Order 90-SAIC-019, DoD Contract No. DCA 100-90-C-0058. November 1993. [This document describes what is necessary from a planning perspective for the United States to establish protection for the Defense Information Infrastructure over the next 20 years. It concentrates on issues of disruption and points out the fundamental points of this book in a very precise and concise manner.]

[64] DISA, DISN, and DISN Switched Services (DSS). Request for Information (RFI). February 12, 1992.

[65] "Defense Information System Network (DISN) Architecture." Final Coordination Draft. May 12, 1993. [This document describes the architecture for the DoD's information networks as they exist today.]

[66] DISA. "DISN Concept of Operations." Coordinating Draft. August 2, 1993.

[67] DISA. "DISN Security Policy." Draft. March 18, 1993.

[68] Defense Management Report Decision 918. "Defense Information Infrastructure." September 1992. [This DoD directive specifies responsibilities for protection of the Defense Information Infrastructure.]

[69] "Secure Networks." *Proceedings of the Fifth International Computer Virus and Security Conference.* March 1993. [This book is a collection of papers presented at a 1993 conference concentrating on computer virus defenses.]

[70] R. Lefkon, ed. *Data Processing Management Association Annual Computer Virus and Security Conference.* New York, 1992. [This book is a collection of papers presented at a 1992 conference concentrating on computer virus defenses.]

[71] D. E. Denning. *Cryptography and Data Security.* Addison-Wesley, 1982. [This is a very good graduate text on computer security covering most of the important issues prior to computer viruses.]

[72] D. E. Denning. "An Intrusion-Detection Model." IEEE CH2292. [This paper describes issues in automated intrusion detection as a method to detect Trojan horses, computer viruses, and other similar attacks against information systems and networks. It is one of the earliest works in this area.]

[73] D. E. Denning. "The Lattice Model of Secure Information Flow" CACM 19, no. 5 (May 1976):236–43.

[74] Peter F. Drucker. *Post-Capitalist Society. Harper Business,* 1993.

[75] T. Duff. "Viral Attacks on UNIX System Security," Proceedings: Fifth International Computer Virus and Security Conference, March 1992. Abstract only; paper available to participants. [This paper described the distribution of viruses in network automatic software distribution and their reappearance almost a year later, probably from write-only backup storage.]

[76] R. Ernest Dupuy and Trevor N. Dupuy. *The Encyclopedia of Military History.* Harper and Row, 1970: p.1021, doctrine, p.1093, Schweinfurt Raid. [This encyclopedia provides a great deal of detail on the history of military endeavor on Earth.]

[77] Bernard J. Eastlund. "Method and Apparatus for Altering a Region in the Earth's Atmosphere, Ionosphere, and/or Magnetosphere." U.S. Patent 4,686,605, 1987. [This patent describes methods for using high frequency ra-

dio signals, which might be powered with the use of a 42,000 lb. air-mobile MHD generator, to disrupt microwave satellite communications as well as other land-, air-, and sea-based communications.]

[78] Marcus Eliason. "The Sky's the Limit." Associated Press. August 11, 1994. [This article describes the launch of a Chinese communications satellite within 1 degree of two other satellites without permission from international bodies. The satellite is expected to interfere with communications throughout Southeast Asia and is already starting to become a political issue between countries.]

[79] J. Epstein and J. Picciotto. "Trusting X: Issues in Building Trusted X Window Systems—OR—What's not Trusted about X?" Proceedings of the 14th National Computer Security Conference. October 1991:619–629. [States that "... X was explicitly designed to avoid enforcing any policies and, in fact, provides many mechanisms that tend to promote the sharing of data and resources among X applications." Discusses problems with many security issues, including distributed applications, channels between clients, auditing, secure networking, and stating, "It is probably impossible to build a system which bears any resemblance to X that cannot be successfully subjected to denial of service attacks."]

[80] "Network Reliability: A Report to the Nation." *Compendium of Technical Papers.* FCC's Network Reliability Council. June 1993. [This National Research Council report details many of the widely known incidents of network disruption, their causes, and how they are being addressed today. No discussion of malicious disruption is included, and only probabilistic approaches to software errors and omissions are included.]

[81] "FCC Preliminary Report on Network Outages." Common Carrier Bureau. July 1991. [This FCC report describes common carrier network outages and their causes.]

[82] "... FROM THE SEA: Preparing the Naval Service for the 21st Century." September 1992. [This is the Navy's doctrine statement regarding information warfare. It views the information environment as an "infosphere" which is essentially a parallel world to the geosphere.]

[83] G. Faden. "Reconciling CMW Requirements with Those of X11 Applications." Proceedings of the 14th National Computer Security Conference. October 1991:472–478. [Discusses changes made to Sun X Window System to improve security. Concludes, "While there are quite a few additional considerations for applying security to the X protocol, the issues discussed here are representative of the general solution."]

[84] W. Falconer. "Service Assurance in Modern Telecommunications Networks." *IEEE Communications Magazine* (June 1990). [This paper discusses issues in service assurance and the lack of assurance in modern information networks. It is clear from this paper that the statistical methods used to assert availability estimates are fundamentally flawed.]

[85] Dan Farmer and Wietse Venema. "Improving the Security of Your Site by Breaking into It." *The Administrator's Guide to Cracking—101* (available online over the Internet). [This paper details very explicitly how attacks are

carried out, including detailed instructions on how to carry out these attacks on current networks and descriptions of some automated attack tools.]

[86] P. Fellows. "Re: 'Gulf War Virus.'" *RISKS Digest* 13.08 (January 26, 1992). [This on-line article discusses the fact that many SCSI devices, including printers, can change from Target to Initiator mode, seek and write to the boot disk or other disk; and that some SCSI devices can have their firmware downloaded across the SCSI bus. It is in support of the possibility that computer viruses were used by the United States to disrupt Iraqi command and control operations in the Gulf War.]

[87] David Ferbrache. "A Pathology of Computer Viruses." Springer-Verlag, 1992. [This paper attempts to introduce similar techniques to those used in medical science to begin to understand and deal with issues in the study of computer viruses.]

[88] E. A. Feustal. "On the Advantages of Tagged Architecture." IEEE Trans. on Computers C-22, no. 7 (July 1973):644–656. [This paper details a method for associating tags with all information in a computer system at the hardware level. It is the basis for many theoretically strong protection techniques based on the concept of associating protection information with other information for the purposes of deciding on the proper use of that information. These results were also used in Lisp workstations.]

[89] J. Filsinger and J.E. Heaney. "Identifying Generic Safety Requirements." *COMPASS '93*. IEEE Eighth Annual Conference on Computer Assurance 1993:41.

[90] Christoph Fischer. "Research Activities of the Micro-BIT Virus Center— A Virus Preprocessor." *Virus Bulletin.* Second International Conference (September 1992):59–64.

[91] D. A. Fulghum. "EMP Weapons Lead Race for Non-Lethal Technology." *Aviation Week & Space Technology* (May 24, 1993):61. [A Los Alamos EMP generator produced a 12–16 million amp pulse, rise time 400 nanoseconds. 16 ×-40 inch generators have produced about 30 million amps.]

[92] D. A. Fulghum. "ALCMS Given Nonlethal Role." *Aviation Week & Space Technology* (February 22, 1993):20–22. [Cars parked about 300 meters from an EMP generator test had coils, alternators, and other controls disabled. The Soviet Union developed an EMP weapon. Nuclear EMP hardening is ineffective.]

[93] D.A. Futcher, R.L. Sharp, and B.K. Yasaki. "Building a Multi-Level Secure TCP/IP." Proceedings of the 14th National Computer Security Conference (October, 1991):78–87. [Discusses shortcomings of current implementations, including that most TCP/IPs are implemented in the kernel and have access to all kernel data structures, no labeling provisions for sensitivity exist, data of different sensitivity levels is buffered in the kernel, and datagram routing may violate security policy.]

[94] NIST. *Government Network Management Profile (GNMP).* Version 1, December 14, 1992.

[95] Fred Giessler. "Reflexive Control," SAIC's Strategic Assessment Center, July 13, 1993. [This paper discusses the mathematical issues underlying the phe-

nomena of reflexive control. The basic idea of reflexive control is that any system responds to stimuli in particular ways. Attackers can exploit these responses to their advantage if they understand the nature of the reflex reaction well enough.]

[96] Ronald D. Ginn, *Continuity Planning*. Elsevier, 1989:9. [This book describes methods for contingency planning.]

[97] Malcolm Gladwell and Jay Mathews. "'Miraculous' Recovery at Towers; Commodity Exchanges Open Today; Officials Say Bomb Caused Blast." *Washington Post* [This article describes the aftermath of the World Trade Center bombing.]

[98] O. Goldreich, A. Herzberg, and Y. Mansour. "Source to Destination Communication in the Presence of Faults." Proceedings of the Eighth Annual ACM Symposium on Principles of Distributed Computing:85–101. [This paper describes techniques for communication in the presence of faults. It is one of numerous papers on this subject.]

[99] B. D. Gold, R. R. Linde, R. J. Peeler, M. Schaefer, J. F. Scheid, and P. D. Ward. "A Security Retrofit of VM/370." AIFIPS National Computer Conference, 1979:335–344. [This paper describes some of the effort to make an insecure computer system secure through a major retrofit.]

[100] S. Gould. *The Panda's Thumb.* [This book is a collection of lectures that answer many of the questions regarding evolution and the formation of life on Earth.]

[101] "Safety Criteria and Model for Mission-Critical Embedded Software Systems." *IEEE* CH3033-8/91/0000-0069, 1991.

[102] Jim Gray and Daniel P. Siewiorek, "High-Availability Computer Systems." *IEEE Computer* (September 1991):39–48. [This paper describes the state-of-the-art in high availability systems and predicts future trends in this field.]

[103] M. Harrison, W. Ruzzo, and J. Ullman. "Protection in Operating Systems." *CACM* 19 no. 8 (August 1976):461–471. [This paper introduces the first formal mathematical model of protection in computer systems and forms the basis for the subject/object model of computer security. It also proves that determining the protection effects of a given configuration is, in general, undecidable.]

[104] S. Haykin. "Communication Systems." 2nd ed. John Wiley, 1983.

[105] L. Heberlein, G. Dias, K. Levitt, B. Mukherjee, J. Wood, and D. Wolber. "A Network Security Monitor." *IEEE* CH2884, 1990. [This paper describes the operation of a real-time network security monitor which detects certain sorts of attacks against local area networks in real-time.]

[106] Herbert Hecht. "Rare Conditions—An Important Cause of Faults." *IEEE* 0-7803-1251-1/93. 1993. [This paper describes how rare conditions have a substantial effect on availability and why the current methods for assessing faults based on probabilistic models may lead to increased disruption.]

[107] B. W. Henderson. "Boeing Developing Millimeter Wave Radar to Spot Soviet Union's Mobile Missiles." *Aviation Week & Space Technology* (October 8, 1990). [Suggests MMW Radar (30-300 GHz) is capable of looking through foliage. This radar operates at 35 GHz, and 94 GHz components have been built.]

[108] L. J. Hoffman. "Impacts of Information System Vulnerabilities on Society." AIFIPS National Computer Conference. 1982:461–467. [This paper describes the degree to which we have become dependent on computer systems and what we could reasonably expect to result from existing system vulnerabilities.]

[109] Lance J. Hoffman, ed. *Rogue Programs: Viruses, Worms, and Trojan Horses.* VNR, 1990. [This book is a collection of papers on software-induced attacks against computer systems and networks.]

[110] Personal conversations with IBM personnel four months after the BitNet (Christmas card) incident.

[111] ISO IS 8208. "Information Processing Systems—Data Communications—X.25 Packet Layer Protocol for Data Transmission."

[112] ISO Open Systems Interconnect Standard

[113] ISSA. "Guideline for Information Valuation." International Systems Security Association, April 21, 1993. [This unique publication provides a variety of methods for assessing the financial value of information. This is a fundamental problem that has not been adequately addressed in the information environment today.]

[114] J. Rochlis and M. Eichin. "With Microscope and Tweezers: The Worm from MIT's Perspective." *Communications of the Association for Computing Machinery* 32, no. 6 (June 1989). [This paper describes how one team dissected the Internet Virus of 1988 and what that virus contained.]

[115] E. Spafford. "Crisis and Aftermath." *Communications of the Association for Computing Machinery* 32, no. 6 (June 1989). [This paper gives a perspective on the Internet Virus from one of the researchers who was granted access to the source code of the virus soon after it was decompiled.]

[116] Toni Ivergard. *Handbook of Control Room Design and Ergonomics.* Taylor & Francis, 1989. Chapter 8. [This book provides a wide variety of detailed information on the ergonomic issues in control room design.]

[117] JCS Pub 1-02. *DoD Dictionary of Military and Associated Terms.* December 1, 1989. [This is the book you use to understand all of the acronyms and technical words used in all of the other DoD publications. If it's not in there, it's not an official DoD term.]

[118] Joint Pub 1. "Joint Warfare of the U.S. Armed Forces." November 11, 1991:57. [This is the document that describes the U.S. doctrine of warfighting in joint and combined operations.]

[119] D.L. Jobusch and A.E. Oldehoeft. "A Survey of Password Mechanisms: Weaknesses and Potential Improvements, Parts 1 and 2." *Computers and Security* 8:587–604; 675–689. [This paper describes four actual password attacks involving exhaustive dictionary comparison using commercial, system, and optimized dictionaries. Several authentication improvements are given, including use of tokens, biometrics, password system storage policy, constraints on allowable selections, elimination of valid UID cues, pass phrases, password generators with constraints, and password monitor for initial password choice.]

[120] Personal conversations with several well-known experts on this subject.

[121] David Kahn. *The Codebreakers*. Macmillan, 1967:266. [This book documents the history of cryptography and is widely considered the best book of its sort.]

[122] Kaplan. [U.S. Dept. of Justice, Bureau of Justice Statistics]. *Computer Crime— Computer Security Techniques*. Washington, D.C.:U.S. Government Printing Office, 1982. [This is a wonderful resource book on computer security techniques and gives a firm basis for EDP audit from the pre-virus era.]

[123] Bhumip Khasnabish. "A Bound of Deception in Multiuser Computer Networks." *IEEE Journal on Selected Areas in Communications* 7, no. 4 (May 1989). [This paper describes mathematical limitations on the corruption of information in information systems of specific types. As most such papers, the assumptions in this one lead to conclusions of limited value to general purpose systems in widespread use today; however, such bounds are useful in evaluating other systems.]

[124] M. H. Klein. *Department of Defense Trusted Computer System Evaluation Criteria*. DOD-CSC-84-001. Fort Meade, Md.: Department of Defense Computer Security Center, 1983. [This is the widely touted "orange book" Trusted System Evaluation Criteria published by the NSA for evaluating multilevel secure systems for military use. Although it has become a de facto standard, it does not address integrity or many other issues widely held to be of more widespread import.]

[125] A. Klossner. "Re: 'Desert Storm' Viral Myths." *RISKS Digest* 13.07 (January 25, 1992). [This on-line article discusses an example Ethernet LAN where a printer server could mimic a host and submit programs.]

[126] G. Knight. "Cryptanalysts Corner." *Cryptologia* 1 (January 1978):68–74. [This is the first article in a wonderful series of articles that demonstrate how to break many of the most famous historical cryptosystems by exploiting information theory. It's a great starting point for the budding cryptologist.]

[127] Lauren D. Kohn and Kerry A. Blount. "Information Warfare Issues for Distributed Interactive Simulation." September 14, 1993. [This paper discusses some issues in simulating information-based attacks using modern warfare simulators. It is quite limited, but is a good starting point for exploring these issues.]

[128] B. W. Lampson. "A Note on the Confinement Problem." *Communications of the ACM* 16(10) October 1973:613–615. [This famous paper described the covert channel problem for the first time. The implication is that no system that shares resources in a non-fixed fashion can ever provide perfect separation of the sharing parties.]

[129] Steven Levy. *Hackers—Heroes of the Computer Revolution*. Dell, 1984. [This book describes the history of the personal computer coming to prominence from the perspective of the people who were part of it.]

[130] Lundy Lewis. "A Case-Based Reasoning Approach to the Management of Faults in Communications Networks." *IEEE* 11d.3.1.(1993):1422–1429. [This paper describes a system for automated detection and correction of select network faults in which the system learns from examples. It is limited in its

value for malicious attacks, but is quite useful in day-to-day management of network operations.]

[131] R. R. Linde. "Operating System Penetration." AIFIPS National Computer Conference (1975):361–368. [This paper described many of the common techniques for operating systems penetration and how systems could be designed to defend against them.]

[132] Lindsey, Robert. "The Falcon and the Snowman: A pair of dishonorable schoolboys stole top secrets for the KGB." *Life* 2 (October 1979):67(7).

[133] Karen D. Loch, Houston H. Carr, and Merrill E. Warkentin. "Threats to Information Systems: Today's Reality, Yesterday's Understanding." *MIS Quarterly* (June 1992):173–186.

[134] H. O. Lubbes. "High Assurance Computing Software Technology Requirements." Naval Research Laboratory, 1991.

[135] Mark Ludwig. *The Little Black Book of Computer Viruses.* American Eagle Publications, 1991. [This book describes details of how computer viruses operate and introduces several source level programs for computer viruses in DOS-based systems. Many anti-virus researchers believe that this book is the cause of current computer virus strains.]

[136] T. F. Lunt. "Automated Audit Trail Analysis and Intrusion Detection: A Survey." Eleventh National Security Conference. October 1988. [This paper surveys several intrusion detection technologies and reports on the state-of-the-art as of 1988.]

[137] T. F. Lunt and R. Jagannathan. "A Prototype Real-Time Intrusion-Detection Expert System." IEE Symposium on Security and Privacy, April 1988. [This paper describes the IDES real-time intrusion detection system.]

[138] T.F. Lunt. "A Survey of Intrusion Detection Techniques." *Computers and Security* 12:405–418. [This paper describes tools for automating audit data inspection which can operate off-line or in real-time to detect several types of attacks both from outside and inside the system.]

[139] Edward Luttwak. *Strategy: The Logic of War and Peace.* Belknap Press, 1987.

[140] MIL-HDBK-419. "Grounding, Bonding, and Shielding for Electronic Equipment and Facilities." 2 (January 21, 1982). [This military specification details the grounding and shielding requirements for electronic equipment and facilities.]

[141] DoD, MIL-STD-2045-3800. "Network Management for DoD Communications." Draft. January 4, 1993. [This draft standard describes the methods used for managing DoD networks. It notably lacks adequate protection for integrity and availability of information networks under malicious attack.]

[142] Lt. Leo S. Mackay. "Naval Aviation, Information, and the Future." *Naval War College Review* XLV, no. 2, sequence 338 (Spring 1992).

[143] Wayne Madsen. "The Intelligence Agency Threat to Data Privacy and Security." pending publication in *The Journal of Intelligence and Counter-Intelligence,* 1993.

[144] John McAfee and Colin Haynes. *Computer Viruses, Worms, Data Diddlers, Killer Programs, and Other Threats to Your System.* St. Martin's Press, 1989. [This simplistic book on computer viruses and defenses details some of the

many attacks underway today and how management has worked to solve these problems. It contains a lot of questionable information, so the reader should beware.]

[145] McGrath, Peter. "A Family of Spies." *Newsweek* 105 (June 10, 1985):32(5).

[146] E. J. McCauley and P. J. Drongowski. "KSOS—The Design of a Secure Operating System." AIFIPS National Computer Conference, (1979):345–353. [This paper describes one of the early operating systems designed in the 1970s to maintain secrecy.]

[147] Messmer, Ellen, "Group Warns of Growing Security Woes on Internet." *Network World* 11, no. 13 (March 28, 1994):9. [Describes the CERT team's announcements about break-ins throughout the Internet.]

[148] D. Minoli. "Cost Implications of Survivability of Terrestrial Networks under Malicious Failure." *IEEE Transactions on Communications* 28, no. 9 (September 1980):1668–1674. [This paper describes the difference in cost if we attempt to defend against intentional disruption of communications networks as opposed to the cost of defending against random failures. The costs of redundancy increase almost exponentially for malicious attacks, which demonstrates clearly the inadequacy of statistical methods for providing availability measures under malicious attack.]

[149] Robert Molloy and Raja Parasuraman, "Monitoring Automation Failures: Effects of Automation Reliability and Task Complexity." Proc Human Factors Society. Annual meeting, 1992.

[150] Mary Mosquera. "Telephones," Washington news, Washington (UPI) March 7, 1992.

[151] J.M. Musacchio and A. Rozen. "Countering Terrorist Threats." *Civil Engineering* (June 1989):62–64. [This article concerns protection of bank computer centers, advising that several terrorist pamphlets say computers represent the essence of capitalism and should therefore be destroyed. Terrorists are credited with attacking approximately 30 computer centers in Europe from 1979 to 1989.]

[152] NCSD 3-8. "Provisioning of Emergency Power in Support of NS/EP Telecommunications." April 2, 1991.

[153] R. H. Brown, Chair. "National Information Infrastructure Agenda for Action." Information Infrastructure Task Force. September 15, 1993. [This is the call to action for the development of a National Information Infrastructure as introduced by the Clinton administration.]

[154] NIST. "The Industry/Government Open System Specification." Draft. January 1993. [This specification details the so-called open system architecture to be used for interconnection information systems in the National Information Infrastructure.]

[155] "National Military Strategy Document" (NMSD). FY1994-1999. Annex C (Command, Control, Communications, and Computer Systems). [This document defines the national military strategy of the United States through 1999 for C4I. It details the doctrine of information warfare and places it in the context of strategic plans.]

[156] National Research Council. "Growing Vulnerability of the Public Switched Networks: Implications for National Security Emergency Preparedness." National Academy Press, 1989. [This is a very detailed analysis of vulnerabilities in information networks and the implications of these vulnerabilities to national preparedness. It is full of good detailed examples of problems, the lack of attention paid to them, and the implications of this lack of attention.]

[157] National Research Council. "Computers at Risk: Safe Computing in the Information Age." National Academy Press, 1991. [This is a detailed report on the lack of protection in modern information systems and networks throughout the United States. It supports many of the contentions in this book about our inadequate attention to this issue, and details many examples.]

[158] National Science Foundation statistics available via Internet from "nis.nsf.net."

[159] *Compton's Interactive Encyclopedia.* 1994. [Nero, the last Roman emperor descended from Julius Caesar. He also won the reputation of being a demented and depraved tyrant, the ruler who "fiddled while Rome burned" and who instigated the first persecution of Christians; however, Nero's unsavory reputation is almost wholly undeserved. . . . He was not in Rome when the city burned in 64, nor did he inaugurate a persecution of Christians because of the fire.]

[160] Perter G. Neumann, "The Computer-Related Risk of the Year: Weak Links and Correlated Events." *COMPASS '91* (Computer Assurance). NIST. June 25–27, 1991. [This paper describes some of the subtle problems we encounter in modern information systems and networks and how seemingly minor problems have become major risks.]

[161] Office of the Inspector General. October 2, 1992 Audit Report No. 93-002. Project 1FD-0043. [This report details some of the major lapses in protection in DoD information centers upon which we rely for all aspects of our military capability. It includes many detailed examples of how policy, procedure, technical safeguards, and other lapses combine to make an environment that should support mission-critical operations vulnerable to accidental and malicious attacks of all sorts.]

[162] OSD(C3I). Letter, "Review of Multilevel Security Capabilities." October 25, 1992.

[163] "Open Systems Environment (OSE) Profile for Imminent Acquisitions (Part 10 of 10 parts) Security Services." Draft. [This eternal draft specification for protection in open systems defines a number of areas of service, but lacks sufficient detail to allow any utility as a standard. It is essentially a wish list of protection features that might be nice in some situations.]

[164] Peter Schweizer. *Friendly Spies.* Atlantic Monthly Press, 1993. [While some elements of this book have been questioned by other reporters, other elements are strongly supported by written sources both before and since publication.] and *Computers and Security* 9, no. 6:515.

[165] Bob Pekarske. "Restoration in a Flash—Using DS3 Cross-connects." *Telephony.* September 10, 1990. [This paper describes the techniques used to compensate for network failures in certain telephone switching systems in a

matter of a milisecond. The paper points out that without this rapid response, the failed node would cause other nodes to fail, causing a domino effect on the entire national communications networks.]

[166] Esther Pessin. "Pirate." New York (UPI). April 29, 1986. [HBO on January 15 became the first major cable channel to scramble its signals to prevent satellite dish owners from picking up HBO programming for free and the interruption which appeared during a movie early Sunday apparently was a protest of the policy. The hacker dubbed himself "Captain Midnight" and broke into the film "The Falcon and the Snowman" with a message that flickered on television screens across the nation for anywhere from 10 seconds to more than a minute. The cable raider broke into HBO with a multicolor test pattern and a five-line message printed in white letters: "Good evening HBO From Captain Midnight $12.95/month? No way! Showtime/Movie Channel beware."]

[167] J. Peterzell. "Spying and Sabotage by Computer." *Time* (March 20, 1989):25–26. [Quotes unnamed sources that the NSA and CIA have experimented with the disruption of other nations' computers using viruses and other destructive programs, and that both the United States and other countries have accessed classified information in foreign computer systems. Also cites that up to 90 percent of known computer security breaches are from corporate or government insiders, and that one of every 15,000 key operators had sold or given away classified information.]

[168] Merrill L. Pierce, Jr. "Established Architecture Keys Marine Data." *The First Information War*. 153.

[169] G.J. Popek, M. Kampe, C.S. Kline, A. Stoughton, M. Urban, and E.J. Walton. "UCLA Secure Unix." AIFIPS. National Computer Conference 1979:355–364. [This paper describes a secure implementation of the Unix operating system in which much of the implementation was proven correct mathematically.]

[170] Karl Popper. *Logik der Forschung*. 1935 (English translation in 1959, *The Logic of Scientific Discovery*) [This famous philosophy of science work is widely considered a breakthrough in scientific thinking.]

[171] "C4I for the Warrior." June 12, 1992. [This document details the Joint Staff's view of how information technology will be in future military operations. It makes several major assumptions (such as the security of multilevel secure operating systems) that have not been realized, and uses these as a basis for planning how future wars will be fought.]

[172] C. Preston. Personal conversation with computer manufacturer engineer. August 1991. [An engineer described contractor bringing virus-infected disks into a computer production facility to use in quality and function check.]

[173] A quick experiment for UV and IR emissions from a monitor through nylon tarp/tent material showed low or no UV from the monitor, and detectable visible light or IR from the monitor, but no details of the screen unless the fabric was very close to the monitor face.

[174] C. Preston. "Computer Virus Protection." 1993. Seminar Manual by Charles M. Preston, Information Integrity.

[175] P. Proctor. "A Computer Misuse Detection System." [This paper describes the combination of expert systems for known attack detection and statistical deviation detection for behavioral change detection as a method for automated misuse detection and demonstrates how many of the current network-based attacks are detected and countered in real-time by these mechanisms.]

[176] Paul Proctor. "White Paper to Implement Computer Misuse Detection on the Operational Support System (OSS)." 1993. [This paper describes a misuse detection system and how it can be used to protect systems and networks against many current attacks.]

[177] RS-252-A. "Standard Microwave Transmission Systems." Electronic Industries Association, 1972.

[178] Y. Radai. "Integrity Checking for Anti-Viral Purposes—Theory and Practice." (submission imminent) [A paper on integrity in information systems.]

[179] Marcus J. Ranum. "A Network Firewall." Washington Open Systems Resource Center. Greenbelt, MD (June 12, 1992). [In this paper, a method for detecting and limiting the scope of attacks from over the Internet is implemented.]

[180] D. Pescovitz. "Reality Check." *Wired* (April 1994):31. [This short piece shows the results of an industry survey on the real timetable for upgraded information technologies.]

[181] risks@csl.sri.com

[182] R. L. Rivest, A. Shamir, and L. Adleman. "A Method for Obtaining Digital Signatures and Public-Key Cryptosystems." Comm. of the ACM (February 1978) 21, no. 2:120–126. [This famous paper introduced the best known and only unbroken class of public key cryptosystems. It forms the basis for almost all current public key systems.]

[183] K.H. Roberts and D.M. Rousseau. "Research in Nearly Failure-Free, High-Reliability Organizations: Having the Bubble." IEEE Trans. on Engineering Management, 5–89:132–139.

[184] Unclassified extract of "1979 Project SECA", 1979.

[185] (Ames) may have sold information to the Russians about the government's secret key-escrow technology used in Clipper Chip chip sets and Capstone Tessera cards. *Security Insider Report*. Seminole, Fla.

[186] "SONATA" [OP-094 booklet] [SEW designated by the Chief of Naval Operations as a Navy warfare mission in 1989.]

[187] "Summary of SunOS Security Patches," CIAC D-20. August 6, 1993. [Cites security vulnerabilities in all versions of SunOS, including unauthorized access to systems and files, and denial of service.]

[188] Tom Schmitz. "Hacker Forces Sun to Cut Off Outside Access Computer System is Shut Down in an Effort to Stop Possible Sabotage of a Product." *San Jose Mercury News (SJ)* July 31, 1993.

[189] Winn Schwartau. *Terminal Compromise*. InterPact Press, 1991. (also available via Internet) [This fictional work plays out a scenario in which computer viruses are used to bring down the United States. Although the book has

many problems, it demonstrates that many people are contemplating these issues from many different perspectives.]

[190] U. Feige, A. Shamir, and M. Tennenholtz. "The Noisy Oracle Problem." Advances in Cryptology. *CRYPTO '88 Proceedings*: 284–96.

[191] John H. Shannon and David A. Rosenthal. "Electronic Mail and Privacy: Can the conflicts be resolved?" *Business Forum* 18, no. 1,2 (Winter/Spring 1993):31–34, [Oliver North, the now famous Marine officer at the heart of the Iran-Contra scandal, used an electronic mail system to communicate with staff at the White House. When it was apparent that he would be charged with illegal activity, he shredded paper documents and purged e-mail messages that might be incriminating. Unbeknownst to him, messages on the e-mail system were routinely copied by a backup procedure. It was from these backup tapes that evidence was retrieved and used against him in both the Senate hearings and criminal proceedings.]

[192] C. Shannon. "A Mathematical Theory of Communications." *Bell Systems Technical Journal.* 3, no. 27, (July 1948). [This is perhaps the most famous and seminal paper in the information sciences. In this paper, Shannon described the first practical syntactic information theory, which formed the basis for a vast array of developments in the information sciences from the design of computer instruction sets to the integrity of satellite communications and beyond. It is hard to overestimate the impact of this work.]

[193] C. Shannon. "Communications Theory of Secrecy Systems." *Bell Systems Technical Journal* (1949):656–715. [In this paper, Shannon applied his information theory to breaking all of the known ciphers up till that date and provided a proof that the only theoretically unbreakable cryptosystem was the so-called *perfect* cipher. This paper also introduced the concepts of diffusion and confusion, and introduced the concept of work load which is the basis for using imperfect cryptosystems today.]

[194] M.L. Shannon. *Don't Bug Me*. Paladin Press, 1992. [The author reports an experiment in which a screen-text to Morse code program was running and he was able to decode the screen listings at several frequencies using a short whip antenna outside the building housing the personal computer.]

[195] J F Shoch and J A Hupp. "The 'Worm' Programs—Early Experience with a Distributed Computation." *CACM* (March 1982):172–180. [This was a famous paper that first described the Xerox "worm" experiments for parallel processing on a distributed computing network.]

[196] Daniel P. Siewiorek, M. Y. Hsiao, David Rennels, James Gray, and Thomas Williams. "Ultradependable Architectures." *Annual Review of Computer Science 1990* 4:503–15. [This paper describes many of the most sophisticated techniques available for providing high availability and integrity in information systems and networks. It is particularly useful in understanding the limits of today's technology.]

[197] Daniel P. Siewiorek and Robert S. Swarz. *The Theory and Practice of Reliable System Design*. Digital Press, 1982, [This book describes many of the underlying techniques and much of the well understood theory of high-reliability computer system design.]

[198] Frank Simon. "Liste der militaerischen Rechner im ARPA-Internet." from the Chaos Computer Club directory. University of Ulm, Germany. system date 4-19-91. Shown in directory of Chaos Computer Club files titled LIES-MICH, system date 5-1 4-91.

[199] H. Simon. "The Sciences of the Artificial."

[200] Robert M. Slade. "Antiviral Contact List." (computer file) 1993.

[201] Jean M. Slupik. "Integrating Tactical and Strategic Switching." *The First Information War.* 148.

[202] P. Smulders. "The Threat of Information Theft by Reception of Electromagnetic Radiation from RS-232 Cables." *Computers and Security* 9:53–58. [In some cases there was enough radiation from shielded RS-232 cables to receive and reconstruct data using a whip antenna and broadcast AM/FM receiver several meters away from the cable.]

[203] S. R. Snapp, J. Brentano, G. V. Dias, T. L. Goan, L. T. Heberlein, CL Ho, K. N. Levitt, B. Mukherjee, S. E. Smaha, T. Grance, D. M. Teal, and D. Mansur. "DIDS (Distributed Intrusion Detection System)—Motivation, Architecture, and an Early Prototype." Proceedings of the 14th National Computer Security Conference, October 1991:167–176. [Sets out several scenarios in which detection of attacks depends on information from multiple sources: doorknob attacks where multiple login trials are below the threshold on each system; chain and parallel attacks; and network browsing, where multiple files are examined on several different computers during a short period, and where the level on each machine is below an alarm threshold.]

[204] H. Spencer. "Predicting System Reliability." *RISKS Digest* 11.14 (February 20, 1991). [States that OS kernel software is rarely stress tested under truly severe operational loads. Example given is the system failure of a kernel flaw from an interrupt in a window 100 nanoseconds long on a RISC processor. Programmers had assumed incrementing an integer in memory was an atomic operation, somewhat true on single-processor CISC, rarely true in multiprocessors or RISC.]

[205] J. Stanley. "Re: 'Desert Storm' Viral Myths." *RISKS Digest* 13.07 (January 25, 1992). [Discusses the fact that a networked Ethernet printer sees all data, including passwords and logins, and could possibly login and submit a program.]

[206] Robert D. Steele. "War and Peace in the Age of Information." Superintendent's Guest Lecture, Naval Postgraduate School. August 1993. [In this paper, Steele describes how the United States could be crippled militarily by a few people with a relatively small amount of money in a fairly short period of time.]

[207] Donald V. Steward. *Software Engineering with Systems Analysis and Design.* Brooks/Cole Publishing Company, 1987:26.

[208] C. Stoll. *The Cookoo's Egg.* 1991. [In this widely read book, Cliff Stoll describes the trials and tribulations he went through when he found a 75 cent accounting error on his computer system and looked deeper only to find that he had detected an international spy that was invading government computer systems throughout the United States.]

[209] C. Stoll. "An Epidemiology of Viruses & Network Worms." Proceedings of the 12th National Computer Security Conference. October 1990:369–377. [By gathering times of first infection from the Morris Internet Virus, an exponential spread rate appears, taking only about four hours to go from 15 percent to 90 percent of the 2,600 sample-estimated total.]

[210] Mary E. Thyfault, Stephanie Stahlwith, and Joseph C. Panetteri. "Weak Links." *Information Week* (August 10, 1992):26–31.

[211] From Times Staff and Wire Reports, Tuesday November 5, 1991, Home ed., Business Page: 2 Pt. D Col. 1, [Computer Saboteur Pleads Guilty: Michael John Lauffenburger, 31, a former General Dynamics computer programmer who planted a destructive logic bomb in one of the San Diego defense contractor's mainframe computers, pleaded guilty to one count of attempted computer tampering. He faces up to one year in prison and a fine of $100,000.]

[212] M. A. Titov, A. G. Ivanov, and G. K. Moskatov. "An Adaptive Approach to Designing Antivirus Systems." unpublished, 1992.

[213] Alvin Tofler and Heidi Tofler. "War, Wealth, and a New Era in History." *World Monitor* (May 1991).

[214] Alvin Tofler and Heidi Tofler. *War and AntiWar.* Little Brown, 1993. [In this book, the Toflers describe a view of the future in which the information age has completely taken over the industrial age and the agricultural age. It is a fascinating book which explores the concept that war is no longer just for the big and powerful.]

[215] Data communications trade magazines.

[216] A. Turing. "On Computable Numbers, with an Application to the Entscheidungsproblem." *London Math Soc.* Ser 2. 1936. [This is the famous paper that shows that any problem that can be solved by any general purpose computer can also be solved by any other general purpose computer, given enough time and space. It also shows that a large class of problems can never be solved by a computer. The so-called Halting problem, in particular, is proven unsolvable.]

[217] G. Turner. "I Spy." *Computerworld* (October 26, 1992):129–130.

[218] J. Allen, B. Heltai, A. Koenig, D. Snow, and J. Watson. "VCTV: A Video-On-Demand Market Test." *AT&T Technical Journal* (Jan/Feb 1993). [This paper describes details of market tests of video-on-demand service by many of the largest companies in the cable and telephone business. It also describes how AT&T has been able to use existing telephone wire infrastructure to operate 1.2 million baud digital transmissions.]

[219] M.E. van Valkenburg, ed. *Reference Data for Engineers: Radio, Electronics, Computer, and Communications.* 8th ed. SAMS, 1993:12.37. [Details radiated and conducted computer equipment emission limits for FCC Class B and other standards.]

[220] W. van Eck. "Electromagnetic Radiation from Video Display Units: An Eavesdropping Risk?" *Computers and Security* 4:269–286. [Demonstrates how $200 worth of electronics hardware available off-the-shelf can be used to observe

output on video display terminals from a distance and details experimental results using this technique. A realistic system of this sort can now be assembled from used components for about $1,000.]

[221] Bob Violino and Joseph C. Panetteri. "Tempting Fate." *Information Week* (October 4, 1993):42–52.

[222] "PSI tells BBS Advertiser to Stop." *Wall Street Journal* (June 22, 1994):B5. [In this article, the results of a law firm advertising over the Internet are described. One of the side effects was massive electronic mail overloads for the Internet provider.]

[223] Washington news. "Court-phone." Washington (UPI) January 8, 1990. [The court refused to hear a case brought by Scott Tyler, of Dixon, Iowa, and members of his family against his neighbors and Scott County officials who listened in on his cordless telephone conversations for months in 1983. The eavesdropping eventually resulted in criminal charges against Tyler.]

[224] CIA sources told the *Washington Times* that Mr. Ames used his CIA computer to make unauthorized entries into computers within the espionage branch and downloaded information about the CIA's operations in Europe, including the identity of undercover agents posing as businessmen. *The Washington Times* (March 16, 1994):A3.

[225] Wayner, Peter, "Should Encryption Be Regulated?" *Byte* (May 1993) 18:129(5) [U.S. law enforcement agencies are pressing to ban or limit the private use of computerized encryption systems.]

[226] SAIC. "Threats and Defenses for WCCS." August 1993. [This paper explores protection requirements for a military Command and Control computer network.]

[227] *The Meriam-Webster Dictionary. 1974.*

[228] G.H. Whidden. "The Ear." Technical Services Agency. 2.12 and 3.1 (1988–89). [Speculatively discusses the design and placement of a transmitter in a personal computer, that transmits display information in short bursts at irregular intervals, and only if information on the video display has changed.]

[229] "Commission Studies: State of the Art of Electronic Surveillance." National Commission for the Review of Federal and State Laws Relating to Wiretapping and Electronic Surveillance. 1976. [Details numerous methods of audio surveillance with transmitters, the smallest being the size of an aspirin tablet including battery and microphone, commercially available; mentions use of passive resonant cavities modulating an outside-supplied microwave beam. A current video camera has a rugged metal case and lens, both low-level visible light and good IR sensitivity, that measures $34 \times 26 \times 22$ mm. A video modulator/transmitter PC board available for $50 from a Canadian company measures about 2×2 inches. Such cameras and transmitters are readily available built into clocks, lamps, and other objects.]

[230] "Top Ten U.S. Infrastructure Targets." *Wired.* November 1993. [This article describes one author's view of the most tempting targets in the United States.]

[231] R.W. Wolverton. "Software Costing." TRW Systems. In *Handbook of Software Engineering*. ed. C.R Vick and C.V. Ramamoorthy. Van Nostrand Reinhold, 1984:469–493, cites R.O. Lewis, "The Cost of an Error: A Retrospective Look at Safeguard Software." Science Applications International Corporation, Inc. Prepared under Contract DA660-76-C-0011. Huntsville, AL (March 1977).

[232] "Soft Kill." (Interactive CD-ROM), Xiphias, 1993.

[233] Moses, et al., *The Holy Bible* Joshua 2:1, 2:24, 6:1–3 (The battle of Jericho), ... (The Macabees versus the Philistines).

[234] "EDPACS." December 1993.

Glossary

AAA: American Automobile Association

active-tapping: Observing, introducing, and/or modifying information in a medium

ADP: Automatic data processing

AIDS: Acquired Immune Deficiency Syndrome

AP: Associated Press

arrays: Sequences of memory locations used to store lists

ATM: Automated teller machine

AT&T: American Telephone and Telegraph Company

Availability: MTTF/(MTTF+MTTR)

backhoe: An automotive digging device with a narrow scoop in the back and a plough in the front

Bandwidth: A frequency range

Basic: A computer language

bugs: Errors or omissions

CD: Compact disk

CD-ROM: Compact disk read only memory

CEO: Chief executive office

CERT: Computer emergency response team

CIA: Central Intelligence Agency

CMDS: Computer misuse detection system

CMW: Compartmented Mode Workstation

CO: Central office

COTS: Commercial off-the-shelf

CPA: Certified public accountant

CP-M: An early small-computer operating system

CRC: Cyclic redundancy code

Cryptography: Secret writing

DAC: Discretionary access control

DAT: Digital audio tape

DBase: A popular database management program

debugging: The process of removing bugs

DEC: Digital Equipment Corporation

digital-diode: A device which allows information to flow in one direction only

DII: Defense Information Infrastructure

DISA: Defense Information Systems Agency

DISN: Defense Information Systems Network

DoD: Department of Defense

DOS: Disk Operating System

E-mail: Electronic mail

EDI: Electronic data interchange

EDP: Electronic data processing

EFT: Electronic funds transfer

EMI: Electromagnetic interference

EMP: Electromagnetic pulse

Ethernet: The current dominant local area network technology

FAA: Federal Aviation Administration

FAX: Facsimile

FBI: Federal Bureau of Investigation

FCC: Federal Communications Commission

firewall: A protective barrier

FTP: File Transfer Protocol

fungibles: Things of cash equivalent value

GNMP: Government Network Management Profile

GOTS: Government off-the-shelf

GPS: Global Positioning System

GWEN: Ground Wave Emergency Network

HEMP: High-altitude electromagnetic pulse

HERF: High-energy radio frequency

IBM: Formerly known as International Business Machines

Internet: The network connecting millions of computers throughout the world

IRS: Internal Revenue Service
ISDN: Integrated services digital network
ISO: International Standards Organization
IT: Information technology
ITSEC: Information Technology Security Evaluation Criteria
jamming: Interfering with signals
LAN: Local area network
LANtastic: A local area network software product
MAC: Mandatory access control
mainframe: A computer compatible with IBM large computer systems
MLS: Multi-level secure
modem: Modulator/Demodulator
MRE: Meal ready to eat
MTTF: Mean time to failure
MTTR: Mean time to repair
NCSC: National Computer Security Center
NFS: Network File System
NII: National Information Infrastructure
NRC: National Research Council
NSA: National Security Agency
NSF: National Science Foundation
NSFnet: National Science Foundation Network
NWAN: National wide area network
OCR: Optical character recognition
Oracle: A software database program
OS-2: Another PC-based operating system
OSD: Office of the Secretary of Defense
OSI: Open Systems Interconnect
Outsourcing: Having outside vendors provide services
PBX: Private Branch Exchange
PC: IBM-compatible personal computer
peer-to-peer: Equivalent users on multiple computers
PGP: Pretty good privacy
PIN: Personal identification number
Protocol: A standardized syntax and semantics for communication
RACF: Access Control Facility
RF: Radio Frequency
RSA: A public key cryptosystem created by Rivest Shamir Adleman

RWAN: Regional wide area network
SOP: Standard operating orocedure
T1: 1 million bits per second digital telephonic connection
TCI: Telecommunication Incorporated
TCP/IP: Terminal Control Protocol/Internet Protocol
Tempest: Electromagnetic emanations
Trojan-horse: A device that performs an unexpected function
TS: Top Secret
U: Unclassified
UIC: Universal industry code
ultrasonic: High-frequency sound waves (not humanly audible)
UNIX: A multiuser operating system common in the NII
UPC: Universal product code
UPI: United Press International
USAF: United States Air Force
USPS: United States Postal Service
VAX: A computer made by Digital Equipment Corporation
VCR: Video cassette recorder
Virus: A program that reproduces
VMS: Digital Equipment Corporations VAX Operating System
WAN: Wide area network
Windows: PC-based operating system
WPA: Works Project Administration
WWMCCS: World Wide Military Command and Control System
X11: A networked graphical user interface

Index

747, 30
800, 98
911, 20
8080, 85
8086, 85
68000, 86
80386, 87

A Generation of PC Programmers, 86
A Lot of People Disrupt Information
    Systems, 6
Achilles heel, 32
Activists, 63
Africa Corps, 87
Aggravating Factors, 177
AIDS, 30, 53, 60
air traffic control, 19, 76
Alcatel, 68
allies' transmissions, 87
Alternatives, 170
America OnLine, 63
American Indians, 30
Ames, Aldrch, 57, 66, 88
Analysis Method, 254
AP, 11
Apple, 85
areas covered, 167
Argentina, 70
ARPAnet, 100
ATM, 4
attacks covered up, 88
attacks, combined, 54

auditing, 209, 214, 224, 230, 235, 247,
    263
Australia, 68, 70, 104
Austria, 70
automated telephone attendant, 16
Availability, 248
awareness, 231
Axis, 81

background checks, 221
Backhoes, 34
Backout, 217
backup theft, 50
backups, 37, 213, 227, 246, 250
Bagdad, 15
bandwidth, 200
bang-for-the-buck, 31
Battle of Britain, 87
Battle of Midway, 87
Belgium, 70
Bell, 82
Biba, 82
Biblical, 13
big business, 22
Blackhawk, 70
blackouts, 25
bombing, 223, 224
bond certificates, 62
bounds checking, 94
brakes, antilock, 109
Bribery, 211
Bribes, 45

British. *See* England
Brother, 127
bugging, 211
Bulgaria, 70
burning used floppy disks, 109

cable cuts, 35
cable television, 17
Caelli, Bill, 104
Call forwarding fakery, 51
caller-ID, 51
Canada, 70, 118
CD-ROM, 16, 71, 204
CDs, 16
CERT, 262
change control, 217
channel capacities, 199
Chaos Computer Club, 43, 71
checklists, 165
Chicago, 35, 102
China, 14, 68–70
Christmas Card Virus, 102
CIA, 66
CIS, 70
Civilian Government Dependency, 24
classification scheme, validity of, 56
Clipper, 66
Club Initiates, 60
CNN, 63
CO, 68
coercion, 73
Colombia, 70
command and control, 265
commercial communications
    systems, 203
communication replaces
    transportation, 29
Communication Technologies, 203
competitors, 61
computer, multistate, 84
computer security kicks in, 81
computer viruses, 46
consent decree, 203
consultants, 58
corrosion, 40
corruption, 55, 245
COs, 205
cost factors, combined, 157

cost increases dramatically with
    life-cycle phase, 151
cost increases with coverage and
    assurance, 156
cost increases with immediacy, 154
cost of incidents increase with time,
    155
covering table, 254
covering table results, 256
CP-M, 85
CPA, 170
Crack password guessing program,
    213
Crackers, 60
Crackers for Hire, 63
crashes, 5
CRC, 95, 130
critical repairs, 173
criticality of function should be
    properly addressed, 265
Crusades, the, 73
cryptographic, 13, 238
cryptography, a short history, 80, 87
cryptography leashed, 87
Cuba, 13

DAT, 16
data aggregation, 50
data diddling, 47
data exchange, 241
database, 223
David and Goliath, 24, 72
decomissioning, disposal, and
    conversion, 162
deep doodoo, 28
denial, 55, 237
Denmark, 104
Denning, Dorothy, 82
dependencies, 18
dependency effects of the
    information superhighway, 32
dependency on information, 3
deranged people, 64
Desert Shield, 27
Desert Storm, 25
dial-back, 51
dial-in, 215, 220
dial-out, 212

Dickens, Charles, 60
digital diodes, 235
DII, 25, 258
diodes, 242, 246
DISA, 27, 257
diseases, 30
DISN, 76, 259
disruption, 6, 34, 76
distribution, 236, 250
DITSO, 75
documentation, 137, 229
DoD dependency, 25
DOS, 85, 128, 214
drug cartels, 64
dumpster diving, 42
dust, 39

E-mail, 43, 215, 226
E-mail overflow, 43
E-mail spoofing, 52
earthquake, 36
Ebola, Zaire, 30
EDI, 22
education, 232
efficiency trades with adaptability, 31
EFT, 60, 62
Egypt, 80
electronic funds transfer, 209
electronic interference, 40, 48
eliminating accidental events, 129
eliminating attackers, 113
eliminating effects, 132
eliminating motives, 118
eliminating techniques, 120
emanations, 238
emergency measures and long-term
    planning, 160
EMI, 69
EMP, 69
England, 43, 68, 70, 104, 143
Ericsson, 68
errors and omissions, 34
Europe, 87
European Community, 62
executive summary, 173, 185, 193

FAA, 36, 40, 48, 74
Fagin, 60

False update disks, 53
fax, 14, 20, 127
FBI, 2, 66, 88
FCC, 124
fiber optic, 205
fictitious people, 42
field deployment issues, 250
findings, 181, 188, 228
Finland, 70
fire, 35
firewall, 7, 8
flood, 35
force multiplier, 13
forge packets, 95
forgery, 245
France, 61, 68, 70, 74
FreeNet, 43
FTC, 143
FTP, 216
Fujitsu, 68
fun, challenge, and acceptance, 72
future networking enhancements, 249
futuristic visions, 205

gang, 72
Gangs, 60
GAO, 75
gasses, fumes, and cleaning
    chemicals, 39
gateways, 213, 215
gathering or destruction of evidence,
    74
General Motors, 23
German, 18, 43
Germany, 68–72, 87, 102, 104
get a job, 46
GNMP, 76
Goldberg, Rube, 28
Gopher, 12
Gore, Al, 9
government agencies, 66
GPS, 36
Greece, 41, 70
Gulf War, 15, 74, 201
GWEN, 69

hacker, 59, 69, 72
Hamburg, 74, 104

hangup hooking, 51
hardware, 177
hardware and operations, 175
Harrison, 82
Hawaii, 37
HBO, 44
Heat, 39
HEMP, 69
HERF, 146
HERF Attack, 146
hieroglyphics, 80
Hill, Benny, 54
Hitachi, 61, 68
Holland, 70
Hoods, 62
how findings were analyzed, 189
how to protect yourself, 9
Hudson, 25
human engineering, 45
human vulnerability should be
    addressed, 262
humidity, 38
Hungary, 70

IBM, 46, 61, 85
Iceland, 70
IFIP, 68
illegal copies of software, 225
illegal value insertion, 52
implementation and testing, 161
important changes, 175
inadequate maintenance, 38
incident response, 139, 231
India, 69, 70
Indonesia, 70
induced stress failures, 53
information, additional, 228
information advantage, 13
information age, 14
information assurance, 260
information assurance, as an
    unsolvable problem, 195
information assurance is a military
    readiness issue, 257
information assurance is vital, 93
information assurance policies and
    standards are needed, 259

information assurance standards are
    inadequate, 99
information systems are highly
    vulnerable, 5
information warfare, 258
information warriors, 71
infrastructure design, 111
infrastructure interference, 44
infrastructure observation, 44
infrastructure warriors, 67
input overflow, 52
insiders, 57
integrity protection, 245
Intel, 85
Internet, 2, 7, 43, 53, 71, 75, 77, 78, 102,
    203, 215
invalid values on calls, 46
inventory control, 225
Iran-Contra, 73
Iraq, 1, 74
IRS, 2, 31, 129
ISDN, 74, 214
ISO, 99
Israel, 70, 104
Italy, 68
ITSEC, 68

jamming, 235, 237, 249
Japan, 16, 68–70, 87, 104
Johnstown, 35
junk mail, 45
just-in-time, 22, 23, 26

Kennedy, John, 13
Knight, 81
Kremlin, 14

Lampson, 82
LAN, 12, 86, 216, 235, 236
LANs, 77
LaPadula, 82
law enforcement is clueless, 88
leakage, 55
learned shared attack, 147
legal, 231
legal considerations, 143, 231
Lehigh University, 51

login spoofing, 51
logistics, 265
London, 65
long-term limitations, 178
Los Angeles, 116, 125

MAC, 247
Madsen, Wayne, 68
maintenance people, 61
Malasia, 70
Malaysia, 70
Marine Corps, 27
mechanical skew, 37
mental illness, 72
meta-information, 205
Mexico, 70
military or economic advantage, 74
military organizations, 69
misuse detection, 244
MLS, 241, 245, 247
money or profit, 72
monitoring, 246
Morris, 89
Moscow, 104
MREs, 27
MTTF, 55
MTTR, 55

NASA, 11
Nation States and Economic Rivals,
    68
national planning should reflect
    information age warfare, 258
Naval Postgraduate School, 68
NCSC, 50
NEC, 68
Nero, 35
Netherlands, 68
network, 219
network services attacks, 53
New Jersey, 62
New York, 35, 62, 65, 70, 76
New Zealand, 68, 70
NFS, 240
NII, 5
North, Oliver, 74
notice, adequate, 215

Novell, 74, 214, 216
NRC, 98
NSA, 50, 88, 240
NSF, 4, 87, 88
NSFnet, 12
nuclear missiles, 13
NWANs, 205

OCR, 15
one-state computer wins, 85
open microphone listening, 48
operation and maintenance, 162
operational tempo, 26
operations overview, 207
organizational suitability, 145, 232
organized crime, 64
OS/2, 87
outsourcing, 224

pacemaker, 18
packet insertion, 47
packet watching, 47
packets, 204
packets and protocols, 203
paper, shredding of, 109
parity, 95
password guessing, 46
passwords, 75, 92, 215, 218, 226, 227,
    244
Patton, Gen. George, 87
PBX, 68, 124, 156, 215
PBX bugging, 48
PBXs, 52, 219
PC, 85
peer-to-peer, 242
People's Republic of China, 104
perfect systems are infeasible, 96
personnel, 166, 231
personnel issues, 142, 231
PGP, 127
physical protection, 142, 231
physical proximity, 22
physical security, 210
PIN, 49
plagues, 30
plan of action, 232
plans, current, 205

plumbing, 28
Police, 66
political documents, 170
poor assumptions lead to
    disruptions, 97
Popper, Karl, 107
Portugal, 70
power failure, 34
power grid, 6
priorities should be properly
    addressed over time and
    circumstance, 264
priorities should interact properly
    across components, 265
private detectives and reporters, 58
procedures, 229
process, 168
process bypassing, 50
procurement is only part of lifecycle
    cost, 153
Professional thieves, 62
Project rehab, 69
Protection administration, 235, 244
Protection audit, 138, 230
Protection awareness, 143, 231
protection is something you do, not
    something you buy, 3, 7
Protection limit poking, 43
protection management, 133, 228
protection policy, 134, 229
protection posture assessment, 159
protection requires knowledge, 8
protocol, 204
protocol issues, 240
prototype conversion, 239

RACF, 213, 217
Rapid ongoing adaption, 249
reactive protection posture, 108
readiness, 257
Reagan, Ronald, 91
Real-time prioritization should be
    addressed, 264
reflexive control, 103
religious or political beliefs, 73
relocating computers, 37
repair, replace, and remove
    information, 49

Republic of Korea, 69
Republic of South Africa, 70
Revere, Paul, 13
Rome, 35
ROTC, 116
routers, 98
RSA, 81
Rube Goldberg, 28
Russia, 13, 57, 68, 70, 104
Russian embassy, 45
Russian roulette, 60
RWANs, 205

San Francisco, 125
satellites, 201
Scotland Yard, 48
secrecy standards DO NOT address
    information assurance, 94
self-defense, 73
selling (and buying) a posture
    assessment, 170
severe weather, static electricity, air
    conditioning loss, etc., 37
Shannon, Claud, 81
shoulder surfing, 49
Siemens, 68
Singapore, 68
site visit, 207
small business, 21
Smoke, 38
soft-kill, 104
software, 173, 175
solar flares, 36
some widely applicable results,
    150
South Africa, 68, 69
South Pacific, 87
Soviet, 57
Soviet Union, 66
speech understanding, 17
Spies, 65
standards, 229
standards and procedures, 136, 229
strategic needs, 149
Stoll, Cliff, 65, 88
stovepiped, 25
superbugs, 153
Supreme Court, 66

Sutton, Willie, 62
Sweden, 68, 70
switching systems, 199
Switzerland, 70 .
sympathetic vibration, 45
synergistic, 77, 157
system maintenance, 37

T1, 214
tactical needs, 149
Taiwan, 69, 70
tapping, 212, 245
TCP-IP, 240
TCP/IP, 203, 214
TCSEC, 82
technical safeguards, 138, 230
technical vulnerability should be
    assessed, 261
telephone, 7, 200
television, 201
temperature cycling, 39
tempest, 234, 236, 250
tempest problems, 236
terminal servers, 98
terrorists, 65
testing, 38, 73, 140, 211, 231
Thailand, 70
tiger teams, 60
time bombs, 41
toll fraud networks, 50
toll frauds, 221
training, 232, 244
training and education, 144, 232
Trojan horse, 41, 53, 120, 250
TS, 242
Turkey, 70
turnaround, 209
two architectures, 189

UIC, 10
Ukraine, 70
United Kingdom, 87
University of Southern California, 116
UPC, 10
UPI, 11
use or condition bombs, 41
USPS, 129

Van Eck bugging, 47
vandals, 63
VCR, 8
VCR voice, 16
vengeance or justice, 72
Vibration, 40
video, 213
video viewing, 49
Vietnam War, 116
viruses, 70, 77, 82, 213, 216, 223, 225
voice, 213
volcanos, 36
vulnerabilities and protection
    techniques, 234

Walker Family, 88
WAN, 86
Washington, 44
Watergate, 73
we all depend on information
    systems, 5
we must retain flexibility, 259
we need to protect ourselves, 7
we should address current
    weaknesses, 260
we should train for defensive
    information warfare, 266
what are the top priorities?, 195
what the analysis showed, 191
whistle blowers, 59
White Plains, 100
why organizations do get
    assessments, 171
why organizations don't get posture
    assessments, 171
wire closet attacks, 49
World Trade Center, 65
World War II, 18, 29, 81, 87
World Wide Web, 12
WPA, 28, 29, 112
WWMCCS, 68

X-ray, 74
X11, 240

Zaire, 30
zip code, 100

Critical acclaim for Peter Robinson and the Inspector Banks series

'The Alan Banks mystery-suspense novels are the best series on the market. Try one and tell me I'm wrong'
Stephen King

'A powerfully moving work'
Ian Rankin

'Top-notch police procedure'
Jeffery Deaver

'A wonderful novel'
Michael Connelly

'An addictive crime-novel series'
New York Times

'A guaranteed page-turner'
Mirror

'It demonstrates how the crime novel, when done right, can reach parts that other books can't . . . A considerable achievement'
Guardian

'One of the most authentic and atmospheric of crime series'
Independent